"No one is more passionate or informed about classic television than Herbie J Pilato, who is at it again with this truly exhaustive survey of the most influential male stars and producers over three decades. With profiles from the sublime (Rod Serling) to the ridiculous (Don Adams), and a slew of other icons in between, *Dashing, Daring, and Debonair* is comprehensive, enlightening, and a blast to read."—**David Bushman** (Curator of Television, Paley Center for Media)

"Herbie J Pilato writes about classic television not only with a deep knowledge of his subject, but with an equally deep love and respect. If you know nothing about television and its greatest stars, read one of Herbie J's books. If you think you know everything about television and its greatest stars, read one of Herbie J's books. Either way, you will learn something new, fun, and fascinating. *Dashing, Daring, and Debonair* is a brilliant addition to his canon. It belongs in your collection!"—**Melissa Byers** (Digital Content Producer, Television Academy)

"Herbie J Pilato gives a true voice to classic television in the same way historians give voice to classical music, poets, writers, filmmakers, and creators of masterpieces in museums all over the world. Herbie J places television history as defining America where it needs to be, side by side with the greatest artists of all time."—**Pierre Patrick** (talent agent, author of *The Doris Day Companion*)

"There is no one more enthusiastic or knowledgeable than Herbie J Pilato where classic TV is concerned. *Dashing, Daring, and Debonair* not only demonstrates his vast expertise in this realm, but also gives the reader a fresh perspective on the many pop culture icons profiled in this book. Great scholarship married to great fun!"—**Bill Royce** (Emmy Award–winning co-producer of *The Tonight Show with Jay Leno*)

"Herbie J Pilato takes us back in time yet again to remind us of the tremendous impact our favorite TV male icons have had on us as individuals as well as on society at large. From Desi to Van Dyke to Gleason to Roddenberry, each having fulfilled his own special *Dashing, Daring, and Debonair* niche in classic television history. Thumbs up to Herbie J for another great read!"—**David Van Deusen** (publisher of *The Walnut Times*, *The Dick Van Dyke Show* newsletter)

DASHING, DARING, AND DEBONAIR

TV's Top Male Icons
from the
50s, 60s, and 70s

HERBIE J PILATO

TAYLOR TRADE PUBLISHING
Lanham • Boulder • New York • London

TAYLOR TRADE PUBLISHING
An imprint of Rowman & Littlefield
4501 Forbes Boulevard, Suite 200, Lanham, Maryland 20706
www.rowman.com

Distributed by NATIONAL BOOK NETWORK

British Library Cataloguing-in-Publication Information Available

Library of Congress Cataloging-in-Publication Data

Names: Pilato, Herbie J., author.
Title: Dashing, daring, and debonair : TV's top male icons from the 50s, 60s, and 70s / Herbie J Pilato.
Description: Lanham : Taylor Trade Publishing, 2016.
Identifiers: LCCN 2016011412 (print) | LCCN 2016020091 (ebook) | ISBN 9781630760526 (hardback) | ISBN 9781630760533 (e-book)
Subjects: LCSH: Masculinity on television. | Male actors—United States—Biography. | Television actors and actresses—United States—Biography. | Masculinity in popular culture—United States—History—20th century. | Men in popular culture—United States—History—20th century. | BISAC: PERFORMING ARTS / Television / History & Criticism.
Classification: LCC PN1992.8.M38 P55 2016 (print) | LCC PN1992.8.M38 (ebook) | DDC 791.4502/8092273—dc23
LC record available at https://lccn.loc.gov/2016011412

Printed in the United States of America

*In loving memory of Eva Lois Easton-Leaf,
who was everyone's Number One fan on Earth . . .
and who remains so in Heaven.*

"Handsome" means many things to many people. If people consider me handsome, I feel flattered—and have my parents to thank for it. Realistically, it doesn't hurt to be good-looking, especially in this business.

—Richard Chamberlain, best known on television as the dashing Dr. Kildare

Contents

CONTENTS

Foreword
by Adam "Batman" West

"Thank you for making my life just a little bit brighter."

"You are such a happy part of my experience as a human being. You give the world hope."

"You are my hero."

These are just a few of the countless, incredibly kind and heartwarming comments that I have heard over the years since I was first cast as Batman in the 1960s ABC-TV series of the same name.

I never assumed that all these decades later the show's effect or my involvement with it would have remained so strong and steady.

To this day, wherever I travel in the world, I am approached by fans of all ages, who share with me their most sincere memories of growing up with the show.

Time and again, I am humbled by words of appreciation from fans of the show and their ability to recall a certain episode or recite a favorite line of dialogue.

Clearly, my contribution to *Batman* changed my life and somehow, in the process, also altered the lives of those who watched our performances, and those who may have appreciated the absurdities of the juxtapositions inherent in the show; all delivered with a wink or a smile. *Batman* certainly dispelled some choice advice that helped many restless souls to rise up in faith and confront the ignorance of a bully—or what they may have at one time viewed as an insurmountable obstacle.

It's during the many-times astounding encounters with fans that I've realized the unmistakable positive power of television, especially classic TV, which this book so readily examines and documents with specific regard to male heroes from the 50s, 60s, and 70s.

As to those fans of all positive television programming from every era, and as to my "Bat-fans" in particular, I say this:

"Thank *you* for making *my* life just a little bit brighter."

"You are such a happy part of *my* experience as a human being. *You* give the world hope."

"You are *my* hero."

Preface
by Joel Eisenberg (The Chronicles of Ara)

Herbie J Pilato is on to something. Seriously folks. No joke.

"Can you do me a favor," he asks me. "I would like to interview you for my new book?"

"I appreciate the ask," I said. "But I'm insanely busy. What's the book?"

"*Dashing, Daring, and Debonair: TV's Top Male Icons from the 50s, 60s, and 70s,*" he tells me.

"Interesting. Who do you want me talk about?"

"Leonard Nimoy, William Shatner, and Rod Serling."

And that was that. Herbie J and I go back a few years, and he knows full well of my passion for classic televised science fiction. "Done," I tell him.

We did the interview later that same day, but that in itself does not explain why exactly Herbie J Pilato is "on to something" as I mentioned. The real reason? Over the next week he called me again to hear my thoughts about DeForest Kelley, Bruce Lee, Adam West, George Reeves, Henry Winkler, Norman Lear. You get the picture. Once I was in, I was really in, even with my own dance card as full as it's ever been. A recent television sale based on my fantasy book series (*The Chronicles of Ara*), a couple of films in development, and several other projects in various stages, including one with the author of this book . . . but whenever he asked me to contribute I very happily complied.

Herbie J Pilato is on to something because I personally could not tell this man "no," despite my hectic schedule. I couldn't tell him "no" because classic TV in large part ignited my own career passion (and present vocation) as a full-time writer. This is a man who knows full well that many doctors have been inspired by Oscar Goldman and Rudy Wells from *The Six Million Dollar Man*, that inventors in the space program and other technological fields were inspired by Kirk, Spock, and McCoy . . . that writers and other creatives, like myself, were inspired by the sheer artistry of programs like *The Twilight Zone*.

This guy exposed my vulnerabilities! Herbie J Pilato may be smart, he may be a kind-hearted spiritual person but make no mistake, he also knows how to pull those strings. If I couldn't tell him "no" then how about others? If the reader sees this present tome in their local retailer, surely they'll pick it up and resist any temptation to put it down. Right? I hope so.

Here's why: I'm a fan. I've read several of Herbie J's other books with keen interest, and I consider two of them in particular, *The Bionic Book* and *Twitch Upon a Star*, to be among the finest pop-culture tomes ever written. That is not hyperbole; it is, in fact, immense praise from someone who's typically highly critical when it comes to most similarly intended pop culture efforts. The difference is, whereas others may exhibit a strong degree of expertise as it regards specific programs, Herbie J is a human encyclopedia on all things classic television. Or, whereas others may maintain a more cynical outlook toward it all, Herbie J is not only knowledgeable but appreciative. Or maybe he's simply a gift from another planet. Krypton or Vulcan or something.

Regardless, Samantha and Lucy and Colonel Austin and Fonzie and Barbarino and Superman and Gilligan and Gidget and Mr. Spock . . . they would all love the guy.

In this present volume, the male spin-off of Herbie J's *Glamour, Gidgets, and the Girl Next Door*, comprehensive profiles are included of every top male star from TV's initial classic eras. The book is a treasure trove of information and, most of all, great fun.

Herbie J, it's an honor to partake in your latest work. In large part because of all your efforts, classic TV will live forever.

Introduction

Glamour, Gidgets, and the Girl Next Door: Television's Iconic Women from the 50s, 60s, and 70s (Taylor Trade Publishing, 2014) presented a plethora of perspectives on appealing female TV performers from those three classic decades.

Dashing, Daring and Debonair: TV's Top Male Icons from the 50s, 60s, and 70s follows suit by profiling legendary television men of every ilk from the same era. Whether actors, comedians, singers, dancers, or talk show hosts, everyone from George Burns and Milton Berle to Jack Benny and Jackie Gleason to Sid Caesar and Cesar Romero, to Erik Estrada, Lee Majors, and Lou Ferrigno ignited his own particular brand of "man-erisms." In the process, each inspired his own particular brand of audience to cheer him on. Some legendary television men became notable for the classy chassis they drove on screen, such as Gene Barry on *Burke's Law*, David Soul and Paul Michael Glaser on *Starsky & Hutch*, and John Schneider and Tom Wopat as *The Dukes of Hazzard*. Even Peter Falk's rumpled yet lovable Columbo navigated a sporty if not sophisticated vehicle: a tiny 1959 (or 1960) Peugeot 403 two-door convertible that nonetheless remains memorable—but mostly because of who was at the wheel.

Male TV crimefighters have also held viewers' attention over the years with their various props and character traits: the steamy voice juxtaposed with the sticky lollipop that Telly Savalas mouthed as *Kojak*; Rock Hudson's self-deprecating decency as a San Francisco police commissioner on *McMillan & Wife*; James Garner's gutsy affability on *Maverick* and *The Rockford Files*; Craig Stevens's suave gumshoe showmanship as Peter Gunn; and Mike Connors's bold charisma as Mannix.

Many TV men have left their impressions both in front of and behind the cameras. Rod Serling, as host, narrator, and the main creative voice of *The Twilight Zone* and *Night Gallery*, could work an audience like none before him or since. Multi-hyphenate talents Michael Landon and Jack Webb were on the outside looking in, as well as on the inside looking out, each with his own separate unique style. Landon's diverse abilities as actor and director were initially displayed on *Bonanza* and later coupled with producing poise on *Little House on the Prairie* (and on into the 80s with *Highway to Heaven*). Jack weaved his pervasive and persuasive web as director, producer, and performer on two different TV editions of *Dragnet* (as well as one version for the radio and another for the big screen), later supervising the scenes of TV classics like *Emergency!* Each of these men, and more, was distinguished, wise, and insightful, and pursued his TV career with great heart in his own way.

Countless classic television males created and/or interpreted the adoring fathers and father figures, the brothers we never had, the uncles that we always wanted, and the *Six Million Dollar* men from *U.N.C.L.E.* and *Shiloh* who some of us wanted to be and others of us wanted to marry. They were the *Virginians* who journeyed by horse, buggy, or *Wagon Train*, from the western plains through the *Voyage to the Bottom of the Sea*, to the galactic outskirts of *Star Trek*, to up, up, and away as with *Superman*. They were mortals and wizards and gods, our sons and neighbors, cousins and co-workers, and handymen and employees. They weren't really doctors, lawyers, teachers, policemen, detectives, firefighters, spacemen, astronauts or aliens, good ol' boys or cowboys; they just played them on TV.

Some true-to-life siblings, like Ricky and David Nelson on *The Adventures of Ozzie and Harriet*, and Stanley and Barry Livingston on *My Three Sons*, played their TV parts to the hilt; but most were fabricated relatives, friends, and colleagues who somehow seemed real. Jerry Mathers and Tony Dow were not biological brothers away from *Leave It to Beaver*, but they might as well have been, as they remain as close as real siblings today. The duos were dynamic between Adam West and Burt Ward on *Batman*, and Van Williams and Bruce Lee on *Green Hornet*, while millions of viewers looked forward to primetime greetings and "good night" salutations with the fresh-as-apple-peach-and-pumpkin-pie face of Richard Thomas as John-Boy on *The Waltons*. Audiences were enthralled with the hip young studs of *The Mod Squad*, *The Rookies*, and *WKRP in Cincinnati*—as well as the elegant senior reverence of Ricardo Montalban, who presided with such grace over *Fantasy Island*.

Who could deny the smoldering good looks of *Gunsmoke*'s James Arness or his brother Peter Graves and his assorted male colleagues on *Mission: Impossible*? What of the musical majestic genetics passed from Desi Arnaz (*I Love Lucy*) to Desi Arnaz Jr. (*Here's Lucy*), or the dueling youthful M.D.s Richard Chamberlain (*Dr. Kildare*) and Vince Edwards (*Ben Casey*); the mightily coifed medical practitioners played by James Brolin (*Marcus Welby, M.D.*) and Chad Everett (*Medical Center*); or the patriarchal dignity of Robert Young, who set the standard for dads and doctoring from *Father Knows Best* to *Welby*?

Who could peek away from the puka shell status of top teen idols like Bobby Sherman (*Here Come the Brides*) and David Cassidy (*The Partridge Family*), or Barry Williams and Christopher Knight (*The Brady Bunch*)? Who wasn't driven to watch *Route 66* with the riveting George Maharis and Martin Milner, who later partnered with Kent McCord on *Adam-12*? What about the little bit of rock and roll from Donny Osmond on *The Donny & Marie Show*, or the pretty pairing of Shaun Cassidy and Parker Stevenson on *The Hardy Boys*? What of the more historic and dramatically diverse teaming of Robert Culp and Bill Cosby on *I Spy*—or the equally disparate Michael Cole and Clarence Williams III on *The Mod Squad*?

Who could keep a straight face and not embrace with anticipation the sophisticated humor of Johnny Carson on *The Tonight Show*, or the lithe physical comedy of Dick Van Dyke on his self-named weekly sitcom treasure? What of the rubber-faced expressions of those double Darrins Dick York and Dick Sargent, who were equally mind-boggled to perfection by the magic mayhem on *Bewitched*? Who could distrust the eloquent young gents of *77 Sunset Strip*, *Hawaiian Eye*, *Hawaii Five-O*, or *The FBI*? Who could not admire the nice-guy guise of Andy Griffith's Sheriff Andy Taylor, Dwayne Hickman's *Many Loves of Dobie Gillis,* or Ron Howard's "Opie Cunningham" transformation from *The Andy Griffith Show* to *Happy Days*, the latter of which also featured the one and only Fonz—Henry Winkler's legendary library-card-carrying hood-with-a-heart?

These and more memories of small-screen machismo and machinations, and/ or mere mortal men galore are celebrated and explored in *Dashing, Daring, and Debonair*. Combining profiles of real-life personas with TV's best-known male alter egos, this book delivers a unique glimpse into television's manly landscape peppered with everything from moral to misanthropic manliness.

While *Glamour, Gidgets, and the Girl Next Door* focused mostly on youth-geared female TV personalities, *Dashing, Daring, and Debonair* expands the limits by showcasing renowned and formidable male TV icons of every generation and age, heritage and culture, talent and ability: from the quirky, more character-driven personas, to the romantic to the witty and sophisticated roles. Yet, too, this book makes certain to cover the ever-popular teen-to-mid-thirties-to-forties-matinee-idol sector (if not with a profile of every single such young actor, but with at the very least a significant representative from as many TV show groups as possible).

Many of TV's historic males profiled are no longer living, but of those who are, a select group granted exclusive interviews for this book, including Ed Asner (*The Mary Tyler Moore Show/Lou Grant*), Michael Cole (*The Mod Squad*), Dwayne Hickman (*Dobie Gillis*), Billy Gray (*Father Knows Best*), Stanley Livingston (*My Three Sons*), Larry Matthews (*The Dick Van Dyke Show*), Radames Pera (*Kung Fu*), David Selby (*Dark Shadows*), Parker Stevenson (*The Hardy Boys*), Robert Wagner (*It Takes a Thief/Switch*), and Larry Wilcox (*CHiPs*) as well as actress Caryn Richman (*The New Gidget*), Chris York (son of Dick York, the original Darrin on *Bewitched*); writers/producers Larry Brody (*Barnaby Jones/Hawaii Five-0*), Fred Freeman (*The Andy Griffith Show/The Dick Van Dyke Show*), Arnie Kogen (*The Carol Burnett Show/The Donny & Marie Show*), Marty Nadler (*Happy Days/Laverne & Shirley*), and Rick Lertzman (co-author with Williams J. Birnes of *The Life and Times of Mickey Rooney*); comedian and Los Angeles weatherman legend Fritz Coleman; Linda Burton (a close friend to Donny Osmond); the prolific Joel Eisenberg (co-author of *The Chronicles of Ara* and co-creator of its subsequent TV adaptation), who has penned the Preface to this book; and Adam West—the one and only true Batman, who so generously provided the Foreword.

Information about those male icons who have passed away, or who were otherwise unavailable for an interview, was gathered from previous interviews, articles, or profiles that appeared in various other books, publications, online resources, magazines, newspapers, and websites, or from TV talk shows, specials, documentaries, or DVD extras.

Supplementary and key commentary was provided by an A-list of classic TV and film historians and authors, including Jeffrey D. Dalrymple, John S. Drew, James Nuttel, Rob Ray, Steve Randisi, Steve Reeser, Virginia Reeser, Ed Robertson, Mark Simpson, Randy Skretvedt, Professor Jeff Thompson, and David Van Deusen. Particularly insightful perceptions are delivered by the heralded veteran entertainment journalist Ann Hodges, who not only wrote about television for decades for the *Houston Chronicle*, but who was also personal friends with a good portion of the male icons profiled here.

Dashing, Daring, and Debonair is divided into eight main sections, grouping the actors into the categories with which their characters or TV personas are most associated. Each section includes an introductory essay about the given band of performers, which is then followed by chapters that focus on one to several particular personas.

The chapter numbers and listings should not be perceived as rankings of any sort, as this book does not seek to ignite a debate about the relative popularity of these TV men. Some intro sections devote space to certain icons who do not receive full chapter profiles (e.g., Tim Conway, Harvey Korman, and Lyle Waggoner in the introduction to Part 1), as well as referencing a few of the icons who do receive full profiles in those sections.

Due to editorial demands and restrictions, allotted space, or lack of access to certain stars, not every male actor who was ever featured in a TV series or as a leading presence in some capacity is profiled within these pages. Because this book focuses on primetime television programming, those not profiled also include daytime male superstars, and news anchors and journalists, with the exception of Jonathan Frid and David Selby, whose popularity as the lovelorn vampire Barnabas Collins and the lost soul/ghost-man/zombie-turned-werewolf-turned-redeeming-soul Quentin Collins (respectively) on ABC's groundbreaking gothic daytime soap opera, *Dark Shadows*, reached epic heartthrob proportions.

Dashing, Daring, and Debonair: TV's Top Male Icons from the 50s, 60s, and 70s is published in this 50th anniversary of *Batman*, *Dark Shadows*, *Mission: Impossible*, *Family Affair*, *That Girl*, *The Monkees*, and *Star Trek*, all of which feature some of television's finest and most revered male talents. Every effort was made to profile as many of these dynamic men as possible within the confines of limited space—and with the utmost respect and dignity, focusing on what made each TV personality unique in his own way.

Enjoy.

PART I

THE JACKS OF ALL TRADES

Some have it all—and some know how to do it all. When it comes to male TV icons from the 50s, 60s, and 70s, that "it" factor takes many forms. Many manly small screen idols from these eras kept themselves busy by hosting variety series, such as Ed Sullivan, who introduced Elvis and The Beatles to mainstream America with his legendary *Ed Sullivan Show*. Milton Berle, aka Uncle Miltie, headlined *The Milton Berle Show*. Red Skelton twisted and churned his face as the one of TV's first clown princes with *The Red Skelton Show*. Jackie Gleason's contoured expressions and larger-than-life presence was adored on *The Jackie Gleason Show*, a segment of which was titled *The Honeymooners* went on to have a life of its own.

As New York City bus driver Ralph Kramden, Gleason on *The Honeymooners* became TV's first mainstream blue-collar relatively average-looking male character, one who ultimately inspired more to come—including Kevin James's similarly hefty postal delivery truck driver Doug Heffernan on *The King of Queens* (CBS, 1998–2007) as well as the animated Fred Flintstone (voiced by Alan Reed) on *The Flintstones* (ABC, 1960–1966). According to one report, Gleason based most of *The Honeymooners* on the impoverished life he and his mother experienced after his father abandoned their family, and it was this everyman status with which viewers identified. His catchphrases populated the airwaves at the time, including his trademark statements, "How sweet it is!"; "And away we go!"; and "Baby, you're the greatest!"

On CBS, Sunday nights from 1948 to 1971, Sullivan, who died in 1973, popularized his own way of connecting with the audience, utilizing opening phrases such as "Right here on our stage," and "really big show." Sullivan's variety hour exemplified the term in its entirety, with performers of every definition, ranging from circus acts, to every kind of comedian, dancer, and musical performer, to regulars like puppet "Topo Gigio," the tiny Italian mouse who sought to have Ed "kiss me goodnight."

Sullivan, Gleason, Berle, and Skelton also contributed to the overall behind-the-scenes productivity of their particular programs—although certainly not without the stellar assistance of their seasoned writing staffs.

From 1963 to 1964, writer Fred Freeman worked on Gleason's variety show with fellow scribe Marvin Marx, who had penned episodes of *The Honeymooners*. Says Freeman of Gleason: "He did his characters, and I thought he was a genius in his own certain way. Very often we would go into the dressing room for an hour-and-a-half before show time, live cameras and everything, and he'd say [of the show's scripts], 'This is shit. I don't want to do it.' Everyone would panic. And then he would go out and do the things he liked, and pulled it off."

Gleason would "wing it to an extent," adds Freeman, who also confirmed that the performer was not a fan of rehearsals. "Jackie did very little of that."

Years after Gleason's variety series ended, the beloved performer reinvented himself in the 70s as a movie star with a mustache and a dash of elegance via the *Smokey and the Bandit* feature films with fellow male TV icon Burt Reynolds (*Dan August*), as well as female TV icon Sally Field (*Gidget/The Flying Nun*). It was clear why Jackie was dubbed "The Great One" (long before Muhammad Ali delivered a self-spin on that title with "The Greatest"). The sketch-comedy bravado of comedy greats Sid Caesar, Carl Reiner, and Mel Brooks was on full display with their groundbreaking variety series, *Your Show of Shows*. When the variety genre began transmuting into sitcoms, with series hosted by those such as George Burns (*Burns and Allen*) and Jack Benny (*The Jack Benny Program*), nobody did it better than night-club performer Danny Thomas, who turned his live stage act into a long-running hit situation comedy with two names: *Make Room for Daddy*-cum-*The Danny Thomas Show*.

Stand-out talent Nat King Cole paved the way as the first African American to host a weekly television series, variety or otherwise, with *The Nat King Cole Show* in the 50s. Cole's massive charisma was merely heightened by his ability to sing, dance, and charm an audience.

Conversely, Flip Wilson, also African-American, would years later present a more edgy presence in the world of variety with his own brand of breakout humor, some of which was considered relatively contentious by some members of the African-

American community: namely, his personification of the character named Geraldine—his loose-talking, hip-swaying stereotypical take on a very carefree-spirited woman of color.

Redd Foxx, another African-American TV legend, was relatively more brazen than Wilson, if less campy, with his sex appeal—and certainly less musical than Cole. But Redd still played it for all it was worth. And that was a lot. As the star of NBC's hit 70s sitcom, *Sanford and Son* (which costarred Demond Wilson as his only offspring Lamont), he was sexy, and he knew it—and he used it. Redd's very name said it all: foxy. He may have portrayed junkman Fred Sanford on *Son*, but the ladies loved his stylized raspy voice, which he acquired after years of performing in smoky nightclubs around the country. His edgy live act may have been coined controversial, before, during, and after *Sanford & Son*, but his risqué behavior on stage was toned down to just the right size for his TV sitcom (which made him millions), and later, for a short-lived ABC variety series of his own (and which was nowhere near as successful as *Son*).

Many other male icons headlined variety hours, several of which were penned by Arnie Kogen, who offers this insight on the genre during the initial "Golden Era of Television":

> In 1968 when I came to California there were a zillion variety shows. Well, maybe not a zillion. There were 14. It seemed like a zillion. The Smothers Brothers had a variety show and Don Knotts and *Laugh-In* [hosted by Dan Rowan and Dick Martin] and Andy Williams and Red Skelton and Phyllis Diller. There were stars, sketches, musical production numbers, and dazzling celebrity guests. It was a great time for viewers and writers. I was fortunate enough to hook up with a few of the very best: *The Dean Martin Show*, *The Carol Burnett Show*, and *Donny & Marie*. *The Dean Martin Show* was one of the most entertaining variety shows ever. Dean was loose and easy going. He had a great voice, great charm, and great style. And Dean was a very funny guy. Both Dean Martin and Jerry Lewis had variety shows on NBC at the same time in the same year. Ironically enough, Dean [mostly known for his crooning] opened his show with a monologue and Jerry [mostly known for his comedy] opened his show with a song.

With regard to Dick and Tommy Smothers, aka The Smothers Brothers, and their variety series of the same name, scribe Sam Bobrick who, like Kogen, also wrote for the bros, says this daring duo were unique, groundbreaking, and controversial. "And that's why everybody liked them. When they came on they were bigger than anything. They had an edge and this is where their comedy was going. It was political and satirical. And it was fun to write for them. They were all about comedy and satire. They would bring on some wonderful [then-] new musical acts like Simon and Garfunkel. They let The Beatles debut [their song] 'Hey, Jude.' I remember we had Bobbie Gentry, when she was so hot with [her hit] 'Ode to Billy Joe.' There was no other place for these people to go," says Bobrick, who credits Tommy Smothers in particular for bringing the legendary music acts to *The Smothers Brothers Comedy Hour*. "He made it happen."

"I'll tell you what their secret was," Bobrick goes on to reveal. "Their show was one of the few that adults enjoyed with their children. It spoke to both of those demographics. It was funny and it also was on the fringe. It went against *Bonanza* [a massive hit for NBC], but they held their own, and found their audience. Theirs was a well-produced show and it was fun."

Besides his work on the *Brothers* hour, Bobrick is the prolific author of countless other TV shows as well as feature films and live stage productions, including the play *Norman . . . Is That You?*, which he co-wrote with Sam Clark (and which was adapted for the 1976 big-screen movie starring Redd Foxx). But he has a particular penchant for sketch-writing, which he did regularly for *The Smothers Brothers Comedy Hour* and other such shows of their time.

Bobrick recalls one *Brothers* sketch in particular that stands out, and remembers a few of his writing colleagues and some additional male TV icons he appreciated, who inspired him and/or whom he worked with via the *Smothers* show or elsewhere: "I remember when we took on the NRA. That week we were talking about shooting fish in a barrel. [Comedian and writer] Pat Paulsen was great on the show, along with two [other] good writers . . . Al Gordon and Hal Goldman, who used to write for Jack Benny. And Jack Benny was my template. He was, for me, the best comic ever. I just loved his work—he had such an attitude built into him. He had the character and everything. And he always credited Gordon and Goldman. We became very good friends and they were just wonderful guys. It was just a good feeling [working on *The Smothers Brothers Comedy Hour*]."

Years later and in between, the comedic male troika of Tim Conway, Harvey Korman, and the dapper Lyle Waggoner dazzled TV audiences into a tizzy of laughter, granting solid support for eleven years to their leading lady on CBS's *The Carol Burnett Show*. Both Korman and Waggoner left the series for other opportunities (Waggoner went on to play with perfection the stoic Steve Trevor opposite Lynda Carter on the 70s superhero cult TV favorite, *Wonder Woman*, while Korman failed with his own *Harvey Korman Show* sitcom). Conway, who joined the *Burnett Show* as a regular in its mid-term, remained until the end—and shined (yet never found sitcom success of his own, after several attempts).

In October 2011, *Entertainment Weekly* published one of their special "Reunion" issues, which included a re-banding of the *Carol* troupe vets including its name star, stellar supporting performer Vicki Lawrence, and Conway who, before his Burnett gig, had been featured for years on the long-running hit sitcom *McHale's Navy*. "I have fond memories of the show—not *The Carol Burnett Show*, other shows that I've done," Conway dryly joked with tongue in cheek like only he knows how.

Conway, whose memoir, *What's So Funny?: My Hilarious Life*, reached the *New York Times* best-seller list, went on to say that Burnett granted him, Lawrence, Waggoner, and Korman a creative carte blanche, of which he in particular took full advantage. Tim's most popular performances on the show include the frustrated office manager Mr. Tudball (to Burnett's dimwitted secretary Mrs. Wiggins), his general on-the-spot improvs with Korman, and the shuffling Old Man, with which Korman had initially taken issue. Conway commented on it all:

> Carol gave us the opportunity to do whatever we wanted . . . which was always great because we would surprise not only the audience but her, too. There were so many things we did on the air that were never done until we actually did them for taping. One was the Old Man. When we got the script that week, [Korman] said, "Wait a minute. He's not doing an old man. I do the best old man there is." So all week, Harvey is saying, "What are you going to do as an old man?" and I said, "I have no idea." And I didn't. I really didn't do that shuffle with the Old Man until we were actually taping the show. When I started shuffling across the room, I noticed the rug was gathering in front of me and I thought, "Jeez, if they let this go, we're going to be here for three days." But they let it go and it was created out of the air.

The male "creator" spot in television was never just black or white, but rather colored with several innovative shades of gray, painted and mingled and matched with the imaginative brush of both on- and off-screen talent. Behind-the-scene show-runners such as Stirling Silliphant and Herbert B. Leonard (*Route 66*), Leonard Stern (*Get Smart*), Sol Saks and Harry Ackerman (*Bewitched*), Earl Hamner (*The Waltons*), and other all-around TV talents like Jack Webb and Rod Serling put a unique face on shows like Webb's weekly *Dragnet* crime drama, and Serling's eerie *Twilight Zone* and *Night Gallery* anthology programs.

A few other male TV minds proved just as innovative, if not in obvious ways.

Sonny Bono started out as a musical recording artist with his then wife Cher, before teaming with her to make a hit out of *The Sonny & Cher Comedy Hour*, only later to become the mayor of Palm Springs, California, and a US congressman. *Battlestar: Galactica* creator and producer Glen A. Larson also began his career in music—as one of the founding members of the lyrical pop group The Four Preps.

A few of these jacks of all trades—among others—are profiled more closely in the following section.

1

Jack Webb
Dragnet/Adam-12/Emergency!

Just the facts, ma'am.

—Joe Friday, as played by Jack Webb on *Dragnet*

Jack Webb made his mark on television, literally . . . with his Mark VII Limited production company, the logo of which was animated at the close of his hit TV shows, on everything from the original black-and-white and subsequent color *Dragnet* detective series in the 50s and 60s, to the *Adam-12* spin-off, through to the *CHiPs* motorcycle police and *Emergency* medical dramas of the 70s.

Active in Hollywood from 1951 to his death in 1982, Webb produced many of his programs with Universal Television, and the majority of them aired on NBC. As documented on Wikipedia, the Jack Webb estate owns the rights to his library of prolific work, with the exception of the original 1954 feature film version of *Dragnet* (released by Warner Bros., and now owned by Universal Pictures), as well as the 1955 movie *Pete Kelly's Blues*, and 1957's *The D.I.* (both of which are controlled by original distributor Warner Bros.).

Webb commenced his career as a bit actor in late 40s crime dramas during an era when semi-documentary crime feature films were successful. He appeared as a crime lab technician in the hit semi-documentary crime movie *He Walked by Night* (1948), which costarred future TV-lead Richard Basehart (*Voyage to the Bottom of the Sea*). This production allowed Webb the chance to befriend a Los Angeles police sergeant who was the film's technical consultant which, in turn, led to Webb's creation/development

Globe Photos

of the *Dragnet* show, first on radio then television.

According to cinema and TV historian Rob Ray, "Webb was a savvy producer-writer who knew that his career goals would be better attained by working behind the camera, as much as in front of it. He never had much of a budget to work with, which worked to his advantage on radio, where he created *Dragnet*. All he had was imagination and on radio that costs nothing. As a result, *Dragnet* was probably at its best as a radio drama. His use of stark music and imaginative sound effects, coupled with a loyal talented stock company of actors, suited the medium well."

By the early 50s, a TV adaptation of *Dragnet* was inevitable because, as Ray goes on to explain, "That's where all the hit radio shows were going. The budgets remained tight, but the quality of the writing remained high, and Webb was able to utilize that great stock company on the television series."

That company included Webb in his famous stone-faced role as police sergeant Joe Friday, while his first partner on the television show (as on the radio) was Sergeant Ben Romero, as portrayed by Barton Yarborough, who succumbed to heart failure following the completion of just three episodes. The Romero character (who also died of a heart attack, as explained in the December 27, 1951, radio segment, "The Big Sorrow") was initially replaced by Detective Sergeant Ed Jacobs, as played by Barney Phillips, and then Officer Frank Smith, portrayed by Herb Ellis for four episodes, after which Ben Alexander assumed the Smith role for both the TV and radio edition of the series.

Webb retained his glib, glum, and seamless directorial and theatrical style, popularized by the catchphrase, "Just the facts, ma'am." The rigid line deliveries, acting techniques, and storytelling were so uniquely his own that, as Ray observes, radio and television parodists such as Stan Freberg "had a field day doing imitations."

Dragnet remained popular in the new medium of television before running its course toward the end of the 50s. The tumultuous 60s brought on by the Kennedy assassination and the Vietnam War, coupled with the ensuing Generation Gap, proved divisive to the popular culture. TV became the refuge of the conservative politics and cultural outlook personified by the likes of Jack Webb. Thus, his prolific creative mind embraced the opportunity to revive *Dragnet* as a response to, as Ray puts it, "those who would question authority and refer to the police in derogatory terms."

Once the color edition of *Dragnet* debuted in 1967, the stock company of actors largely remained the same, with the addition of Harry Morgan (*M*A*S*H*) as Webb's new on-screen partner Bill Gannon (replacing Smith, as played by Alexander—who was unavailable by the time the show returned to TV). But Webb's conservative "my defenders of the city—right or wrong" outlook, his trademarked expressions (or lack thereof), and coarse directorial style meant that audiences would be divided as to whether the show was what Ray calls "an effective mouthpiece for the Los Angeles Police Department or merely high camp harkening back to an era now hopelessly dead."

The one element that was emphasized more in the 60s version was comedy. The 50s edition may have had its lighter moments, but the later-day *Dragnet* periodically presented entire episodes dealing with Joe Friday just trying to enjoy a quiet evening at home while suffering one distraction after another. Meanwhile, Morgan's Bill Gannon was utilized as more comedic relief for Webb's character, as Bill constantly touted the advantage of being married to the confirmed bachelor Friday. The looks of bemusement on Friday's face at Bill's tales of his life at home offered great comedy relief that balanced out the efficiently told, eternally stark crime dramas.

Audiences looking for this sort of entertainment took to the revived show, and Webb's production team managed to continue their success with the aforementioned mid-60s to early 70s spin-off, *Adam-12*, as well as throughout the rest of the 70s with *Emergency!*

In 1987, Dan Aykroyd—in perfect comedic pitch as Joe Friday (alongside a new detective played by Tom Hanks)—paid big-screen tribute to the Jack Webb legacy with a feature film hit edition of *Dragnet*.

Webb's show business career was always on the upswing, if after a relatively spotty start in other professions. As explained on www.Emergencyfans.com, the multi-hyphenated talent held a pre-entertainment industry position in sales at Silverwoods, a men's clothing store in Los Angeles. Webb had described himself as "a third rate salesman" (even after working a solid five years in the position, with a later promotion to assistant manager). Beyond that, he performed in plays like *The Lightkeeper's Daughter* and *Hiawatha*. "It was easy," he said of the latter. "I stuck some feathers into a headband, took a bath in body make-up." Years later, in reviewing his lead in *Pete Kelly's Blues*, *Time* magazine said Webb played that part like a "cigar store Indian."

During World War II, Webb worked a swing shift at the Byron Jackson steel mill as an electric hacksaw operator, and eventually joined the air force. He spent three and a half years as a pilot trainee, but never attained his wings. The press had somehow perceived him to be a war hero, and later was blamed for fabricating stories of glory, but he never claimed to see any more war action than "the Saturday night crap game at the post."

After being discharged from the air force, he became a radio announcer at station KOG in San Francisco. His early radio career was as he said, "as romantic as playing post office in an old maids' club." He arrived at the station every day at 4:30 a.m., "pushed a button and said 'And now back to New York.'"

From there, Webb met a writer named Dick Breen, who created a radio program called *Pat Novak for Hire*, about a sarcastic detective. Jack was cast in the lead, and performed in it for twenty-three weeks. Breen then took Novak to Hollywood, and Webb followed. As he explained, "For eight or nine weeks I was everybody's hot cake. I played cops, gangsters, burglars and assorted villains on all the major radio shows . . . the future looked so good that I married [future *Emergency!* star] Julie London." The couple separated nine months later in real life, while Webb found additional challenges finding the right roles in reel life or on the stage.

"We stayed apart for a year," he said of London and himself, "then went back together for five years and had two children, and it still wouldn't work."

Webb eventually found something that did work—at least with regard to his acting career when he was cast as Lt. Lee Jones in the 1948 motion picture *He Walked by Night*. One day after filming, Sgt. Marty Wynn, a technical adviser on the movie, approached Webb and granted him extensive access to the Los Angeles Police Department files with the idea of formulating a new radio detective series. Webb rejected the idea, thinking the police radio show genre was already overstocked. Wynn, however, didn't back down, explaining that the other programs were overly dramatized. Months later, Webb ultimately agreed with Wynn—and the life- and career-defining *Dragnet* was born.

2

Desi Arnaz
I Love Lucy/The Lucy-Desi Comedy Hour/
The Mothers-in-Law

I don't think anyone can tell you what it is that makes you a star.

—Desi Arnaz

That laugh. That smile. Those tall, dark, and handsome good looks. That accent. They were each outstanding trademarks of Desi Arnaz—the actor, singer, and musician who was wise enough to marry Lucille Ball—the genius actress, comedian, and performer who would go on to change his life and career forever.

Arnaz was an underrated talent, underrated because he was an excellent musician, a top-rank farceur, a savvy astute businessman, and an all-around extremely good-looking and bright star who, for better or for worse, forever lived in the shadow of his wife. Together they starred in their hit sitcom, *I Love Lucy*, in which he portrayed bandleader Ricky Ricardo for 194 episodes. On and off screen, Arnaz adored Ball and devoted his career to furthering hers, which included reformulating her first name to be more show business–friendly. As he once explained, "I had started calling her 'Lucy' shortly after we met; I didn't like the name 'Lucille.' That's how our television show was called *I Love Lucy* [and] not [*I Love*] *Lucille*."

Born into wealth and influence in Santiago de Cuba, Cuba, on March 2, 1917, Desiderio Alberto Arnaz y de Acha III attended St. Patrick Catholic High School in Miami, Florida, and Saint Leo Prep, near Tampa (to improve his English). His parents were Desiderio Alberto Arnaz II and Dolores de Acha; he was married to Ball from 1940 to 1960, and they had two children: Lucie Arnaz and Desi Arnaz Jr., both of

Globe Photos

whom went on to star in Ball's third hit CBS sitcom, *Here's Lucy*. From 1963 to 1985, Desi Sr. was married to Edith Skimming.

Desi's family fled to the United States after the 1933 Revolution. As a drummer, singer, and bandleader, Desi helped popularize the conga in clubs in Florida and New York. Discovered by the Broadway team of Rodgers and Hart, he starred in the musical *Too Many Girls*. When it was filmed by RKO, Arnaz arrived in Hollywood and met Ball, who first referred to him as "Dizzy." Shortly thereafter, they wed and retained separate careers in different feature films. Desi's film career, primarily in various films at Metro-Goldwyn-Mayer and most memorably in 1943's *Bataan*, never really took off however, as Hollywood did not seem to know what to do with the handsome Cuban. Thus he took to the road with his band and his marriage to Lucille suffered as a result.

When Lucy's radio hit *My Favorite Husband* was to be turned into a television show, she saw this as an opportunity to keep Desi at home and fought to have her husband be her costar. Just as at MGM, CBS was skeptical about a Cuban leading man, but relented. *I Love Lucy* premiered October 15, 1951, and Lucy and Desi became household names. He shared a 1956 Golden Globe award with Lucy for Best TV Show.

In recent years Desi has been belatedly getting more recognition for being an innovative businessman. *I Love Lucy* was the first scripted television program to be shot with three cameras in front of a studio audience on 35 mm film, which increased its value for syndicated reruns (a process Arnaz commandeered with CBS and later Screen Gems executive Harry Ackerman). In 1957, on Howard Hughes's advice, Desi purchased the two RKO studio lots (Gower Street in Hollywood and Culver City) for $6,150,000, a total of sixty-five acres. His and Lucy's Desilu Studios were home to

The Andy Griffith Show, *The Dick Van Dyke Show*, *Star Trek*, *Mission: Impossible*, *Hogan's Heroes*, and many others. Desi personally produced *The Ann Sothern Show*, *The Untouchables*, and *The Mothers-In-Law*, and was delighted when Ball returned to television with her fourth and final sitcom, *Life with Lucy* (ABC, 1986-1987).

"He was really the secret behind Lucy's success from the time they started, particularly on the business side," says Ann Hodges, the legendary television critic for the *Houston Chronicle*. "But he was also very good about learning and applying the production end of the show. I was around both he and Lucy a lot because I was a good friend of their public relations man Charlie Pomeranz, who was with them for years. And I always found Desi to be just delightful, and you would never know that he and Lucy were having any problems; and of course, they never showed that for the press. And I just think that their marriage is what did for them, more than anything else because they were fun with each other. They were obviously well-mated on television and the audience took a liking to that very quickly."

As to what it was exactly about Arnaz that made him so appealing, Hodges says, "He was intelligent . . . and he was good about deferring to Lucy [on camera]. I liked the way that they both interacted on screen. You really hadn't seen [the woman be the star of a series] until Desi appeared with Lucy." Usually, a television show always featured a male lead. Or as Hodges observes, "It had been the man of the house prior to [*I Love Lucy*], and the lady of the house was always pretty much a secondary character. But Lucy played a strong central character."

The secret to the success and appeal of Desi Arnaz on television was his wisdom, ability, discretion, and foresight in being wise enough to know that Lucy was the star of their show.

As to his off-screen life with Lucy, he relayed the following in his memoir, *A Book*: "Little arguments became big arguments. There was really no chance to be away from each other and let things cool off. It was really ironic. For the first ten years of our married life we had both worked like hell, trying to solve the problem of being separated too much."

While Desi was quoted as saying that "I Love Lucy" was more than just the title of their monumental sitcom, Desi and Lucy eventually divorced. Before, during, and after their marriage, Arnaz battled inner demons, but throughout it all produced and supported Ball's professional endeavors, never once taking for granted their good fortune. "The success of *I Love Lucy* is something that happens only once in a lifetime," he had said, ". . . if you are fortunate enough to have it happen at all." Comparing the show's super success to his rocky personal interactions with Ball, he assessed, "Good things do not come easy. The road is lined with pitfalls . . . Nobody bats .500. We all make mistakes."

The ever-dapper Desi Arnaz passed away from lung cancer on December 2, 1986, at the age of sixty-nine, five days before Lucille Ball received the acclaimed Kennedy Center Honor.

3

Nat King Cole
The Nat King Cole Show

The only prejudice I have found anywhere in TV is in some advertising agencies, and there isn't so much prejudice as just fear.

—Nat King Cole

Nat King Cole was indeed a king . . . of hearts, humanity, music, entertainment, and television. His signature Christmas carol is considered *the* Christmas carol: "The Christmas Song." The joyful, warm message of the song clearly represented the type of man he was. He enjoyed his financial success, but managed to retain a fine balance of priorities. As he once said, "I make no claim to being a business genius. You can make so much money in this business that it loses its value."

The Nat King Cole Show became the first TV musical/variety series to be hosted by an African-American male, debuting November 5, 1956, on NBC. According to Wikipedia, Cole's program began as a fifteen-minute pop-oriented show, expanding to a half hour in July 1957. NBC made great strides to keep Cole's show afloat and under budget, as did several of Cole's associates, many of whom (Ella Fitzgerald, Harry Belafonte, Mel Tormé, Peggy Lee, Eartha Kitt) worked for scale (or for free). But no matter: *The Nat King Cole Show* was cancelled mainly because it lacked a national sponsorship. The show's final segment was broadcast December 17, 1957, after which the performer retorted, "Madison Avenue is afraid of the dark."

Heralded for his velvet vocal chords combined with an eloquent verbal style, Cole was born Nathaniel Adams Coles in Montgomery, Alabama, on March 17, 1919. He

Globe Photos

had four siblings: a half-sister, Joyce, and brothers Eddie, Ike, and Freddy, the latter two of whom would also become musical performers. When he was only four, the Cole family relocated to Chicago, Illinois, where his father, Edward, was ordained a Baptist minister. His mother, Perlina Coles, was the church organist; she taught Nat to play, and he performed his first song, "Yes! We Have No Bananas." At age twelve, he began taking formal voice lessons, and soon honed his pristine vocal inflections, ultimately becoming a master of performing jazz, gospel, and classical music.

His family settled in Chicago's Bronzeville neighborhood and, by day, a young Nat studied music with the acclaimed Water Dyette at DuSable High School. At night he sneaked out to the clubs, where he would listen to performers like Louis Armstrong, Earl Hines, and Jimmie Noone. At fifteen years old, he left school to work full-time as a jazz pianist, temporarily partnered with his brother Eddie and, in 1936, made his first professional recording. He later played piano with the national musical touring revue *Shuffle Along*, formed the King Cole Trio, which toured extensively and, in 1943, had a chart-topping hit with his own composition, "That Ain't Right." The next year, "Straighten Up and Fly Right," inspired by one of his dad's sermons, became another hit for the trio, which continued to succeed with other hits like the aforementioned classic "The Christmas Song" and the ballad "(I Love You) For Sentimental Reasons."

By the 50s, Cole performed solo with other hits like "Nature Boy," "Mona Lisa," "Too Young," and "Unforgettable," the latter of which was re-recorded decades later as a "duet" (utilizing contemporary technology) by his daughter Natalie Cole (who succumbed to ongoing health issues at only sixty-five on Decemebr 31, 2015). Before that modern twist, however, Cole worked with other singing sensations like Louis

Armstrong and Ella Fitzgerald, and iconic arrangers including Nelson Riddle. He also met and befriended legends such as the one and only Frank Sinatra.

As an African American, Cole was confronted by prejudice, particularly while touring in the South. In 1956, he had been attacked by white supremacists during a mixed race performance in Alabama, while he was rebuked by fellow African Americans for his less-than-ancillary remarks about racial integration following his performance. Nat said he was just an entertainer, as opposed to a social or political activist. "The whites come to applaud a Negro performer just like the colored do. When you've got the respect for white and colored, you can ease a lot of things."

By the late 50s, his popularity declined only to have it reignited in the early 60s, with country-inspired hits like "Ramblin' Rose" which, in 1962, attained the #2 spot on the Billboard charts. The following spring, Nat released the happy hit, "Those Lazy-Hazy-Crazy Days of Summer" and, in 1964, made his final appearances on the charts with less than super hits like "I Don't Want to Hurt Anymore" and "I Don't Want to See Tomorrow."

The Golden Globe– and Grammy Award–winning Nat King Cole married twice: Nadine Robinson, from 1937 to 1948; and Maria Cole, from 1948 to his demise from lung cancer on February 15, 1965. His music, brought to the mainstream via his iconic television show, became his legacy. "I'm not playing for other musicians. We're trying to reach the guy who works all day and wants to spend a buck at night."

With his massive heart and talent, Nat King Cole touched many more lives than that.

4

Danny Thomas
Make Room for Daddy/The Danny Thomas Show/
Make Room for Granddaddy/The Practice

Success has nothing to do with what you gain in life or accomplish for yourself.
It's what you do for others.

—Danny Thomas

Upon viewing any episode of *Make Room for Daddy*, which eventually transmuted into *The Danny Thomas Show*, it becomes abundantly clear that its star was charm personified—a characteristic he perfected after years of performing live in nightclubs around the country.

Entertainment historian Rob Ray explains:

Is there such a thing as a nightclub entertainer anymore? Danny Thomas wasn't unique, but he was one of the best. Most nightclub entertainers worked smoke-filled rooms telling off-color jokes between the lounge-songs [as did Redd Foxx]. But Danny was family-friendly in venues where that was unusual. He told jokes, recounted amusing anecdotes and it all led into the inevitable song. With his stand-up material, he had the family appeal of Bill Cosby, but he could also deliver a song like a Perry Como with the self-deprecation of Jimmy Durante when it came to his prominent proboscis. When he made the occasional film [*The Jazz Singer* remake of 1952], he proved that he was also a capable dramatic actor. This versatility with its emphasis toward home and family made him a natural for the young, growing medium of television.

Here was the key to his success: He was very loud, but never vulgar and then, on a dime, could turn impossibly sentimental. That old-fashioned sentimentality was of the kind that went out with Jolson. And then puncture that sentimentality at just the moment before it got too thick with a zinger that told you he was in charge at all times.

All of this made him perfect for television because he was family-friendly and had a sentimentality that attracted the family audience, which was the television audience and demographic the networks wanted. But his loud brashness kept the sentimentality in check.

Like Jimmy Durante, a characteristically similar-in-look friend and fellow song, dance, and act man, Danny's larger-than-average nose helped to break the unrealistic, "perfect-looking" Hollywood mold, and he became one of TV's top lyrical everymen. A jack of all trades indeed, Thomas (who passed away in 1991) did it all. As with Dick Van Dyke, yet another notable colleague (along with Carl Reiner and Sheldon Leonard, all with whom Danny produced *The Dick Van Dyke Show*), Thomas performed on stage, in feature films, and on television, where he became the star of his

Globe Photos

lengthy legendary sitcom (which was produced and directed by Leonard). His lifelong charitable leadership of St. Jude's Children's Hospital, which has catered to and remains to care for millions of youths stricken with disease, has forever sealed the very integrity that to this day signifies Danny's humanity.

As he once observed, "All of us are born for a reason, but all of us don't discover why." His original fans were delighted that he arrived on the scene, while new generations continue to enjoy his work via TV reruns, DVD releases, and online streaming. Countless more ill children have continued to be blessed with the assistance of St. Jude's, which today is overseen by his children, Terre, Tony, and Marlo Thomas (of *That Girl* fame, and profiled in *Glamour, Gidgets, and the Girl Next Door*), who he brought into the world with Rose Marie Cassaniti, who he married in 1936.

According to Wikipedia, Thomas was born Amos Muzyad Yakhoob Kairouz on January 6, 1912, in Deerfield, Michigan, to Charles Yakhoob Kairouz and his wife Margaret Taouk, Maronite Catholic immigrants from Lebanon. They raised Danny (and his eight siblings!) in Toledo, Ohio, where he attended St. Francis de Sales Church, Woodward High School, and the University of Toledo. Thomas was confirmed by the Catholic bishop of Toledo, Samuel Stritch, a native of Tennessee and his lifelong spiritual adviser, who later suggested that St. Jude's Hospital be relocated to Memphis.

Decades before, in 1932, Thomas began performing in Detroit on WMBC radio on *The Happy Hour Club*, making his debut under his Anglicized birth name, "Amos Jacobs Kairouz." As noted on www.stjude.org, Danny and his wife Marie later relocated to Detroit and awaited the birth of their first child. He attended Mass at a local church, was inspired to donate his last seven dollars, and then prayed for a way to cover medical expenses. The next day, he was offered a small part that paid ten times the amount he donated and, in the process, he experienced the power of prayer.

Two years later, Danny had attained moderate success as an actor, but still struggled. In 1940, he moved his wife and young child to Chicago and secretly returned to working clubs where the salary was more lucrative. Once more, he turned to the church and this time petitioned specifically to St. Jude Thaddeus, the patron saint of hopeless causes. "Help me find my way in life," he prayed, "and I will build you a shrine."

He combined the names of his two brothers and created the pseudonym "Danny Thomas," and his career soared—with appearances in clubs around the country, motion pictures, and then ultimately television. He kept his pledge to St. Jude and reached out to his fellow Americans of Arabic-speaking heritage. Believing deeply in his cause, Danny felt the support of St. Jude would be a noble way to honor his forefathers who immigrated to America.

His prayer struck a responsive chord. In 1957 one hundred representatives of the Arab-American community met in Chicago to form the American Lebanese Syrian Associated Charities (or ALSAC) with the sole purpose of raising funds to support St. Jude Children's Research Hospital. Since then, with national headquarters in Memphis and regional offices throughout the United States, the ALSAC has assumed full responsibility for all the hospital's fundraising efforts, raising hundreds of millions of dollars annually through benefits and solicitation drives among Americans of all ethnic, religious, and racial backgrounds. Today, it's the nation's second largest healthcare charity and is supported by the efforts of more than one million volunteers.

Thomas not only became a massive star of his own hit sitcom, first titled *Make Room for Daddy*, and then later changed to *The Danny Thomas Show*, but he served as co-producer with Sheldon Leonard (and others) on hit series like *The Real McCoys*, *The Joey Bishop Show*, and *The Dick Van Dyke Show*, the latter on which he also made a cameo appearance for a fantasy-based episode in which Van Dyke's character, Rob Petrie, encountered Thomas—playing a heightened version of himself—in a dream sequence.

David Van Deusen, editor of the *Walnut Times*, the Official Dick Van Dyke Show Newsletter, explains:

Danny Thomas was clearly an entertainment icon as it related to show business and bringing quality product to the early years of television. His cameo role as Kolak in the "It May Look Like a Walnut" installment of *The Dick Van Dyke Show* was unlike any other he had portrayed, and this appearance put his individual "thumbprint" of approval on this sci-fi and fan loved episode. Whether tossing a contaminated walnut or identifying a spot on Rob's necktie with his 20/20/20/20 vision, Danny's resounding production and financial support of the DVD show from the outset was an integral key to the show's success and longevity during the five year run—not to mention the fact that the show has continued to endure and hold up for the past 50 years!

Writer Marty Nadler, who worked for Garry Marshall, a colleague to both Danny and Dick, recalls working with Thomas on *Happy Days*, one of Marshall's many hit TV shows:

When growing up, I watched a lot of television. Milton Berle, Jerry Lewis—and Danny Thomas on *Make Room For Daddy*. And at the age of 8, I decided I wanted to be in this business—and especially comedy. And one of the greatest thrills for me, was years later, I was on the Paramount lot, on the sound stage, giving Danny Thomas notes on an episode of *Happy Days* when he played Richie Cunningham's grandfather.

While Thomas would later regroup his *Room* costars (Marjorie Lord, Rusty Hamer, Angela Cartwright, and others) for an ABC update of the series called *Make Room for Granddaddy*, writer Arnie Kogen remembers working with Danny on an episode of NBC's successful 1988–1995 sitcom *Empty Nest*, titled, "The Mentor." *Nest* starred Richard Mulligan (previously of ABC's 70s hit *Soap*) as Dr. Harry Weston, a Miami pediatrician. The series was a spin-off of NBC's first big Florida-based popular comedy, *The Golden Girls* (1985–1992). Both *Nest* and *Golden* were co-produced by Tony Thomas (via Witt-Thomas-Harris Productions), Danny's son, as was Danny's last TV show: the short-lived 1976-1977 half-hour comedy, *The Practice* (also on NBC with a medical premise—and in which Thomas played a doctor).

Kogen notes Danny's performance on "The Mentor," in particular, as it turned out to be a benchmark in the actor's life and career—for several reasons:

> Harry (Richard Mulligan) has an idol and mentor who he reveres and respects. That veteran doctor is played by Danny Thomas. Turns out the doctor is "losing it." He's older now and can't perform the way he used to. Harry is torn about confronting his idol and telling him. This was Danny Thomas' last appearance on television. He was nominated for an Emmy for this episode.

5

Dick Van Dyke
The Dick Van Dyke Show/The New Dick Van Dyke Show/Van Dyke & Company

I've retired so many times now it's getting to be a habit.

—Dick Van Dyke

According to author and pop-culture historian Rick Lertzman, Dick Van Dyke is a performer "who can do it all . . . sing, dance and is a master of pantomime," one who has "remained a television icon for nearly 60 years."

Lertzman says Van Dyke got his start on television as the host of *The CBS Morning News* from 1955 to 1956, when "Walter Cronkite was his news-person." He then became a Broadway star in the original 1960-1961 stage production of *Bye Bye Birdie* opposite Chita Rivera, where he was directed by Gower Champion, who taught him how to dance. His television work with producer Carl Reiner produced the classic *Dick Van Dyke Show* (CBS, 1961–1966). In casting Dick as TV writer Rob Petrie, Lertzman says, "Reiner provided Van Dyke the showcase to display his diverse and unique talents, alongside his costar—Mary Tyler Moore."

Reiner had planned to play Rob, but producer Sheldon Leonard insisted on recasting. According to Lertzman, Reiner saw Van Dyke on Broadway in *Bye Bye Birdie* and "knew he'd struck gold." *The Dick Van Dyke Show* went on to receive four Emmy Awards for Outstanding Comedy Series, and Van Dyke himself received three for Outstanding Lead Actor in a Comedy Series. After the *Van Dyke Show* ended its successful run, Lertzman adds Dick "spent nearly fifty years dazzling his fans with his versatility" in other creative venues. Some of those include: the 1963 feature film

Globe Photos

adaptation of *Bye Bye Birdie*, followed by the motion pictures *Mary Poppins* (1964), *Chitty Chitty Bang Bang* (1968), and *The Comic* (1969, directed by Carl Reiner); countless TV appearances, such as the groundbreaking 1969 CBS special *Dick Van Dyke and the Other Woman* (costarring Mary Tyler Moore, who was subsequently cast in her own legendary CBS sitcom), *The New Dick Van Dyke Show* (CBS, 1971–1974), the final season on *The Carol Burnett Show* (CBS, 1976-1977), and the long-running medical dramedy, *Diagnosis: Murder* (CBS, 1993–2001), among so many more prolific performances. Lertzman concluded, "Dick Van Dyke remains one of our treasured legends."

David Van Deusen, editor of the *Walnut Times*, agrees, describing Van Dyke as "affable . . . genuine . . . classy . . . legendary. Dick's long tenured career now spans three generations as he continues to act, sing, and dance his way into our hearts—all while still exhibiting that contagious smile and twinkle in his eye. Amazingly limber with the joints certainly made of rubber, Dick's physical prowess is only overshadowed by his charming persona. Dick is not only remarkably talented, but an all-around nice guy. And that's really why we all love him."

Regarding the actor's performance on the *Van Dyke Show*, Van Deusen says: "Rob Petrie was the essence of Dick Van Dyke—thanks in no small part to the writing genius of Carl Reiner," creator, costar, and original lead as Rob Petrie in an initial pilot for the series that did not sell. "Carl allowed Dick to simply portray himself. In Dick's two roles as work colleague and dad, we could all relate easily and comfortably with Rob Petrie. Rob (Dick) and his family and friends would always be welcome in our homes."

"Who wouldn't love to spend an evening with Laura and Buddy and Sally?" Van Deusen adds in referring to Rob's wife and co-working friends on the *Van Dyke Show* (as played by Mary Tyler Moore, Morey Amsterdam, and Rose Marie, respectively).

Larry Matthews, who played little Richie Petrie on *The Dick Van Dyke Show*, explains the appeal of the show's star and his TV dad:

> Dick is a very unassuming person. He's very humble . . . he's kind . . . very appreciative, thankful and mindful of his life experiences. And when you roll all of those things into one, it's going to add up into the amazing and talented human being that he is. He's just simply one of the purest talents ever. He would do stuff on the show that no one could do. In fact, Carl Reiner used to challenge him to do six different things in one scene, like belch, laugh, sneeze, etc. . .all at the same time, and Dick just did it.

Van Dyke's multiple talents, rubbery physicality, and affable personality—on screen and off—was the glue that held together not only his iconic sitcom, but his entire career and life.

Born Richard Wayne Van Dyke on December 13, 1925, in West Plains, Missouri, Dick attended Danville High School, in Danville, Illinois, where he was a member of the drama club. His parents were Loren and Hazel Van Dyke, who later gave birth to Dick's younger brother, Jerry, also an actor. In 1948 Dick married Margie Willett, who was less than thrilled with show business, but who loved her husband dearly. Before their divorce, they had four children: Christian, Barry, Stacy, and Carrie Beth. Subsequently Van Dyke lived with Michelle Triola until her death in 2009, but they never married, and in 2012 he married Arlene Silver.

After the original *Dick Van Dyke Show* folded on CBS in 1966, the actor returned to the network in 1971 with another sitcom called *The New Dick Van Dyke Show*, this time playing Dick Preston, opposite Hope Lange as his wife. This series, like the original Van Dyke program, was created by Reiner, and aired on CBS (originally paired with *The Mary Tyler Moore Show* on Saturday nights). Although a hit with the viewers, the series ended after only three seasons, due to creative differences and a censorship spat between Reiner and the network (about the utterance and/or inclusion of the topic and/or mention of pregnancy by Van Dyke's on-screen daughter, as played by Angela Powell). Reiner then chose to leave the series, and Dick decided he didn't want to continue without him, and declined to sign a new contract.

A few years following, Van Dyke resurfaced on the small screen with the award-winning, if short-lived *Van Dyke and Company* variety show (NBC, 1976), and *The Van Dyke Show* (CBS, 1988), a sitcom in which he costarred with his son, Barry Van Dyke (years before they would re-pair on *Diagnosis: Murder*).

The multitalented performer then appeared on *The Carol Burnett Show*, ultimately replacing Harvey Korman, who finally left the series in its eleventh year to do his own ABC show, after years of threatening to quit. Consequently, Carol needed a solid second banana and, because she had just performed with Van Dyke in a live stage production, he agreed to do her show only if his position would be substantial. Frustrated from a creative standpoint, and because of his long commute from Arizona (where he was by then living, and from where he had filmed *The New Dick Van Dyke Show* and *Van Dyke & Company*), Van Dyke left the Burnett series after Thanksgiving of 1977.

However, Dick Van Dyke was never derailed. At the age of sixteen, he was a radio announcer at a Danville radio station. His first network TV appearance was with Dennis James on James's *Chance of a Lifetime* in 1954. He won a Tony award for *Bye Bye Birdie* and it launched him to stardom. In 1963, he was cast in the movie based on the play. Van Dyke won acclaim for his role as Bert the Chimney Sweep in the film *Mary Poppins* (1964), even though the Cockney accent he used was not as well received. In Britain, a "Dick Van Dyke accent" is an accepted slang term for an American's unsuccessful attempt to speak with a British accent. However, this fact hasn't hurt Van Dyke's popularity in England.

Dick battled alcoholism during the run of his iconic original TV show, delivered a groundbreaking performance as an alcoholic in the 1974 TV-movie *The Morning After*, and years later went public with his real-life drinking problem to give hope to others. "At the time," he said, ". . . there was such a strange perception about alcoholism that people had serious character flaws . . . They had weak wills or something. They had this image of . . . a guy laying in on the street and skid row, whereas it can happen to any normal, average middle-class guy."

In 2004, Rob Petrie, Van Dyke's character on *The Dick Van Dyke Show*, ranked #22 in *TV Guide*'s list of the "50 Greatest TV Dads of All Time." Van Dyke received the Screen Actors Guild's Life Achievement Award on January 27, 2013.

He once said, "I never wanted to be an actor and to this day I don't. I can't get a handle on it. An actor wants to become someone else. I am a song-and-dance man and I enjoy being myself, which is all I can do." As to his famous "trip" over the ottoman in the opening credits of *The Dick Van Dyke Show*, he said, "I didn't realize how many different kinds of falls I did in that show. At this banquet recently, they showed a little clip of all my falls. I said, *No wonder there's arthritis in my spine*."

While his humorous take on his very serious pain is admirable, his astounding talent has been nothing but a gain for anyone who has been fortunate enough to view his grace on stage, film, or television—all performances that he made sure would be family-oriented.

"When I started having kids," he decided, "I don't want to do anything they can't watch."

Writer Fred Freeman worked in the Golden Age of Television—with countless performers of every age, style, and talent range. For Freeman and his writing colleagues, the word "likable" was a term network executives would frequently utilize in their quest to find the ideal television performer, male or female. As he observes, "[The TV actor] has to be someone the audience wants into their living room. It has to be someone who either amuses them, or they're fascinated by."

Dick Van Dyke certainly fit that description.

"He's fabulous," Freeman said. "He's one of those people who have that personality that everybody loves . . . He wonders why the whole fuss was about his talent. When he did the original *Van Dyke Show*, he was confused by it. He wondered why they hired him. He didn't know how good he was."

6

Johnny Carson
The Tonight Show Starring Johnny Carson

If it weren't for Philo T. Farnsworth, inventor of television, we'd still be eating frozen radio dinners.

—Johnny Carson

Steve Allen, Jack Paar, Merv Griffin, Mike Douglas, David Frost, Dick Cavett, Phil Donahue, David Susskind, Joey Bishop, Regis Philbin, Phil Donahue. These are the talk show princes of television. But there was and remains only one king in the history of the genre: Johnny Carson, who virtually returned to his loyal viewing subjects on January 1, 2016, when Antenna TV began airing select episodes of *The Tonight Show Starring Johnny Carson*.

Johnny's historic edition of *The Tonight Show* (which was formerly hosted by Allen and Paar), originally aired on NBC between October 1, 1962, and Carson's retirement on May 22, 1992. It and was initially broadcast from New York before he relocated to Burbank in 1972.

In the realm of talk show hosts, male or female, late-night, daytime, or otherwise, Carson stood out from the pack. Following a four-year stint as the initial host of the game show *Who Do You Trust?* (ABC, 1957–1963; Woody Woodbury took over when Johnny left in 1962), Carson went on to commandeer *The Tonight Show* with his trademark sense of style, sophistication, and humor like no other before or since. The pencil-flipping, the Johnny Carson coffee mugs, and the Johnny Carson mugging, the double-takes into the camera; all of it and more became the stuff of legends, particularly, the respect he had for his guests.

Each show opened with the rousing musical rendition of the *Tonight* theme (composed by Paul Anka and performed by Doc Severinson and the NBC Orchestra), followed by the equally famous "Here's Johnny" introduction by Ed McMahon (Carson's right-hand man, loyal friend, and former co-host of *Who Do You Trust?*). With shoulders back, a stoic stance, bravado, and confidence extraordinaire, the talk-fest icon then took over with his one-of-a-kind monologue ("Attention: K-Mart shoppers!"), then periodically appeared in legendary skits featuring character creations including (but not limited to): Art Fern (the "Tea Time" movie announcer), Carnac the Magnificent (the flippant psychic who answered questions before they were asked), and Aunt Blabby (a crusty female senior), each of whom interacted with or played off McMahon.

Globe Photos

After that, it was all about the guests, be they celebrities, comedians, everyday folks, or animals, the latter of which were gathered from the San Diego Zoo (for what became some of the most popular segments in *Tonight Show* history).

A key component of Carson's appeal as a host—to his guests, the studio audience, and the viewers at home—was his charming ability to make all feel welcome. He consistently displayed a measure of decorum and veneration for all parties concerned (even during jovial trademark skits like "Stump the Band" with the studio audience, McMahon, and Severinson and his elite musical ensemble).

Johnny never verbally abused, attacked, or insulted anyone for a laugh, nor attempted to detract from or top his guest's general humor, anecdote, or specific joke. He presented satirical interpretations of musical guests and their most popular songs (such as Willie Nelson's "To All the Girls I Loved Before"), but refrained from joining them on stage for a song or dance refrain. Instead, he was determined to deflect the spotlight, granting his guests their moment to shine, whether they were fellow icons like Bob Hope or an aspiring young comedian on national television for the first time. He was particularly encouraging to new comics just starting out or who he deemed particularly talented.Carson joked and laughed with his guests but, as the old adage goes, never at them. He was a true master of ceremonies in every sense of the term.

Fritz Coleman, comedian, and LA's iconic TV weatherman from KNBC Channel 4 (which taped in the famous NBC Burbank Studios that also housed Carson's *Tonight Show* and later *The Tonight Show with Jay Leno*), was a frequent guest on Johnny's show. As he recalls, "Everything about Johnny was as smooth as expensive scotch . . . his smile . . . his baritone timbre . . . Nebraska twinkle . . . his lightning speed reacting to a guest or a moment. When I was a teenager . . . I realized that being that fast and funny did two things: It made people like you. It gave you power over a group. Very intoxicating.

"I think Johnny was the best audience a comedian could have," Coleman continues. "The greats of all eras would agree. Buddy Hackett. Jerry Seinfeld. Don Rickles. Shecky Greene. Even . . . the late Sam Kinison. As out there as Sam was . . . he convulsed Johnny a few times. His ability to be a great audience came from his ability as a great comedian. He sensed the moments. He freely admitted that he learned from Jack Benny. If he laughs . . . the audience laughs . . . and . . . if the audience laughs . . . he looks good."

Coleman, in fact, has several fond memories of working with Carson and company, one of which transpired in the pre-high-tech-mobile-devices-80s, while walking with a home video recorder down the *Tonight* studio hallway. At one point, Coleman approached Severinson and asked if he would wish his parents "Happy 50th Anniversary" into his video camera. Without skipping a beat, the band-leader replied, "Bring your camera to rehearsal at 2 o'clock!"

Coleman did so and, as he recalls, "The entire *Tonight Show Orchestra* played 'Happy Anniversary Dorothy and Fred'"—a magical occurrence that transpired only with Johnny's approval, further confirming his classy grace and dignity.

Years later, during Carson's final week on the air, Coleman again "wandered down" to the *Tonight Show* studio to coordinate a "chance run-in" with Johnny before his final sign-off. Fritz walked up the stairway to Johnny's makeup room, just as the talk-show icon was descending. At that moment, Coleman "just blurted out the truth of my whole comic existence," speaking words to the late-night royalty that went something like this: "Johnny! I wanted to be on television because of you. You've been a hero. Being a guest on your show was the greatest experience of my life. Thank you!"

According to Coleman, Carson was extremely shy about chance encounters, "pathologically shy," he muses, "with weathermen who had wandered into a restricted area of the building."

While Carson did not slow down that day in passing the now-veteran comedian and then-novice TV personality, he did reply with a cordial, if simple "Thanks, Fritz!" and continued walking.

That was Carson, affable—but elusive.

His was not a perfect life. Born October 23, 1925, in Corning, Iowa, to Homer Lloyd "Kit" Carson, a power company manager, and Ruth (Hook) Carson, of Irish descent, Johnny and his younger brother (Dick Carson, a TV director who later helmed *The Merv Griffin Show* and game shows like *Wheel of Fortune*) were raised close by in Avoca, Clarinda, and Red Oak in southwest Iowa before the family relocated to Norfolk, Nebraska, when he was just eight years old. It was there and then the seeds of his penchant for entertaining (and much "alter" performing as Carnac the Magician) were planted. When he was twelve, he discovered a book about magic at a friend's house and immediately purchased a mail-order magician's kit. Afterwards, little Johnny honed his performance skills and card tricks on family.

Years later, he became a family man himself, marrying several times (Jody Wolcott, 1949 to 1963; Joanne Copeland, 1963 to 1972; Joanna Holland, 1972 to 1985; and Alexis Maas, from 1987 until his death from emphysema at age 80 on January 23, 2005). He lost his son Richard (one of three, including Cory and Kitt) in a tragic car accident in 1991.

While Johnny received countless awards for his contributions to the entertainment industry (including six Emmys, the Governor's Award, a Peabody [1985], the People's Choice for Favorite Talk Show Host, the Presidential Medal of Freedom [1992], and a Kennedy Center Honor [1993]), his career was not without its bumps in the road. His bond with Monday-night guest host Joan Rivers was broken after she left to do her own late-night show for Fox, and his friend and colleague David Letterman was displeased when Leno won the *Tonight* gig after Carson's exit. But he made millions of dollars, lived a full life, had a genius mind for diverse business branding (owning and operating a successful eponymous clothing line), and made millions of people happy during his long television career.

From near or far, he always found time to be respectful, even as one of the busiest and most popular TV stars of his generation. With his recent return to late-night television, make that "several generations."

Echoing the sentiment of countless other Johnny Carson fans across the nation and around the world, Fritz Coleman concludes, "I'm beyond happy that the old episodes are back on. It's beyond nostalgia. It's keeping the memory of the master alive."

7

Rod Serling
The Twilight Zone/Night Gallery

Next stop — *The Twilight Zone*.

— Rod Serling

Submitted for your approval, Exhibit A: Rod Serling.

From the beginning, the popularity of *The Twilight Zone* (CBS, 1959–1964), Rod Serling's most prized creative property, and *Night Gallery* (NBC, 1969–1973, its more horror-geared and relatively less optimistic cousin), depended upon his endless reservoir of ideas, originally inspired by his obsession with the past and his preoccupation with aging, mixed in with a measure of courage and faith and a few survival techniques he learned in the army (which served him well during various creative battles with network executives regarding the artistic vision for *Zone*). One word emerges when most think of Serling: passion. As one of the most literate and talented men to work in television, he possessed a compelling drive for the written word, for the ideals he held dear, and for humanity in general. He found himself working in an industry where his kind of ardor could be and many times was perceived as trouble-making — on screen and off. He had things to say, comments to make about the Human Condition and the Condition of the World as it existed in the mid–twentieth century. Iconic television anthology series such as *Kraft Television Theater*, *Playhouse 90*, and the *Hallmark Hall of Fame* were also his kind of programming.

Joel Eisenberg is also a lifelong fan of Rod Serling, whom he calls "a hero and personal inspiration."

Eisenberg discovered Serling and *The Twilight Zone*, though, by way of his favorite film as a youngster: *Planet of the Apes*, for which Serling penned the screenplay. Eisenberg discovered the *Zone* by reading an *Apes* Marvel magazine that mentioned Serling's most famous TV series. "I watched and, like so many, was hooked," Eisenberg says. "Firstly, as to the man himself: What grace, what stature! What poise and intelligence when he hosted the show! And then *Night Gallery* and I had the same thoughts. And the scripts he wrote," including Eisenberg's "all-time favorite anything for television," the original *Playhouse 90* TV adaptation of *Requiem for a Heavyweight*, starring Jack Palance as an emotionally, physically, and psychologically impaired boxer—which was followed by the 1962 feature film version starring Anthony Quinn. Both productions, Eisenberg intones, "make me cry to this day. I'm a writer in part because of Rod Serling. He was a man who never compromised his art and that, I believe, only made him that much more impactful. An amazing man, and an amazing writer. We lost him far too early."

Serling was born Rodman Edward Serling on December 25, 1924, to a Jewish family in Syracuse, New York. When he was two years old, his family moved to the quiet college town of Binghamton, New York, where his father, Sam, opened a grocery store. Following graduation from Binghamton High School, Serling enlisted in the army during World War II, intending to battle the Nazis in Europe. But instead, he became a paratrooper in the Pacific Theater. Serling injured his knee and wrist at the Battle of Leyte in the Philippines and was released from service with a Purple Heart and emotional scars that, according to www.biography.com, "would haunt him for the rest of his days."

Serling's emotional return from the war was complicated by the traumatic loss of his father, who died suddenly of a heart attack. Such experiences would later prove influential for his life and work, while the seeds of his literary career were also planted during his time at Antioch College in Ohio.

From 1951 to 1955, Serling composed over seventy teleplays, including "Patterns," which aired January 12, 1955, on *Kraft Television Theatre*. The story was about a power struggle between a ruthless president of a major organization, an aging vice-president who's pressured into resigning, and a new young executive brought in to replace him. As time would tell, this story may have eerily foreshadowed the frequent producer changes that took place behind the scenes on *The Twilight Zone*. For the moment, Serling followed the success of "Patterns" with scripts for more of TV's most respected anthology shows, such as *Desilu Playhouse*, which ultimately produced what became his script for "The Time Element."

Serling had originally penned "Element" as a time-travel story for a show called *The Storm* back in 1951. But six years later, he expanded the story to sixty minutes and submitted it to CBS where it caught the eye of Bert Granet, producer of the *Desilu Playhouse*. "Element" finally aired on November 24, 1958, and became a massive hit. Thanks to its popularity and positive reviews by the critics, it became clear to CBS—and others—that Serling was a genius. The *New York Times* review, by Jack Gould, was especially complimentary: "Rod Serling is one of the pioneer television writers who still stays in the medium even though he is as articulate as video's expatriates about TV's limitations."

PhotoFest

He developed and sold CBS on the idea of *The Twilight Zone*, which the network purchased and aired from 1959 to 1964. Although Serling was not nearly as pleased or creatively involved with his second hit anthology series, *Night Gallery* (NBC, 1969–1973), to some extent he used both programs to camouflage and transform his creative intensity into the marketable concept of science fiction and fantasy. He fought the tough fight for what he believed was right and achieved far more wins than losses in the process.

With monumental tenacity, Serling on a daily basis sought and gained reign over his creation, all the while delivering top-notch scripts at a frenetic pace. With a strong desire to succeed, and an intense need for creative control, Serling became a foreboding presence and a critically acclaimed talent despite his small stature (he was only 5'5"). He took a no-holds-barred approach to getting his product on the air and settled for nothing less than optimum product along the way. He protected his turf, circumvented the well-charted waters of TV production, and opposed the demands of network executives, with a back-door approach to realizing the fruition of his "other-worldly" dreams. Serling believed in his vision and rarely kowtowed to editorial invasion, fiercely guarding the end results of his *Zone*.

His *Twilight Zone* showcased weekly excursions into an unknown, yet familiar territory featuring multidimensional characters who were introduced with arresting aplomb, many granted a second chance against the odds—much like Serling himself. Although almost cancelled twice before its original network demise, *The Twilight Zone* stayed afloat due to Serling's tactful maneuvers around Hollywood minds that were uncertain of anything—and everything—related to his *Zone*—except his undying passion for the series.

According to Ann Hodges, "Rod Serling was brilliant, and his mind worked in a strange, kind of macabre way that only he could come up with all these wonderful thrillers [*Twilight Zone* episodes] that always ended with twists." So much so, that the audience would never know how the story would conclude. "He had a special talent for surprise endings," says Hodges, "and I don't think there's been anyone since who's had that special knack . . . "

While Serling was the creative genius behind the camera of *The Twilight Zone*, as well as *Night Gallery*, he also hosted both programs. His overtly thick eyebrows and somewhat slight stature certainly wouldn't classify him as handsome in the traditional sense, but his intense bravado, stellar mind and talent, and uniquely stilted vocal tones enhanced his appeal, and contributed to his camera-ready appearance. As Hodges sees it, Serling's on-screen persona on *Zone* and *Gallery* allowed for a certain "authenticity" that granted the viewers accessibility to the fanciful stories that were being told. In the process, both programs became more than just sci-fi/fantasy shows, not just because of Serling's genius mind, but due to his welcoming presence as on-screen host.

"You really liked the characters he presented [and many times created] on his shows," Hodges explains. "You wanted them to succeed . . . to reach their objectives, whatever they may have been. You became interested in their lives, cared about who they were and the differences between them" because of Serling's visible introductions and equally fascinating epilogues.

Hodges concludes, "He made those characters real."

In the end Serling proved to be a mere mortal like the rest of us, leaving this world too young, at only fifty years old, never reaching the twilight of *his* years, though not before he explored the senior mentality in episodes of his shows.

As Serling once said, each episode was to be "complete in itself." The series was not, he clarified, "an assembly line operation. Each show is a carefully conceived and wrought piece of drama, cast with competent people, directed by creative, quality-conscious guys and shot with an eye toward mood and reality."

Zone ended production in January 1964 and was cancelled. CBS president Jim Aubrey claimed he was tired of the show and had been tired of it since the end of the second season. *Twilight Zone* was not what it used to be—and Serling was unhappy with it for quite some time. So he agreed to close up shop.

After *The Twilight Zone* folded, Serling continued writing screenplays such as *Planet of the Apes*, released theatrically in 1968. He returned to Antioch College, as a professor, and rallied against the Vietnam War.

He died in Rochester, New York, on June 28, 1975, from complications from bypass surgery. He left behind his wife, Anne, daughters Ann and Jodi—and a treasure trove of densely inspirational and influential TV episodes, the full depth of which may never be fully measured.

8

Gene Roddenberry
Star Trek

It is the struggle itself that is most important. We must strive to be more than we are. It does not matter that we will not reach our ultimate goal. The effort itself yields its own reward.

—Gene Roddenberry

The Great Bird of the Galaxy. That's how the iconic Gene Roddenberry, who died October 4, 1991, is mostly remembered. As the creator of the original *Star Trek*, its initial TV follow-up, *Star Trek: The Next Generation*, and ultimately the subsequent and ongoing legacy of sequels and remakes for both the big and small screen, Roddenberry's uplifting and majestic vision of the future will forever live long and prosper. Roddenberry was a recipient of the Distinguished Flying Cross for his actions in the U.S. Army Air Corps in the Pacific Theater of World War II, and he would also become one of the first people to be "buried" in space. It all seemed to fit.

A genius of mind and spirit, Roddenberry created *Star Trek*, which became more than just a TV series or a multimedia franchise. The original and additional incarnations of the series have served as inspiration for countless TV viewers, moviegoers, Hollywood insiders, and humanity. As Roddenberry once said:

Star Trek was an attempt to say that humanity will reach maturity and wisdom on the day that it begins not just to tolerate, but take a special delight in differences in ideas and differences in life forms. [. . .] If we cannot learn to actually enjoy those small differences, to take a positive delight in those small differences between our own kind—here on this planet, then we do not deserve to go out into space and meet the diversity that is almost certainly out there."

Ann Hodges says Roddenberry "keyed into something that audiences were hungry for at that time": the science-fiction/fantasy genre. "They loved *Star Trek*, and they loved what he had to say with that show, and how he said it. He was smart. He knew how to present the material, and he did it in a way that was believable. He also had an eye for casting. He knew how to cast particular characters that would appeal to the mainstream audience."

Gene was born Eugene Wesley Roddenberry on August 19, 1921, in El Paso, Texas, and raised in Los Angeles, California. He joined the Army Air Corps after studying law enforcement at Los Angeles City College and flew eighty-nine missions during World War II, earning the Distinguished Flying Cross and the Air Medal. While stationed in the South Pacific, he contributed stories and poetry to publications. After the war, Roddenberry took a job as a commercial pilot for Pan American World Airlines before moving back to Los Angeles to pursue a career as a television writer.

Roddenberry had worked as a Los Angeles Police Department spokesman and as a speechwriter for Chief William H. Parker in the early 1950s as he attempted to gain a foothold in the entertainment industry. Fortunately, the LAPD regularly consulted for fellow male-icon Jack Webb's police series *Dragnet,* giving Roddenberry the chance to develop his writing style. His first TV credit was for a segment of *Mr. District Attorney*, followed by episodes of *West Point*, *Naked City*, and *Have Gun, Will Travel*, for which he won his first Emmy Award.

In the mid-60s, Roddenberry began to develop a sci-fi series that he pitched as *Wagon Train* set in space. His original unaired pilot for this series, "The

PhotoFest

Cage" (starring Jeffrey "*King of Kings*" Hunter as a pre–William Shatner captain) was rejected by NBC as "too cerebral," but he took a second shot at the concept in the fall of 1966 with the first aired episode of *Star Trek*, titled, "Where No Man Has Gone." Hunter was replaced with Shatner, and Leonard Nimoy, who played Mr. Spock in "The Cage," returned for "Gone."

The series aired only seventy-nine episodes over three seasons on NBC, before becoming nothing less than a sensation in syndication—and on to the mammoth expansion in all media that it has turned into. After this initial *Trek* was cancelled in 1969, Roddenberry stuck with the science-fiction theme as a writer and producer for TV-movie/pilots like *Genesis II* (1973), *Planet Earth* (1974), and *The Questor Tapes* (1974). Meanwhile, *Star Trek* was enjoying a surge in popularity thanks to syndicated reruns and an animated version, and in 1975 Roddenberry was tapped to revive the franchise under the name *Star Trek: Phase II*. Executives elected to rush a feature-length film into production, and in 1979, the special effects–laden *Star Trek: The Motion Picture* opened to mixed reviews. Five sequels with the original cast followed, though Roddenberry had limited involvement after the first film as an "executive consultant."

Renowned writer Larry Brody worked for Roddenberry on the animated *Star Trek* series, original episodes of which NBC aired from 1973 to 1975 (ultimately completing the historic "five-year mission" of the Enterprise that commenced on the original live-action series, where it was aborted after only three years). Says Brody:

> Gene was amazing. Huge energy and the biggest ego of anyone I've ever met—but it seemed completely justifiable in light of his talent and influence and totally unassuming. That is, he wasn't pretending to be better than anyone else, he *was* better at what he did than almost everyone else—and he loved being so damn good at it that you couldn't help but admire him for it.
>
> If I had to compare Gene Roddenberry to a fictional character, it would be to the Doctor on *Doctor Who*. A supreme manipulator whose goal was to solve his problems utilizing the talents of those around him—which meant that he had to help them become the absolute best *they* could be. The great thing about Gene was that even when he messed with you or screwed you over you didn't care . . . because it was so much fun watching him do it.

9

Norman Lear
All in the Family/Maude/Good Times/The Jeffersons

We gravitated to issues and shows and causes that made people care.

—Norman Lear

Norman Lear has long been regarded as one of the medium's most influential producers when it comes to trend-setting, ahead-of-its-time comedy—and here are several reasons why.

Lear's "reality-based" scripted shows (as opposed to what later came to be known as unscripted "reality shows") were some of TV's most popular and groundbreaking series, specifically throughout the 70s and early 80s, beginning with *All in the Family* and *Maude*, *Family*'s first spin-off, which begot *Good Times* and *The Jeffersons*, *Family*'s second spin-off—all on CBS—along with *One Day at a Time* and NBC's *Sanford & Son*. Each of these programs, videotaped in front of a live audience, stretched the boundaries of what would eventually transform television programming.

Before that happened, the family of characters from *All in the Family*, *Maude*, and the rest of Lear's best engaged in credible conversations covering timely, realistic topics such as prejudice, abortion, homosexuality, and divorce. If it was controversial in the 70s and early 80s, one of Lear's shows was sure to address it.

Family presented Carroll O'Connor as the bigoted Archie Bunker, and Jean Stapleton as his long-suffering, angelic, if scatterbrained wife Edith. The eclectic Sherman Hemsley was the white-man-taunting George Jefferson, who on *The Jeffersons* was paired with Louise (delightfully played by Isabel Sanford), his long-suffering,

Globe Photos

angelic, more clear-thinking wife. As former neighbors to the Bunkers in Queens, New York, George and Louise (aka "Weezie") "moved on up to the East Side" of Manhattan, where his dry-cleaning business expanded. Never one to mince words, George always had issues with Archie's ignorance, and understandably so. Once upon a better life, however, his own lack of couth became spastically evident, especially when his son Lionel (alternately played by the unrelated Michael Evans and Damon Evans, the former of whom went on to create *Good Times*) fell in love with girlfriend Jenny (Melinda Tolbert), the biracial daughter of her interracial parents (Franklin Cover and Roxie Roker, real-life mom to music genius Lenny Kravitz).

Shows like *The Jeffersons* and *Maude* not only helped us forget our troubles, but in many ways, reflected those troubles—sometimes, as writer Amanda Marcotte observed, in a manner that might be deemed objectionable today. In May 2009, shortly after the death of Bea Arthur, *Maude*'s lead, Marcotte penned the essay, "No Cop-Outs: 37 Years Ago, *Maude* Got the Abortion Experience Right," which was published on the RH Reality Check website.

"Watching 70s-era sitcoms when you're used to a steady diet of 21st century sitcoms is a disconcerting experience," Marcotte wrote. "Old-fashioned ingredients like the three-camera sound stage set-up, the laugh track, and the three extra minutes of programming (instead of commercials) distinguish the experience from watching something like *30 Rock* or *The Office*. But what really shocks is the humor. A character with a new and unwanted pregnancy might tell her husband, as he makes a drink, 'Make mine a double. I'm drinking for two now.' No matter how edgy sitcoms are supposed to be in our century, I doubt anyone would dare put that joke on-screen these days.

"Of course," she clarified, "barely anyone would dare make a joke like that back then either . . . Envelope-pushing went to another level with *Maude*," which in 1972, aired a two-part episode, titled "Maude's Dilemma," in which Arthur's leading lady of liberty opts to terminate an unintended pregnancy.

As Marcotte went on to explain, Maude lived in New York State, where abortion was legal in 1972. "You'd think that something that happens to over a million women a year would merit more than one portrayal in the thirty-seven years since Maude terminated her pregnancy, but in [the world of TV], abortion is rarer than coffee shop employees who can afford enormous Manhattan apartments."

For Joel Eisenberg, *All in the Family* "is the single greatest sitcom of all time, along with *Taxi*. My words and I'm sticking to it."

Eisenberg cried when Archie cried following the death of his beloved Edith. Although *All in the Family* was based on a U.K. sitcom, *Till Death Do Us Part*, Eisenberg says, "Lear did that show one better and scorched America with the wittiest, and most shocking, comedy ever on television. And then there was *Maude*, and *Good Times*, and *The Jeffersons*, and so on."

"So many spin-offs," says Eisenberg, who "loved them all," and their accompanying catchphrases.

"Eat your heart out, Arthur," Maude would say at least once per episode to her beleaguered husband played by Bill Macy.

"Now that we're done with the birds and the bees, let's get down to some black-eyed peas, I'm starved!" once blasted Michael Evans, the character played by the energetic Ralph Carter on *Good Times*. Evans was named after that show's co-creator, actor Michael Evans, who became Lear's colleague and friend via his role as Lionel on *All in the Family* and *The Jeffersons*. On *Times*, Carter's Michael was known as "the militant midget," a line Eisenberg then repeated around his house "for years," he says, "nearly driving my poor parents crazy. I didn't quite know why at the time, but lines in Lear sitcoms were just so memorable."

All in the Family, in particular, proved to be "such a barrier-buster" for Eisenberg. "The black Sammy Davis Jr. kissing the racist Archie Bunker for a photo, a tension-filled dinner conversation between a war veteran and the pacifist Michael Stivic . . . a rape, a transvestite, the Ku Klux Klan . . . not your average TV fare. Shocking and yet immensely poignant. And then Edith. Jean Stapleton. 'Dingbat.' How could anyone not love Edith? When she passed, we felt Archie's pain. Even now, just thinking about that moment, the eyes water. Still, all these years later. As for Carrol O'Connor's Archie? He was utterly authentic in that role, which for me remains my all-time favorite characterization in any sitcom ever."

"In the end," he says, "we have one man to thank for the plateau of 1970's television: Norman Lear. He was just that astounding a producer, a man with his finger firmly on the pulse of American sensitivities."

Norman was born to Herman Lear and Jeanette Seicol on July 27, 1922, in New Haven, Connecticut. He married three times: Charlotte Lear, Frances Lear, and his present spouse, Lyn Lear, the latter of whom he wed in 1987. His children include Madeline Lear, Benjamin Lear, Maggie Lear, Kate Lear, Brianna Lear, and Ellen Lear.

Lear summarized his life this way, on the front page of his website in promotion of his memoir, *Even This I Get to Experience* (Penguin Press, 2014):

In my ninety-plus years I've lived a multitude of lives. In the course of all these lives, I had a front-row seat at the birth of television; wrote, produced, created or developed more than a hundred shows; had nine on the air at the same time; founded the 300,000-member liberal advocacy group People for the American Way; was labeled the "No. 1 enemy of the American family" by Jerry Falwell; made it onto Richard Nixon's "Enemies List"; was presented with the National Medal of the Arts by President Clinton; purchased an original copy of the Declaration of Independence and toured it for ten years in all fifty states; blew a fortune in a series of bad investments in failing businesses; and reached a point where I was informed we might even have to sell our home. Having heard that we'd fallen into such dire straits, my son-in-law phoned me and asked how I was feeling. My answer was, "Terrible, of course," but then I added, "but I must be crazy, because despite all that's happened, I keep hearing this inner voice saying, 'Even *this* I get to experience.'"

10

Sonny Bono
The Sonny & Cher Comedy Hour/The Sonny Comedy Hour

Don't cling to fame. You're just borrowing it. It's like money. You're going to die, and somebody else is going to get it.

—Sonny Bono

Sonny Bono is a not-so-obvious selection to include in a discussion of valued male prototypes of television. But nonetheless he is included here because his talents, though relatively "hidden" to the mainstream viewer, were nonetheless massive, diverse, and significant—beyond television.

With then-wife Cher, Bono hosted the very popular *Sonny & Cher Comedy Hour* on CBS from 1971 to 1974. After both their marriage and their show ended, nearly simultaneously, each partner returned the following year to host their own variety show: Cher came back to CBS, and Sonny resurfaced on ABC. While Cher continued to glitter with elegance on *Cher*, Bono failed to find his singular niche with *The Sonny Comedy Hour*.

However, Bono was no bozo in real life. His on-stage buffoonery alongside "straight-man" wife Cher carried their original show with a kind of combination of Martin and Lewis synergy; and before that, he managed their recording career with the right amount of zeal and business acumen. But it was on the small screen where Bono blanketed his quiet genius and guidance by playing the clown prince to his then–TV queen wife. He proved to be the brains and savvy behind the personal and professional marriage surrounding and including their original show, much the same way Desi

Globe Photos

Arnaz coordinated the success of his *I Love Lucy* sitcom with his legendary spouse Lucille Ball.

As Bono once said, "People underestimate me, but I've always been a stretch runner." And, "I'm a maverick. I've always been a maverick."

Born Salvatore Phillip Bono on February 16, 1935, in Detroit, Michigan, the sincerely modest personality was educated at Inglewood High School in California (but did not graduate). His parents were Santo Bono and Zena "Jean" La Valle. Before Cher, he was married to Donna Rankin (from 1954 to 1962), and post-Cher, his wives were Susie Coelho (1981–1984), and Mary Whitaker (1986–1998). His children include Christine, Chastity (Chaz), Chesare, and Chianna.

A songwriter, arranger, and record producer, Bono initially achieved commercial success as part of Sonny & Cher, the musical duo not the TV show. While their hit singles "I Got You Babe" and "The Beat Goes On" granted Cher more attention as a performer, Sonny was the man behind the woman. In November 1987, years after their divorce, Sonny and Cher—the separate people—performed "I Got You Babe" one last time on *Late Night With David Letterman*, which was a more emotional performance for him than her.

On film Sonny acted in John Waters's cult classic *Hairspray* (1988). He later appeared on ABC's *Lois & Clark: The New Adventures of Superman* (1993) as a mayor, and appeared as himself in a dream sequence on *The Golden Girls* (1990). Frustrated with local bureaucracy, Sonny in real life became mayor of Palm Springs and served from 1988 to 1992. In 1994 he was elected to the U.S. House to represent the 44th Congressional District. His political accomplishments and memorials due to his spearheading and sponsorship of various projects are: the Sonny Bono Copyright Term Extension Act, the Palm Springs International Film Festival, a park at the restored lake, the Salton Sea, and a star on the Palm Springs Walk of Stars. He is the only member of Congress to have scored a #1 pop single on the US Billboard Hot 100 Chart. His headstone epitaph reads: "And the Beat Goes On."

As to why his marriage to Cher went south, Bono once said, "You lose the relationship and suddenly you're a business. I look at Sonny and Cher almost like two other people . . ."

On January 5, 1998, Bono died of injuries from a tragic skiing accident in South Lake Tahoe, California. At his memorial service in Palm Springs, Cher delivered a riveting and emotional public eulogy—one of the first such celebrity eulogies to be televised—long before twenty-four-hour news, YouTube, smartphones, streaming, and other technological devices and platforms helped to popularize such presentations.

11

Ron Howard
The Andy Griffith Show / The Smith Family / Happy Days

It was always my dream to be a director. A lot of it had to do with controlling my own destiny, because as a young actor you feel at everyone's disposal. But I wanted to become a leader in the business.

—Ron Howard

As will be explored later with Ricky Nelson and *The Adventures of Ozzie and Harriet*, the television world watched Ron Howard grow to maturity—first as little Opie Taylor on *The Andy Griffith Show* and, in his teen years, as Richie Cunningham on *Happy Days*. But rather than attempt the difficult transition from child star to adult actor, Ron went behind the camera to become one of the preeminent Oscar-winning directors of our time. Perhaps one could have anticipated his later enormous success as a filmmaker of taste and intelligence by his pedigree. Like an early version of Jodie Foster (whose brother Buddy Foster took Ron's place on *Mayberry RFD*, the *Griffith* sequel that CBS aired from 1968 to 1971), Howard always seemed to know how to deal with the vicissitudes of longtime success in Hollywood by being well grounded in a supportive family, filled with love and respect. As such, he is a rarity in Hollywood.

Entertainment journalist Peggy Herz observed in 1974, "It's hard to figure Ron Howard. He seems too nice to be real. He isn't obnoxious about it; he's just a pleasant, level-headed young man who happens to be a veteran actor at the age of 20. He's been working regularly since he was four years old—yet he seems to have no ego problems or big-shot complexes."

That analysis, of course, took place over forty years ago, just as Howard's then-new series, *Happy Days*, was enjoying its second full season on ABC, a few short months after it concluded its first half-year (the series originally aired from January 1974 to May 1984).

On *Days*, Howard played fresh-faced teenager Richie Cunningham, a role he originated on an episode of *Love, American Style*, titled "Love and the Happy Day," which served as a backdoor pilot for the show that went on to introduce the mainstream audience to another male icon in the guise of Henry Winkler as Arthur "The Fonz" or "Fonzie" Fonzarelli.

In retrospect, that was exactly Herz's point. *Days* was originally envisioned as a star vehicle for Howard who, a few years before, had finished his lengthy run as little Opie Taylor on *The Andy Griffith Show*. Viewers had become so familiar with both Opie and Richie that when Howard hosted *Saturday Night Live* on October 9, 1982, then Not-Ready-For-Prime-Time Player Eddie Murphy referred to Ron in a sketch as "Opie Cunningham," combining the first and last names of the actor's most famous roles.

Although Howard found great success as an actor, his career aspirations reached behind the camera—as a director. Howard has since excelled in his chosen endeavor, at the helm of major motion pictures ranging from *Cocoon*

Globe Photos

(1985) to *A Beautiful Mind* (2001). His first directorial effort on screen was a TV-movie titled *Skyward* (1982), starring none other than cinematic legend Bette Davis.

It was a good start to what has become an amazing second career.

Today, Howard is respected and regarded as an equal among colleagues like Steven Spielberg and George Lucas, the latter of whom directed him as an actor in the 1973 feature film, *American Graffiti*, which many mistakenly believe served as a big-screen pilot for the small-screen *Happy Days*. While Ron portrayed a high school senior of the 1960s in *Graffiti*, he started out playing a high school sophomore in the 1950s on *Days*. As Ron said in 1974, "*American Graffiti* is about. . . . kids making a decision . . . *Happy Days* is about a family. *Graffiti* is about the end of an era; *Happy Days* is about the middle of an era."

Ron was born in Duncan, Oklahoma, on March 1, 1954, to Rance and Jean (Speegle) Howard, both actors. His family later moved to Los Angeles, where he attended high school and later the University of Southern California, which he had to leave when *Happy* soared to success.

Years before *Days*, Ron made his stage debut, if ever so briefly—and without pay—at a mere two years old when his parents were performing in a live production of *The Seven Year Itch* in Baltimore. His first professionally paid gig transpired when at four, he appeared alongside Yul Brynner and Deborah Kerr in the 1959 feature film *The Journey*.

Two years later, he was cast as Opie on *The Andy Griffith Show*. As he once recalled, "I was in that series until I was 14. I've always enjoyed working. If I hadn't enjoyed it, I wouldn't have done it—and my parents wouldn't have let me. I always had the option of turning down work." But when he wasn't working, he missed it. "That's when I knew for sure I wanted to be in the [entertainment] business."

Between the *Griffith Show* and *Happy Days*, Howard appeared in a few films for Walt Disney, and had a regular role on ABC's short-lived Henry Fonda series, *The Smith Family*, in which he played the eldest son. Howard also did TV guest appearances on shows like *Daniel Boone*, *Gunsmoke*, *The FBI*, *The Waltons*, and *Gentle Ben*, the latter of which starred his younger brother Clint Howard.

Through it all, life for the young Howard brothers was kept in balance by their father, Rance Howard, who along with his wife, made sure their sons retained a life beyond Hollywood. "I owe my Dad an awful lot," Ron said. "He helped me a great deal with my acting; then he took time to come to the set when I was working and help me understand what the director wanted of me. I'm always interested in watching other people's acting techniques—and here again my father has been tremendously influential. That's one reason why I think I did well in this industry as a kid. Having someone like Dad who knows the [ropes] and who will work with you is invaluable." Both his parents, Ron said, helped keep set priorities for his life and career. "They believe in simplicity to the hilt."

Actor Tom Bosley, Ron's TV father on *Happy Days*, also helped him keep things in perspective when the show was in its infancy. According to Howard, Bosley believed *Days'* success transpired because over thirty million viewers were ready for a series that dealt in a humorous way with subject matter beyond the life and death scenarios that were running rampant on television at the time. "We deal with happy days," Howard said, "not with the problems of the 1950s. We call back times that people remember as being pleasant."

While playing Richie, Ron didn't mind being typecast as a high school student in the 50s. As he told Peggy Herz, "I can relate to those days. I'm not convinced the 1950s were much different from the late 1960s and early 1970s when I was in high school. The problems are basically the same—first cars, dating, getting a job, trying to do well in school."

However, Ron didn't believe that *Happy* family life or the peer group, as portrayed on *Days* by Winkler and other cast-mates like Anson Williams as Potsie or Donny Most as Ralph Malph, was as important when he attended real high school. "Peer pressure did exist," he said, "but it didn't carry the power that it seemed to have carried in the 1950s."

He told Herz:

Someday, I'd like to be a director. Writing, too, has become more of an interest to me. A director has to be able to write. Half of making a film is rewriting and restructuring—that's why writing is so important.

A male icon not just of television but in every aspect of the entertainment industry, Ron Howard has for decades retained the family values and priorities that were instilled in him years before by his real-life parents and TV dad. He's been married to the same woman, Cheryl Howard, since 1975, and they are the proud parents of Paige Carlyle Howard, Reed Howard, Jocelyn Howard, and the eldest, Bryce Dallas Howard, an accomplished actress in her own right.

12

John Ritter
The Waltons/Three's Company

Me—a TV star? I've got to be the luckiest guy in the world.

—John Ritter

John Ritter became a television star gradually over time on two very different series: first as the country preacher Reverend Matthew Fordwick in the initial (and prime) years of the one-hour family drama *The Waltons* (CBS, 1972–1982), and later on *Three's Company* (ABC, 1977–1984), the half-hour farcical sitcom in which he portrayed the fumbling and aptly named Jack Tripper, who pretended to be gay to appease his landlord (Norman Fell) so he could live with two women (Suzanne Somers and Joyce DeWitt).

From playing a reverend on *The Waltons* to performing in the completely irreverent *Three's Company*, Ritter once said, "Most people don't know that I am an accomplished dramatic actor . . . But I've performed in several Shakespeare productions including 'Hamlet,' except in this version, Hamlet lives in an apartment with two women, and has to pretend he's gay so that the landlord won't evict him."

Another time, he also observed wryly, "If I found a cure for a huge disease, while I was hobbling up onstage to accept the Nobel Prize they'd be playing the theme song ('Come and Knock on Our Door') from *Three's Company*."

In yet another moment, he concluded, like only he could, "I knew when I grew up, I always wanted to be a liar, and if you're in television, you're lying because you're just pretending to be yourself much like I'm doing now."

According to a biography written by Gary Richard Collins II for www.imdb.com, Tex Ritter, the legendary country singer/actor, and actress Dorothy Fay were married in 1941. Their first child, Tom, was diagnosed with cerebral palsy. John was born Jonathan Southworth Ritter in Burbank, California, on September 17, 1948. Like his parents, John pursued a career in the entertainment industry, first attending Hollywood High School, where he was elected student body president.

John later attended the University of Southern California where he majored in psychology and minored in architecture. In 1966, he made his television debut as a contestant on *The Dating Game*, where he won a vacation to Lake Havasu, Arizona. Soon after, Ritter began taking acting classes with Nina

Globe Photos

Foch and changed his major to theater arts, graduating in 1971 with a bachelor of fine arts in drama. He also honed his craft with Stella Adler at the Harvey Lembeck Comedy Workshop and, between 1968 and 1969, performed in various stage productions in England, Scotland, Holland, and Germany.

John's first major acting role as a fictional character was as a campus revolutionary in ABC's *Dan August* series starring fellow male icon Burt Reynolds and future *Three's Company* costar Norman Fell. From there he performed his periodic gig on *The Waltons* and subsequent appearances on *Medical Center*, *M*A*S*H*, *The Bob Newhart Show*, *The Streets of San Francisco*, *Kojak*, *Rhoda*, and *The Mary Tyler Moore Show*. While working on *The Waltons*, his father passed away, only twenty-four hours after New Year's Day in 1974. In late 1975, ABC optioned the rights for *Three's Company*, which was based on the British hit show, *Man About the House*, and John was chosen to portray Jack Tripper, besting other actors, including a young Billy Crystal (who later played TV's first major male gay character via ABC's satirical prime-time *Soap* serial).

Ritter also performed in feature films such as *Nickelodeon* (1976), *Breakfast in Bed* (1977), *Americathon* (1979), *Hero at Large* (1980), and *They All Laughed* (1981). In 1980, *Company* was sold into syndication, and became a ratings phenomenon. At the height of his success, Ritter won a Golden Globe in 1983 for Best Performance by an Actor, following his second nomination for Best TV Actor in a Musical-Comedy Series. One year later, he won the Emmy Award for Outstanding Lead Actor in a Comedy Series (after being nominated twice again).

By its eighth year, *Three's Company* began to drop in the ratings and was can-celled in the spring of 1984. The following fall John returned as Jack Tripper in the one-season spin-off *Three's a Crowd*, which costarred Mary Cadorette and Robert Manden (also of *Soap*). Beyond his work on *Company* and in feature films, Ritter, who ultimately became known for his physical humor, also found success with more camouflaged voiceover work as in animated films such as *The Flight of Dragons* (1982), and in PBS-TV's *Clifford, the Big Red Dog* (2000), for which he was nominated for a Daytime Emmy Award three consecutive times, totaling seven Emmy nominations in his thirty-five-year career.

Other work included John's Emmy-winning and Golden Globe–nominated single-season performance as the lead on *Hooperman* (ABC, 1987-1988), which became one of TV's first half-hour dramedies—and for which he also won a People's Choice Award. He continued doing more big-screen movies like *Skin Deep* (1989), playing a womanizing, alcoholic writer, and in two *Problem Child* movies (1990-1991), as the surrogate father of a relatively modern-day *Dennis the Menace*. In 1992, he performed in *Noises Off* and *Stay Tuned* before returning to the small-screen in the sitcom *Hearts Afire* (which also featured Billy Bob Thornton).

Although *Fire* was well written, the series struggled to find viewers, and left the air in 1995. During its production, however, John found feature film time to play Ward Nelson in *North* (1994), and to perform (once more) with Thornton in *Sling Blade* (1996), in which he portrayed the gay manager of a department store.

In 1999, John was nominated as Outstanding Guest Actor in a Comedy Series for playing George Madison on an episode of *Ally McBeal*. In 2002 and 2003, he played his final TV role as the beloved father Paul Hennessey on ABC's *8 Simple Rules for Dating My Daughter*, which was based on the popular book of the same name. As the head of a family, Paul was more mature and responsible than the single, carefree-spirited Jack Tripper from *Three's Company*. But in his spousal portrayal opposite TV wife Katey Sagal (formerly of *Married with Children*), Ritter's charm remained intact. John's Paul on *Rules* kept a close eye over their three children (including a pre–*Big Bang Theory's*

Kaley Cuoco), as the comedic series, with its serious overtones (addressing curfews, sex, drugs, and more), won devoted viewers, a People's Choice Award for Best New Comedy, and a Favorite Comedy Series accolade from the Family Awards.

In 2003, Ritter also starred in his second-to-last film *Manhood*. On September 11 of that year, he felt ill during *Rules* rehearsals on the Disney lot in Burbank, California. He was rushed into the emergency room across Buena Vista Street to Providence St. Joseph Medical Center, where he was mistakenly treated for a heart attack. He underwent surgery and died from an undiagnosed aortic dissection (a tear in the wall of the aorta), just six days shy of his fifty-fifth birthday. A prince of a performer, and a stellar human being, John left behind his second wife, Amy Yasbeck (1999–2003), first wife Nancy Morgan (1977–1996), and children, actor Jason Ritter (TV's *Parenthood*, among other shows and films), Tyler, Carly, and Stella Ritter.

13

Robin Williams
Mork & Mindy

Nanu-nanu.

—Mork, as portrayed by Robin Williams on *Mork & Mindy*

Around the same time as John Ritter's rocket to fame, Robin Williams also became a television star, but this time, overnight—with his portrayal of an alien named Mork (from Ork), first in a dream sequence in a 1978 episode of ABC's *Happy Days*, which gave birth to that same network's spin-off show *Mork & Mindy* (which costarred Pam Dawber, married to male TV icon Mark Harmon, then of NBC's medical drama *St. Elsewhere*, today of CBS's *NCIS*).

Williams was born Robin McLaurin Williams in St. Luke's Hospital in Chicago, Illinois, on July 21, 1951. His mother, Laurie McLaurin, was a former model from Jackson, Mississippi; her great-grandfather was Mississippi senator and governor Anselm J. McLaurin. Robin's father, Robert Fitzgerald Williams, was a senior executive in Ford Motor Company's Lincoln-Mercury Division. Robin, along with his two elder half-brothers, Robert Todd Williams and McLaurin Smith-Williams, stemmed from an English, Welsh, Irish, Scottish, German, and French ancestry. While his mother studied Christian Science, Robin was raised as an Episcopalian, later authoring the humorous list, *Top Ten Reasons To Be An Episcopalian*. During an interview on TV's *Inside the Actors Studio* in 2001, he said his mother was an initial inspiration for his sense of humor, noting that he would make her laugh to gain attention.

Robin attended public elementary school at Gorton Elementary School (now Gorton Community Center) and middle school at Deer Path Junior High School (now Deer Path Middle School), both in Lake Forest, Illinois. Although considered a school class clown, he described himself as a quiet child who did not conquer his shyness until he enrolled in his high school drama department.

In late 1963, when he was just twelve years old, his father was transferred to Detroit. The family resided in a forty-room farmhouse on twenty acres in suburban Bloomfield Hills, Michigan, where he attended the private Detroit Country Day School, where he excelled in academics and athletics (on the soccer and wrestling teams), and was voted class president.

PhotoFest

Because his father was away much of the time, and his mother also worked, Robin was cared for by the family's maid, who was his main companion. When he was sixteen, his father took early retirement and the family relocated to Tiburon, California. Williams then attended Redwood High School in nearby Larkspur, from which he graduated in 1969, and he was named "Most Likely Not to Succeed" and "Funniest" by his classmates. He later attended Claremont Men's College in Claremont, California, to study political science, only to then later drop out to pursue acting. Williams subsequently studied theater for three years at the College of Marin, a community college in Kentfield, California.

According to Marin drama professor James Dunn, the depth of Williams's talent first became evident when he was cast in the musical *Oliver!* as Fagin. Williams was known to improvise during his time in Marin's drama program, putting cast members in hysterics. Dunn called his wife after one late rehearsal to tell her that Williams "was going to be something special."

In 1973, Robin attained a full scholarship to New York's Juilliard School, in New York City. He was one of only twenty students, including *Superman* star Christopher Reeve (with whom Robin remained close friends until Reeve's tragic death in 2003, following a paralyzing horseback riding accident in 1995). Shortly thereafter, Williams commenced his stand-up act, which led to a career-changing guest-spot on *Happy Days* and *Mork & Mindy*.

As with John Ritter, Williams left us much too soon, yet even more tragically: He committed suicide on August 11, 2014—approximately one year after his last TV series, CBS's *The Crazy Ones*, failed to find an audience. Ritter utilized his rubbery physicality to performance perfection and, as a result, helped to return to TV the beloved slapstick-type humor made famous by the legendary likes of Lucille Ball (who was, in turn, a huge fan of the actor's jovial style). In like manner, Williams employed his elastic facial expressions and genius improvisational skills, the likes of which had not been seen on TV since the 50s (and the days of Sid Caesar on *Your Show of Shows*).

Williams was found dead in his Tiburon, California, home with a belt looped around his neck, and the other end wedged between a closet door and the doorframe. As pathologist Dr. Cyril Wecht observed in December 2014, the oxygen to Williams's brain was cut off, and he "lost consciousness within a few seconds and died minutes later." According to Wecht, the actor had also sliced his wrists with a pocket knife. The coroner also reported that Williams had a form of dementia that causes hallucinations and makes victims hear voices. But Robin was unaware that he was challenged by this issue. It was then that his third wife, Susan Schneider, disclosed that he was secretly battling Parkinson's disease and struggling financially.

Years before, he began his career as a stand-up comedian who was discovered by *Happy Days* producer Garry Marshall and, upon leaving Marshall's *Mork & Mindy*, went on to become a respected feature film star of comedic movies like *Good Morning, Vietnam* (1987) and *Mrs. Doubtfire* (1993), as well as dramas such as *Awakenings* (1990) and *Good Will Hunting* (1997), for which he earned an Academy Award for Best Supporting Actor.

As Williams once said, "Acting is different from stand-up. It gives you this ability to enter into another character, to create another person." With further regard to his switch in performance style, he said, "I was only a leading man for a minute; now I'm a character actor."

"For me," he added at another time, "comedy starts as a spew, a kind of explosion, and then you sculpt it from there, if at all. It comes out of a deeper, darker side. Maybe it comes from anger, because I'm outraged by cruel absurdities, the hypocrisy that exists everywhere, even within yourself—where it's hardest to see."

Williams started performing for his mother and chose comedy because as he noted, "that was the only stage that I could find. It was the pure idea of being on stage. That was the only thing that interested me, along with learning the craft and working, and just being in productions with people." He used to think the worst thing in life was to end up "being alone."

At times, he believed the audience would discover his success to be "a fluke" or that he just didn't possess the "it" factor or that he "never had it at all." Pop-culture historian Rick Lertzman concludes that Williams "was a one-of-a-kind comedian who brought great frenetic energy and improvisational skills to the small screen."

In the December 18, 2014, edition of the "Roc Weekend" supplement for the *Democrat and Chronicle* newspaper of Rochester, New York, entertainment journalist Jack Garner further summed up Robin Williams's talent, life, and career with this brief review of the *Mork & Mindy* DVD release of the entire series:

> In the late 70s, when I tried to watch this wacky spin-off of *Happy Days*, about an alien from Ork who lands in Boulder, Colorado, I found it too silly for my taste. Since then, I (and the rest of the world) warmed to the cutting-edge, high-energy of Robin Williams . . . I now find the series very funny, and a generous time capsule of early Robin, which is more desirable than ever, given the comedian's tragic death . . . Comic dialogue seems to explode out of his mind. Some, I'm sure, is improvised, and other lines *seem* improvised, even if in the fourth (and final) season, when Jonathan Winters (Robin's most obvious mentor and muse) joined the cast. Now all four seasons are packed in a delightful box set, with extras like insane gag reels, and the two *Happy Days* shows that inspired the spin-off.

PART II

DARRINS, DOBIES, DONS, AND BOBS

In the history of entertainment, classic TV and beyond, Bob Hope is considered the most affable male personality. As several contemporary comedians and performers observed in a special presentation about his life for the Turner Classic Movies TV network in 2014, Hope (who died in 2003) was both silly and sophisticated. "Everyone wanted to be [like] Bob Hope," said notable writer/actor Buck Henry, who commenced his career as one of the scribes for the *Get Smart* TV sitcom.

Like his contemporaries Jack Benny and George Burns—and many iconic talents before the golden age of radio and the advent of film and television, Hope began performing live on stage in the era of vaudeville. From there he went on to radio, then teamed with Bing Crosby (and Dorothy Lamour) for their long list of "Road" motion pictures, including *Road to Utopia* (1945) and *Road to Rio* (1947), among others. Hope soon ventured into television with first his weekly variety show, followed by his periodic specials, the Christmas editions of which were spent overseas entertaining the troops during the Korean and Vietnam Wars (following his same path for those brave soldiers of World War II). Hope's special mix of humor and sophistication was easy to watch, especially for TV viewers, as he became the ultimate "guest" in their living rooms across the country.

A similar male TV type was created by Bob Cummings in shows like *Love That Bob*, which became *The Bob Cummings Show*, and later in *My Living Doll* (with Julie Newmar). Dwayne Hickman also portrayed a variation on the Hope persona and admitted to employing on his *Many Loves of Dobie Gillis* sitcom the "Now cut that out" delivery technique that he learned from Cummings when the two appeared on *Love That Bob* (Cummings, of course, had initially borrowed that line of delivery from originator Jack Benny).

Other affable male TV types over the years included Dick York and Dick Sargent as mortal Darrin Stephens married to supernatural sweetheart Elizabeth Montgomery's twitchy-witch Samantha; Larry Hagman and Bill Daily on *I Dream of Jeannie*; Andy Griffith and Don Knotts on *The Andy Griffith Show*; Don Adams on *Get Smart*; and a more sedate and subtle affability with Bob Newhart on *The Bob Newhart Show*.

A closer look at some of these gentlemen of distinguished humor follows.

14

Bob Crane
Hogan's Heroes/The Bob Crane Show

Darren McGavin
Riverboat/Kolchak: The Night Stalker

> Maybe you have to brush with death before you can really reflect on life, on the people and times that really meant something to you.
>
> —Karl Kolchak, as played by Darren McGavin on *Kolchak: The Night Stalker*

One lived a relatively scary life off screen; the other found himself in scary situations on screen.

From 1965 to 1971, Bob Crane starred as Colonel Robert E. Hogan on *Hogan's Heroes*, a military comedy slightly inspired by the 1953 feature film, *Stalag 17*.

From 1972 to 1975, Darren McGavin portrayed mystery investigator Karl Kolchak, first in a series of ABC TV-movies (*The Night Stalker*, 1972; *The Night Strangler*, 1973), followed by a spin-off series, awkwardly titled *Kolchak: The Night Stalker*.

Crane, born June 13, 1928, lived a short tragic life, and died an even more tragic death. Three years after the demise of his short-lived NBC series *The Bob Crane Show*, the actor was found on June 29, 1978, bludgeoned to death by a weapon that was never found though, according to various reports, investigators believed it to be a camera tripod (an electrical cord had been tied around his neck).

McGavin, born May 7, 1922, went on to experience a huge resurgence in his career with the 1983 feature film holiday release of *A Christmas Story*, which has now become a TV classic, many-times screened in succession over a twenty-four-hour period on networks like TNT.

Bob Crane
Sylvia Norris/Globe Photos

Both gentlemen attained their male TV icon status due to their likable performances in their most famous small-screen roles. McGavin, for one, played the crumpled-garbed Kolchak with such down-to-earth, yet frenetic appeal, that his show's supernatural premise became secondary to the star's charismatic performance. Meanwhile, Crane's Colonel Hogan, with his sneaky, and not-so-squeaky-clean smile and comedic care-free spirit, was ultimately camouflaging the actor's real-life melodramas.

According to Wikipedia, in June 1978, Crane was residing in the Winfield Place Apartments in Scottsdale, Arizona, while performing in the *Beginner's Luck* live stage production at the Windmill Dinner Theatre. On the afternoon of June 29, Crane's costar Victoria Ann Berry found his body in his apartment after he failed to show up for a lunch meeting. He left behind second wife, Sigrid Valdis (to whom he was wed from 1970 to 1978); his first wife, Anne Terzian (1949 to 1970); and children Robert Scott, Robert David, Deborah Ann, Karen Leslie, and Ana Marie Crane.

To this day, the ultimate cause of his death remains a mystery.

Darren McGavin, whose TV character loved a mystery on *Kolchak*, passed away on February 25, 2006. As explained on his website, www.darrenmcgavin.net/, now operated by his widow, actress Kathie Brown McGavin, the actor's roles beyond *Kolchak* and *A Christmas Story* were numerous, each "superbly crafted nuisances." According to Brown:

Darren slithered his way across the big screen in [1955's] *The Man with the Golden Arm*, stealing scenes as easily as his character sold narcotics. Donning a cowboy hat and casually slipping between the centuries, Darren guest-starred on *Gunsmoke*, playing outlaw Lon Gorman (with future *Stalker* costar Simon Oakland at his side) in an episode titled "Hostage." Later, as gunfighter Joe Bascom, Darren would be nurtured back to health by France Nuyen in one of the most outstanding guest-star episodes that sacred series ever produced in its long, distinguished twenty-year run.

Darren matched wits with Barbara Bain and Martin Landau in *Mission: Impossible*, briefly replaced Tony Franciosa on *The Name of the Game*, rode a hot air balloon over the Civil War in Disney's [TV show] *High Flying Spy*, drove race cars, represented the United States in a one-on-one duel with Mako in [one of] the first ever, made-for-TV film[s], *The Challenge* . . . [and] won an Emmy for his recurring role on *Murphy Brown* [in which he played father to series star Candice Bergen].

Darren McGavin
Globe Photos

Bob Crane and Darren McGavin clearly lived and died two different lives—but their theatrical abilities elevated their place in the memories of millions of classic TV fans, allowing each the status of one of television's top male icons.

15

Dwayne Hickman and Bob Denver
The Many Loves of Dobie Gillis/Gilligan's Island

I have often been told that I have many of the same mannerisms as Jack Benny and certainly Bob Cummings.

—Dwayne Hickman

The Many Loves of Dobie Gillis made stars out of Dwayne Hickman and Bob Denver; and while Hickman would later become a television programming executive for CBS, Denver found additional on-screen fame as the lead in Sherwood Schwartz's *Gilligan's Island*. A young *Loves* semi-regular named Warren Beatty also didn't do so badly for himself. But it was Hickman and Denver who are best remembered from this landmark series.

As Hickman relayed to *TV Gold* magazine in 1986, he landed the *Gillis* lead as a direct result of his previous work on *The Bob Cummings Show*. The *Dobie* series was based on a collection of short stories by Max Shulman, and 20th Century Fox subsequently wanted to produce a TV pilot. Once the series actually aired, Hickman told *TV Gold*, "it was a one . . . or two day film show," depending on the length of the episode, the number of sets, guest-stars, etc. "Monday we would rehearse. Tuesday we would rehearse again, and (we) would film on Wednesday. Thursday we usually had off, and Friday we would go in and read the next [week's] script."

One memorable aspect of the series for Hickman was the diverse array of guest-performers that it featured. "We had an awful lot of exciting young people who [went on to] become big stars," including Beatty, who played Milton Armitage (in the first eighteen episodes), Tuesday Weld (Thalia Meninger), who was "wonderful, and just starting out," Hickman remembered. Sheila James, who played Zelda Gilroy "was great. . . . Bill Bixby got his first job on the show. Ryan O'Neal had one of his first jobs there. Marlo Thomas was on one [episode]; Ron Ely [TV's *Tarzan*] was on another. A whole bunch of people got their start there!"

Born May 18, 1934, in Los Angeles, California, Hickman attended Loyola University (now Loyola Marymount), in LA. He married three times: Carol Christensen (1963–1972), Joanne Papile (1977–1981), and Joan Roberts (1983 to present), and he has two children.

Dwayne made his first appearance in the 1940 movie, *The Grapes of Wrath*. He had no lines, while his elder sibling,

Dwayne Hickman
Globe Photos

Darrell, had a small part. As he once said, "Even as a small child I never felt that I should have to compete with anyone—even my older brother."

Still, Dwayne seemed destined to be in the show business shadow of his brother until television beckoned. He played Bob Cummings's nephew on *The Bob Cummings Show* (1955) and then, at the age of twenty-five, *The Many Loves of Dobie Gillis* came along. *Dobie Gillis* was about a high school teen who stood by and emulated Auguste Rodin's statue of *The Thinker* and addressed the audience with thoughtful reflections on life and love followed by living examples. "Dobie was so well written and ahead of its time," he said.

After 148 episodes from 1959 to 1963, Hickman returned to film in *Cat Ballou* (1965) with Jane Fonda and Lee Marvin, but unavoidable typecasting led to 1965 roles in *Ski Party*, *How To Stuff a Wild Bikini*, and *Dr. Goldfoot and the Bikini Machine*. So the actor found work behind the scenes, notably as a programming executive for CBS (from 1977 to 1988). He directed episodes of that network's *Designing Women*, ABC's *Head of the Class*, and other programs.

Bob Denver
PhotoFest

However, Hickman has continued to connect with the *Gillis* persona via public appearances, and a 1994 autobiography *Forever Dobie*. He even returned to the role in a 1977 pilot *Whatever Happened to Dobie Gillis?*—as well as in *Bring Me the Head of Dobie Gillis*, a 1988 TV-movie. As he once said, "The *Dobie Gillis* show was the first show that I'm aware of that was not about the family. It was about the teenagers, the kids, the kids' life from a teenager's point of view . . . Parents were part of the show, but they weren't the driving force . . ."

As beatnik Maynard G. Krebs, Bob Denver was certainly an integral part not only of the *Gillis* series—but of its general success. The editors of *TV Gold* magazine explained it all in 1986:

[Max] Schulman [*sic*] tried for years to get the books going as a TV series, but it was only after he changed Dobie from a college student to a high-school student and added the character of Maynard G. Krebs did it become a reality. [This character] was the perfect counterpoint to Dobie. While Dobie worshipped the female form, Maynard would shriek "Girls!" when confronted with anything remotely female, including Dobie's mother ("Like no offense, Mrs. G," who was played by Florida Friebus).

Born January 9, 1935, in New Rochelle, New York, Denver, like Hickman, also attended Loyola University in Los Angeles, California (now Loyola Marymount University). He wed four times: Maggie Ryan (1960–1966), Jean Webber (1967–1970), Carole Abrahams (1972–1975), and Dreama Perry (1979–2005), and he had four children: Patrick, Megan, Emily, and Colin; and one grandchild: Elana.

Denver switched from a potential career in law to acting and made his film debut in a bit part in the 1959 Sal Mineo film *A Private's Affair*. That same year he was cast as Krebs on *Gillis*, which he played for four years. In 1964 he was cast as the title character in *Gilligan's Island*, portraying the bumbling shipwrecked sailor in all ninety-seven episodes (through 1967), often playing scenes with the Skipper (Alan Hale Jr.) that were reminiscent of Laurel and Hardy.

On Broadway, on January 12, 1970, he was the first replacement for Woody Allen in the role of Allan Felix in *Play It Again, Sam* at the Broadhurst Theatre. From 1973 to 1974 Denver was the title character in *Dusty's Trail*, a sitcom about seven pioneers who are separated from their wagon train, a sort of western variation on Gilligan. In later years, Denver reprised the role of Gilligan many times: in the TV movies *Rescue from Gilligan's Island* (1978), *The Castaways on Gilligan's Island* (1979), and *The Harlem Globetrotters on Gilligan's Island* (1981), on two animated series *The New Adventures of Gilligan* (1974–1977) and *Gilligan's Planet* (1982-1983), plus "Gilligan" guest appearances on *The New Gidget* (1986), *ALF* (1986), *Baywatch* (1989), and *Meego* (1997).

Denver died September 2, 2005, at Wake Forest University Baptist Medical Center, Winston-Salem, North Carolina, of complications from cancer treatment. He will forever be fondly remembered as who Hale's Skipper might have referred to as "Everyone's 'Little Buddy'."

16

Andy Griffith and Don Knotts
The Andy Griffith Show

> There are some things beyond the ken of mortal man that shouldn't be tampered with. We don't know everything, Andy.
>
> —Deputy Barney Fife, as played by Don Knotts on *The Andy Griffith Show*

When it comes to the iconic television status of Andy Griffith and Don Knotts, it's difficult to talk about one without addressing the other. They are irrevocably intertwined due to their monumental pairing on *The Andy Griffith Show*, which originally aired on CBS from 1960 to 1968—and which remains one of the most popular TV series of all time.

Entertainment journalist Rick Lertzman sums up it up this way:

Andy was a film and stage star before he was offered a television series by producer Sheldon Leonard in 1960. Andy, who started his career as a stand-up comedian, showed great stage presence on Broadway in the starring role of country bumpkin Will Stockdale in "No Time for Sergeants." He later starred in the [1958] film version. He showed his great range as an actor portraying the dark character of Lonesome Rhodes in Elia Kazan's "A Face in the Crowd" (1957). In one of television's first spin-offs (from *The Danny Thomas Show*), he portrayed the laconic sheriff of Mayberry, Andy Taylor in *The Andy Griffith Show*. While he started out as the comic lead, he eventually morphed into more of a straight-man for Don Knotts.

As Knotts bumbling character of [Deputy] Barney Fife was expanded, Griffith showed his great versatility by toning his character down. While Knotts won five

Emmys for his role, Griffith was sadly never nominated. Griffith appeared in films and several short-lived series until he starred as wily southern attorney Ben Matlock in the long running TV series, *Matlock* [on which Knotts periodically appeared, following his regular gig as Mr. Furley on *Three's Company*].

As to Griffith's appeal in particular, legendary television critic Ann Hodges says the actor was "delightful because he, like James Garner, played who he was. With *The Andy Griffith Show*, he touched a chord in everybody's heart whether or not you were from a small-town [like Mayberry presented on the *Griffith* series]. I think he kind of looked at that and said, 'Oh, what a great way to grow up . . . and what a great town [Mayberry] to live in.'"

Hodges goes on to explain how Griffith, the actor, injected all the qualities of who he was as a human being into the show, which represented everything that was "good and kind, with heart-warming stories of family and friendship. One of the most redeeming and endearing qualities of the Sheriff Andy Taylor character, was that no matter what, no matter how challenging it was to be a friend to someone so high maintenance like Deputy Barney Fife, as played by Don Knotts, Andy was always such a true and loyal friend."

Taylor's loyalty, concludes Hodges, was one of his "great qualities . . . and he was a diplomat, certainly with his son, Opie [played by little Ronny Howard], and even with his Aunt Bee [Frances Bavier], who was another great character . . . so many people have an Aunt Bee, or they wished they had one."

Writer Sam Bobrick, who penned several segments of the *Griffith* series with Bill Idelson, with whom he was partnered for three years, adds:

When I wrote for *The Andy Griffith Show* Andy and Don were easy to work with, and I liked them. I enjoyed it. It was a good experience. But once Don

Clockwise from left: Andy Griffith, Ron Howard, Jim Nabors, Don Knotts
CBS/PhotoFest

left, I had a difficult time writing for the show. He could never be replaced. But the ratings stayed up, so that was nice.

Fred Freeman, a colleague of Bobrick's, also wrote for *Griffith*, and he, too, appreciated the personable qualities of the show's star. "He would sit in on story meetings. Intelligent. Not real showbiz at all, but very serious about what he was doing."

According to Freeman, a good portion of what defined Andy Taylor, the character, was also embodied by Andy Griffith, the actor. "There are other sides to people, sometimes not so good. But Andy was always terrific [on screen and off]."

Griffith was also smart enough to know a good thing when he saw it, which is why Freeman believes the actor called upon his friend, Don Knotts, to join him on *The Andy Griffith Show* as Barney Fife. "Andy was smart in the same way Mary Tyler Moore was smart, or as any actor or comedian is smart: they know they don't have to be the funny one all the time. Mary Tyler Moore was a great straight man (woman) on her [*Mary Tyler Moore Show*], and Andy, too, just like Mary, knew to surround himself with an A-list of supporting talent on [his *Andy Griffith Show*]. That's what Jack Benny did. He was the butt of all the jokes. That, to me, is a smart actor, a smart person. It was good performances and it was real. Don Knotts fit in perfectly [with Andy on *Griffith*]. He was the more broad character. He was terrific."

Freeman says *The Andy Griffith Show* remains successful and "down-to-earth realistic television" due to the chemistry between Griffith and Knotts:

Don was funny. I think so many shows are successful because of the relationships between the characters on screen. The background can be one thing. The small town. But with *The Andy Griffith Show* it was all about Andy and Don, as well as little Ronny Howard [as Andy's son Opie]. The people [viewers] could identify to a degree with the problems that Andy had with his Opie. Those are identifiable things treated in a more realistic way.

The Andy Griffith Show was unique because it was filmed like a movie, and not in front of a studio audience as were many shows of the day, including *Make Room for Daddy*, from whence it sprang. There were also a large number of on-location shoots on the series. Both the movie-style filming and the location shoots were mandated by Griffith, thinking these techniques would add to the realism and longevity of the series. He clearly was correct on both accounts.

Andy Griffith was born to Geneva Nunn Griffith and Carl Lee Griffith on June 1, 1926, and died at age eighty-six on July 3, 2012. He was married three times: Barbara

Griffith (1949–1972), Solica Casuto (1975–1981), and Cindy Knight (1983–2012). He had two children: Andy Griffith Jr. and Dixie Griffith.

Don Knotts was born July 21, 1924, and died at age eighty-one on February 24, 2006. Like Griffith, he was married three times: Kathryn Metz (1947–1966), Loralee Czuchna (1974–1983), and Frances Yarborough (2002–2006); and he had two children: Karen and Thomas Knotts.

Like many prestigious male TV icons, Andy and Don's most substantial legacy is the joy millions of viewers have received—and millions more will receive forever—from their performances, specifically the laughter they left behind with *The Andy Griffith Show*.

17

Dick York and Dick Sargent
Bewitched

I thought Dick Sargent did a marvelous job as Darrin on *Bewitched*.

—Dick York

It is without a doubt the biggest double-casting controversy in the history of classic television: Dick York and Dick Sargent's dual turn as mortal ad-man Darrin Stephens, married to Elizabeth Montgomery's adorable witch-with-a-twitch Samantha on *Bewitched*, which originally aired on ABC from 1964 to 1972.

The actors resembled each other, acted in a similar fashion, and yet were very different. Cast as Darrin before Sargent, York played the character with animated aplomb while many viewers believed that Sargent, who just so happened to be gay, portrayed a kinder-gentler Darrin. Montgomery explained it all quite diplomatically in *The Bewitched Book*, which was later revised a few times as *Bewitched Forever*. By the time Sargent came to play Darrin, she said, the character was not as startled by Samantha's magic (or her other-worldly characters):

Darrin was becoming a more easygoing presence. The show's situation almost became funnier. He would lapse into this kind of complacence and maybe into something that he just might enjoy for a minute or two. It was almost as if Darrin grew as the relationship developed. He didn't have to be on his guard as much. So, when he was suddenly confronted by witchcraft, the newness of the marriage was gone. It wasn't as shocking an experience as it was in the show's first season.

Sargent expanded on Montgomery's thoughts. "To tell you the truth," he said, "I think there was a stronger sense of warmth between Samantha and Darrin when I did the show. Liz and I were more kissy-kissy."

Dick York, ever the gentleman, always felt tagged as the neurotic, hyperactive Darrin, and wanted desperately to stop playing him as "so damned mad at Samantha all the time." York felt, "Why should [Darrin] come home and start raising hell every day?" As an actor, York found himself frequently frustrated with exploring ways to justify the character's somewhat off-putting behavior. As he explained in *The Bewitched Book*, "I knew when I would come home from a long-day's shooting on the

Dick York
ABC/PhotoFest

show, I wouldn't want to start ragging on my wife . . . So, I thought it was terribly selfish of Darrin to do the same with Samantha."

Born September 4, 1928, in Fort Wayne, Indiana, York believed the seeds of his acting career were sown in his Depression-era childhood in Chicago, where he later moved with his own family, and where he began his career in radio in the late 1930s. He did several network and local shows, such as *Junior Junction, Jack Armstrong: The All American Boy*, and *That Brewster Boy*. A student of St. Paul University, York moved to New York in 1950 and started making various TV appearances, including *Alfred Hitchcock Presents, The Twilight Zone*, and the TV version of *Going My Way* (with Gene Kelly). He began *Bewitched* in the fall of 1964 and left in the spring of 1969 due to increasing pain from an injury he endured years before on the 1959 movie set of *They Came To Cordura*. He retired from acting until the early 1980s, when he began making guest appearances on TV-movies like *High School, USA* and weekly series such as *Fantasy Island* and *Simon & Simon* (the latter on which his theatrical talents shined, while playing a ruthless, very non-Darrin-like character).

As to his general perspective on acting, according to his son, Chris York, the original Darrin once said, "Real things are generally too much to bear . . . that's why the essence of good acting, I suppose, is just going to the point where the audience can feel it without them being embarrassed about it."

Chris goes on to explain his father's take on playing Darrin in particular:

First and foremost because it was a love story between a man and a woman, a woman who had some extraordinary baggage, number one being a meddling mother. The magic was almost secondary to the mother's influence on their lives. He knew there was a reactionary character on the show and how he handled each situation would dictate the success or the failure of each episode. That came from his theater training knowing that you only have a limited time on stage and you better give your best performance each and every time. Darrin needed to have an understandable irritated reaction to things that happened to him but the audience had to know that no matter what predicament he was put in at the end of the day he would still be deeply in love with Samantha.

With regard to his father's take on Dick Sargent taking over the role in the fall of 1969, Chris adds:

My Dad felt that Sargent did a very fine job as Darrin on *Bewitched* and thought that he was unjustly criticized because not only was he trying to replace a character on the television show but also replacing an actor who had his own way of interpreting the role of Samantha's husband. It would be basically a no-win situation for almost anyone. Dick Sargent [performed] the best way he knew how with professionalism, integrity and class.

Dick Sargent said he had first won the role of Darrin before York. But the actor who played the "second Darrin" said he was under contract with Universal (to do *The Tammy Grimes Show*; her character was named "Tamantha," and Grimes was ABC's first choice for Samantha on *Bewitched*, but she declined). In 1999, however, *Bewitched* producer/director William Asher (married to Montgomery during the original run of *Bewitched*) said York was always the first choice for Darrin.

Like York, Sargent enjoyed a long list of roles before and after playing Darrin (including TV gigs such as *The Six Million Dollar Man*, *Here's Lucy*, and *Trapper John, M.D.*), as well as feature films including *Hardcore* (in 1976, with George C. Scott).

York was married to Joan Alt from 1951 to his demise from emphysema in 1992. They had five children: Mandy, Christopher, Stacy, Matthew, and Kim York.

Sargent, born April 19, 1930, in Carmel, California, was with his partner Albert Williams from 1986 to his death on July 8, 1994, from prostate cancer (and not AIDS, as has been periodically and falsely reported).

Since 2002, Mark Simpson, a life-long *Bewitched* enthusiast and authority, has organized the acclaimed *Bewitched Fan Fare* events, which are attended by the show's devotees from all over the world. As far as he's concerned, both York and Sargent delivered top-notch performances and splits evenly a twin-character-interpretation that remains beloved in the magical male icon history of TV from the 50s, 60s, and 70s. Simpson concludes and breaks down the Darrin-divide this way:

Despite claims otherwise, William Asher stated that Dick York was the first choice to play the part of Darrin Stephens. His comic timing and chemistry with Elizabeth Montgomery and the

Dick Sargent with Elizabeth Montgomery
ABC/PhotoFest

rest of the cast is undeniable. He was brilliant, especially considering that he was in constant pain from a severe back injury throughout his entire time on the show. You would never know it from his performance, which was considerably under-rated. He was definitely not given the credit he deserved. He was Darrin Stephens. He made the role, and the feel of the show changed without him.

Dick Sargent, who was originally considered for the part along with Richard Crenna, was chosen to replace York after he was forced to leave following Season 5. The comparison of the two actors is still talked about today, more than 46 years later. I feel that Sargent portrayed Darrin admirably. It had to have been hard for him to take over a character that someone else had played for 5 years, especially when he was expected to act like Dick York. After a while, when the producers realized that didn't work and let him act like himself, he became more comfortable in the role and, in my opinion, made it his own. The chemistry with Liz was different. Not bad, but different, and the show even had a different feel, but he went on to do a commendable job as Darrin for the final 3 years.

18

Larry Hagman
I Dream of Jeannie/Dallas

Here you have this unapologetic character who is mean and nasty and ruthless and does it all with an evil grin. I think people related to J.R. . . . because we all have someone we know exactly like him. Everyone in the world knows a J.R.

—Larry Hagman

Like his most famous television persona, John Ross (J. R.) Ewing from TV's *Dallas*, Larry Hagman, who died November 23, 2012, was a straight shooter. He always gave credit where credit was due. "Good acting is all in the writing," he once observed. "If it isn't on the page, then it really won't make any difference. You cannot act on force of personality alone."

Hagman portrayed J. R. for 356 episodes of the original *Dallas* series, which aired on CBS from 1978 to 1991. His most memorable moment while working on the show transpired in 1980 when J. R. was shot. "The rest is a blur," he said.

Likability is a key factor to the appeal of any performer playing any character, be that character defined as "good" or "evil." Hagman made two legendary marks in the world of classic television from the 50s, 60s, and 70s. Besides likably playing the unlikable J. R. on *Dallas*, Hagman likably played the likable Major Anthony Nelson on *I Dream of Jeannie*, which provided a platform for him to portray a very physical and comedic role—a marked contrast to J. R.

Fred Freeman says, "It's difficult to define what makes a performer likable on-screen. But when it comes to Larry Hagman, his likability shines."

Even though Hagman's J. R. character on *Dallas* is ultimately unlikable (and a little dastardly, too!), the actor's performance in the role was extremely likable. TV viewers loved to hate J. R. It was quite a departure from playing the very-Darrin-on-*Bewitched*-like character of Major Anthony Nelson on *I Dream of Jeannie*, a transition which is a testament to Hagman's talents as an actor. In comparing Hagman to another legendary actor, this time, of the big screen, Freeman says: "Jack Nicholson can play a lovable idiot just like Larry did with J.R. Either way, the actor has to bring a certain vulnerability to their performance. That's the other key word alongside likability."

Born September 21, 1931, in Fort Wayne, Texas, to actress Mary Martin (famous for *Peter Pan* on Broadway and

Globe Photos

later TV), and Benjamin Jack Hagman, Larry was married to Maj Axelsson from 1954 to his death from cancer in 2012. They had two children: Heidi and Preston.

Hagman had reunited with former *Jeannie* costar Eden for an arc of original *Dallas* episodes, as well as in TV-movies like 1971's *A Howling in the Woods*, and for personal appearances alongside their other *Dream* costar Bill Daily, who played Major Roger Healy on that beloved series.

"I think Larry was wonderful," beams Ann Hodges, "but of course I'm prejudiced because he was one of my best friends. But I believe he was able to pull off just about anything . . . any character he was cast to play."

The first time Hodges noticed Hagman was on a daytime TV serial, when he was "playing a little bit of a wicked character." Hodges thought to herself, "I bet he's going to do well." Hagman did. "He didn't stay there too long, before he was cast opposite Barbara Eden on *Jeannie*. And of course he was terrific in that, and I thought he and Barbara Eden were just great on-screen together. But what I think what really helped Larry always was the fact that he had what we [in Texas] like to call the 'Texas gleam' in his eyes. And it's a little wicked gleam," Hodges chuckles, "but it's not so wicked that it's off-putting; it's like he's teasing you. And he always had it . . . before and during JR. And he also knew so well the type of oil baron family characters that he played on *Dallas*. He knew oil men, because he came from Wuterford, Texas, where there were a lot of oil men. But he was able to pull that off even as the villain. He was one you loved to hate."

19

Don Adams
Get Smart

Missed it by *this much*!

—Maxwell Smart, as played by Don Adams on *Get Smart*

It's one thing to make an impression based upon one's physical appeal. It's an entirely different scenario when someone is considered attractive due to his or her sense of humor. That's a true testament to sincere, long-lasting appeal.

With regard to actor Don Adams, his main small-screen attraction was a double-edged sword. He was sharp on both ends; handsome as all get-out, and witty beyond belief. Or as his character Maxwell Smart on *Get Smart* (NBC, 1966 to 1971), might have wondered, "Would you believe?"

Carl Birkmeyer, editor of www.wouldyoubelieve.com, explains what it was like to have the "great pleasure" of meeting Adams at the *Get Smart* Gathering, a cast and crew reunion of Don's series that was held in 2003 (and that included lovely *Smart* costar Barbara "Agent 99" Feldon). Birkmeyer noted that Don was recovering from a broken hip and was in pain that night, however, "Don was funny, gracious and grateful to see the outpouring of love and respect he received that night from his friends, co-workers, and fans. Even though he was uncomfortable, Don sat and posed for pictures with all of the fans present, as he wanted to give something back to all of us, not realizing that he had been doing that for years. When he left the restaurant that night, Don received a standing ovation that brought a tear to his eye. I believe at that moment he knew for certain that he had made a positive impact on all of our lives, even if all we did was know him from TV. That night, and that moment meant a great deal to Don, as he realized just how much we all loved him. I'd like to share with you a small part of the speech that I gave that night for Don and the cast and crew."

There's not a week that goes by that I don't receive a wonderful message from another fan, telling me how much [they] loved the show and what an impact it has had on [their] life. Women to whom 99 was their very first strong role models. Writers who got into the industry because *Get Smart* inspired them. Ordinary people who use the powerfully strong and honest character of Max as a role model to "fight rottenness."

The term hero gets bandied about a lot these days, with firefighters, soldiers, and police officers all hearing that term routinely. And those people are heroes. But there's another type of hero, the everyday hero. The person who through his or her efforts the world is a better place for each of us. I'm talking about people who make us laugh and make us smile and create a world special in our lives. That's you, the people who created *Get Smart*. Yes, it's just a TV show, but it's a TV show that by its quality and its humanity has made our lives just a little better. Put a smile on our face the day we really needed one. A TV show that gave us a family that we still hold dear. The reason this show is so important to us is because it's got a little piece of all of you in it. The humanity and grace that Don and the rest of the cast and crew put into this show lives on and permeates all our lives. Two nights before the *Gathering* [reunion] the Museum of Radio and Television held a tribute to *Get Smart*. Once again, Don was witty and entertaining, even recreating a scene from the show with Bernie Kopell. One of the many great points Don made (and I'm paraphrasing) was that through *Get Smart* he would be forever young, handsome, funny and creative and what a great thing that was for all of the cast and crew. He was right and wrong. Right because the Don Adams from *Get Smart* will live forever, entertaining new generations of fans. Wrong because he was 80-years-old that night and Don was still handsome, funny, creative, and talented.

That's how I'll choose to remember him, as a man who gave part of himself to entertain all of us.

Born Donald James Yarmy on April 13, 1923, in Manhattan, New York, Adams was educated at DeWitt Clinton High School in New York City. His parents were William Yarmy and Consuelo Deiter; he had a brother, Richard (known as actor Dick Yarmy). He married three times (Adelaide Adams, 1947–1960; Dorothy Bracken, 1960–1976; and Judy Luciano,1977–1990), resulting in seven children (Caroline, Christine, Catherine, Cecily, Stacey, Sean, and Beige).

Adams began his career as Don Yarmy, an aspiring stand-up comic and, after marrying Adelaide, changed his name to Don Adams, retaining it even after they divorced (for auditions, which were often held in alphabetical order).

Adams's big break arrived with his *Smart* role as Agent 86, Maxwell Smart. The show was devised by Mel Brooks and Buck Henry, partially due to the success of the spy genre (brought on by the James Bond feature films), and as an antidote to sitcoms that tended to end with a moral or message. *Get Smart* was satire at its TV finest, and Adams won three consecutive Emmys (1967–1969) for his participation as the inept yet endearing secret Agent 86. By 1970, after a five-year run, Adams had starred in 138 episodes as well as writing

NBC/Globe Photos

two and directing thirteen. His trademark voice inflections came from exaggerating William Powell's interrogative tone in *The Thin Man* films.

Voiceover work for animated characters was a special talent of Adams (who died September 25, 2005, at Cedars-Sinai Medical Center, Los Angeles, of a pulmonary infection). Prior to *Smart* he delivered top vocal techniques to *Tennessee Tuxedo* (1963–1966) and later (from 1983 to 1986) as *Inspector Gadget*. He reprised his Smart performance in the 1980 feature film *The Nude Bomb*, the 1989 TV-movie *Get Smart, Again!* and, in 1995, with a seven-episode ABC reboot (with Feldon and Andy Dick as their spy-son) titled, *Get Smart, Again*.

Adams never thought the original series had a chance. "I didn't think the pilot came together well," he said.

The pilot may have been initially weak, but the show and Don Adams remain forever strong—in the hearts and minds of millions of television fans the world over.

20

Ted Bessell
That Girl

> Donald Hollinger made me a name.
>
> —Ted Bessell

It's been nearly twenty years since Ted Bessell died on October 6, 1996 (at age sixty-one) in Los Angeles from an aortic aneurysm. On that day, the entertainment industry—and the world—lost to a heart attack a beloved and talented human being.

The versatile actor, producer, and director was best known as the fictional *Newsview* news magazine writer and boyfriend Don Hollinger to Marlo Thomas's Ann Marie on TV's classic *That Girl* sitcom (ABC, 1966–1971). But he's also forever remembered as just a great guy of the real world.

Ted was born Howard Weston Bessell Jr., on March 20, 1935, in Queens, New York. He attended Georgetown University and the University of Colorado. His parents were Howard and Jo Bessell. He was married to Janeen A. Dara from 1963 until 1967, when the union was annulled. He was married to Linnell S. Nobori from 1982 to his death in 1996. He had two children: Sarah and Mary Bessell.

Some benchmark moments from his life and career before and after *That Girl*: At age twelve he performed a piano recital at Carnegie Hall. In 1961 he played an elevator operator in the feature film *Lover Come Back.* He was a semi-regular on *Gomer Pyle, U.S.M.C.*; played Mike Reynolds in the short-lived series *Me and the Chimp* (CBS, 1972); and was Joe Warner, Mary's boyfriend, on two episodes of *The Mary Tyler Moore Show* (1975). He played Harry Jenkins in the brief series *Good Time*

Harry (1980), and Gen. Oliver Mansfield, husband of Julie Mansfield, president of the United States (Patty Duke), in the short-lived Fox series *Hail to the Chief* (1985). By the late 80s, he had largely abandoned acting and became a television director, sharing an Emmy in 1989 for directing an episode of Fox television's *Tracey Ullman Show*.

Before Bessell died, *That Girl* was scheduled to be honored with an all-star tribute in Los Angeles at the Museum of Television and Radio on October 11, 1996. Instead, the remaining cast and crew from the show, including Thomas and Bernie Kopell (who played Don's best friend and co-worker Jerry Bauman), mourned the loss of their friend whom they affectionately referred to as Teddy.

Bessell was accessible, such that he was unaffected by his celebrity, and came to grips with his Hollinger persona—by which he first felt stereotyped. After *That Girl* folded, it was a challenge for him to win other roles and be at peace with the character. "Donald Hollinger made me a name but took away the heart of me," he said in 1989, when he labeled the part a creative "imposition."

ABC/PhotoFest

However, due to the renewed interest and affection shown to *That Girl* via Nick at Nite and TV Land, Bessell began to realize his importance and endearing contribution to television's grand hall of fame. At the time of his death, he was scheduled to direct the *Bewitched* feature film, which at the time was being produced only by Parkway Productions, headed by Penny Marshall (his good friend, who had also attended his tribute in 1996).

The lingering impression Bessell left with everyone he met was his complete lack of arrogance. Anyone who portrayed so consoling, warm-hearted, and supportive a character as Don Hollinger, with such credibility would have to be as sincere in real life.

The fondest vision that many *That Girl* fans have of Bessell rests with their first view of his on-screen character's initial meeting with aspiring actress Ann Marie in the show's pilot. Thinking she was under assault (when she was actually filming a commercial in Hollinger's *Newsview* building), Don, with his briefcase as a weapon, comes along and slams the head of an actor who he believes to be Ann's assailant. After she explains the situation, and seeks to alleviate an already-stressful situation, Don realizes his mistake, deeply regrets it, and labels himself, "Captain Dumb Dumb."

The line was priceless, and Bessell's delivery of it was done with all the charm and likability that any one actor could muster. At that moment, Ann fell in love with Donald Hollinger, along with the rest of us. As Marlo Thomas herself once noted, "Our show was called *That Girl*, but we all knew *that guy* was a huge part of our success."

Had Ted Bessell lived, he not only would have directed the *Bewitched* feature film, but a TV-movie adaptation of *That Girl*—with Bessell and Thomas reprising their roles. Bessell was very much looking forward to the movie. "I wanted to see what happened to those characters," he said in 1996. Although the original *Girl* sitcom completed its run with Don and Ann engaged to be wed, Bessell envisioned the couple breaking up but eventually exchanging vows. "They would have remained friends," he said. "And I think they would have gotten back together again. He probably would have married [someone else after he and Ann broke their engagement], and she might have done well as an actress."

Bessell concluded about redoing *Girl* to *TV Guide* shortly before he died, "As long as we're still alive and kicking, I think it's a mistake not to do it."

Instead, it became a dreadful mistake that Ted Bessell left us too soon. *That Girl* may still one day be remade. But it just won't be the same without Bessell and Thomas; and regarding Bessell's involvement with the *Bewitched* feature film, his good friend Penny Marshall was devastated upon learning of his death.

"He was a great force behind a lot of creative people," she said at the time.

Good souls usually are.

21

Clifton Davis and Sherman Hemsley
That's My Mama/The Jeffersons/Amen

. . . never can say good-bye.

— As sung by Clifton Davis

Sherman Hemsley was a force of nature. Clifton Davis remains the calm in the storm. Both gentlemen were born with multiple talents, of equal measure, if on different levels.

These two TV legends initially gained fame separately on the small screen in two different half-hour situation comedies, then they found it together on the same sitcom. Hemsley was introduced to television audiences as George Jefferson by way of Norman Lear's groundbreaking show *All in the Family*, followed by the spin-off series, *The Jeffersons*, which costarred Isabel Sanford as his wife. Davis first came to television as the star of his own weekly variety show costarring Melba Moore, and then later as the lead male on the ABC sitcom, *That's My Mama*.

Davis and Hemsley then combined their polar opposite, but equally energetic talents (Hemsley was manic; Davis was even-keeled) in the 80s on the NBC religious-geared sitcom, *Amen*. Hemsley portrayed church deacon Ernest Frey. Davis was Reverend Reuben Gregory, the church minister. It was a match made in heaven—at least for TV.

Today, Davis is a real-life licensed minister (for the St. Luke Baptist Church in New York City). He was born in Chicago, Illinois, the son of Thelma van Putten Langhorn, a nurse, and Toussaint L'Ouverture Davis, also a Baptist minister. He was raised in Mastic, New York. In an article he penned for the book *Chicken Soup for the Teenage*

Soul, Davis addressed the prejudice he confronted being raised in the pre–Civil Rights Act era.

Before finding success in front of the camera, Davis worked as a songwriter, most famously composing the hit song, "Never Can Say Goodbye" for The Jackson 5. Then came his costarring TV variety show gig with Melba Moore, followed by his role as Clifton Curtis on *Mama*, which aired in the mid-70s. The show also featured Theresa Merritt, Theodore Wilson, and Ted Lange, the latter of whom would reach a measure of male TV icon status himself as Isaac, the bartender, on *The Love Boat*.

A triple heart bypass survivor, Davis participated in several celebrity TV sports and game competitions in the 70s. In 1977, he appeared in the feature film *Scott Joplin* and, in 1999, the movie *Any Given Sunday*.

Clifton Davis, left; Sherman Hemsley, right

NBC/PhotoFest

A theatrically trained actor, Davis has appeared in live productions in Toronto and on Broadway's *Aladdin* as the Sultan of Agrabah. He attained a BA in theology from Oakwood University and a master of divinity degree from Andrews University. For nearly thirty years he's been involved with Youthville, USA, a children's services organization, while he cofounded Welcome Christian Center in Huntington Beach, California, for which he served as co-pastor. Every year, he hosts The Most Soulful Sound, a gospel choir competition (based in Raleigh, North Carolina), and a celebrity golf tournament (in Elizabeth City, North Carolina, at Elizabeth City State University, where he was vice chancellor for institutional advancement).

Since the end of 2005, Davis has held the position of executive director for Welcome America, a nonprofit organization located in Philadelphia, Pennsylvania, that produces the nation's largest annual Fourth of July event.

Davis is a frequent guest host on Trinity Broadcasting Network and, from 2000 to 2008, he emceed the *Gospel Superfest* TV show (syndicated by United Television).

Hemsley was born Sherman Alexander Hemsley on February 1, 1938. Besides his TV roles on *The Jeffersons* and *Amen*, he offered his voice as Earl Sinclair's loud-mouth employer, a triceratops named B. P. Richfield, on the Jim Henson ABC sitcom from the early 90s called *Dinosaurs*.

Hemsley was born and raised around 22nd and Christian Streets in South Philadelphia by his mother, who worked in a lamp factory. According to Wikipedia, he did not meet his father until he was fourteen. He dropped out of school in tenth grade and joined the US Air Force, where he served for four years. After that, he returned to Philadelphia, where he was employed by the post office during the day while taking evening classes at the Academy of Dramatic Arts. Many stage roles followed and led to Norman Lear casting him in his most iconic role of George Jefferson on *All in the Family*.

Hemsley once described his TV alter (and massive) ego George Jefferson as "pompous and feisty." As the diminutive-in-size-actor with the larger-than-life presence later explained in a 2003 interview for the Archive of American Television, playing George "was really hard . . . because—rude, I don't like to be that way. But it was the character. I had to do it. I had to be true to the character. If I was to pull back something, then it just wouldn't work."

Work, it did. When Hemsley succumbed to lung cancer in 2012, approximately 150 people attended his memorial service at the Cielo Vista Church in El Paso, Texas. As noted by various press reports, mourners were amused by the random clips from *The Jeffersons* that were screened during the service displaying Sherman as George, feisty and bigoted as ever. "He helped us to laugh, gave us an opportunity to forget the troubles, the stresses of life," El Paso Fire Department Fellowship chaplain Sam Faraone said during the eulogy.

With catch phrases like "Say wha'?" and "Weezy" forever embedded in the American psyche, along with his trademark walk and confidence as George Jefferson, Sherman Hemsley, who died July 24, 2012, leaves behind a unique comedic legacy that continues to dissolve racial barriers with his own special brand of cool.

22

Bob Newhart
The Bob Newhart Show

I've been told to speed up my delivery when I perform. But if I lose the stammer, I'm just another slightly amusing accountant.

—Bob Newhart

"Hello": one simple word in one little sentence that is stated in the beginning of the opening credit sequence for TV's classic Saturday night staple in the 70s, *The Bob Newhart Show*. Such a tiny term has held so much power and charisma for such a small-in-stature but larger-than-life presence. Yet, that is the secret to Newhart's monumental appeal: subtlety.

No male icon in TV history has ever held stilted conversations, in person or on the telephone, quite like Newhart, who remains without a doubt one of the most likable actors to ever hit the small screen with his massive talent.

After several attempts at sitcom stardom, decades of live and recorded performances, and frequent guest appearances on TV variety series like *The Dean Martin Show*, Newhart found his niche and audience via his voice on *The Bob Newhart Show*, which debuted in 1972—two years after the premiere of *The Mary Tyler Moore Show*, whose female lead co-produced (with then-husband Grant Tinker) both sitcoms (among several others) for CBS and other networks. It was Newhart's slight stammer and self-deprecating humor, combined with his affable awkward social interaction that sealed his appeal with the viewer.

Rick Lertzman summarizes Newhart's career:

Bob's rise to fame began with his hit comedy album "The Button-Down Mind of Bob Newhart." When Emmy producer Bob Finkel showcased him on the Emmys in 1961, he was a nationwide hit. After a short-lived (but Emmy winning) variety show, he was featured in films like *Catch-22* (among others), on television—and in nightclubs. His sardonic, dry, stammering delivery made him unique among stand-up comedians. He brought that same deadpan style to his *Bob Newhart Show* and, later on the same network, a second sitcom, simply called *Newhart*. Bob was the "Everyman" that viewers always identified with. He recently won an Emmy for his appearance on the popular *The Big Bang Theory*. For over 50 years, Bob has been a comedy icon.

Globe Photos

On his first hit *Newhart Show*, Bob portrayed Dr. Robert Hartley, a psychologist, opposite Suzanne Pleshette as his wife, Emily, a schoolteacher; Bill Daily as their next-door neighbor Howard Borden, an airline pilot in uniform (the actor had worn similar garb a few seasons before as astronaut Major Roger Healy on *I Dream of Jeannie*); Marcia Wallace as his secretary; Peter Bonerz as a dental colleague on the same floor; and various A-list supporting actors portraying a host of clients (with various psychological "issues").

The series remained in the top twenty for its entire six-year run, a hit in its final season (even after the demise and absence of its strong lead-in *The Mary Tyler Moore Show*). But it was at the close of the show's first season that Newhart made an observation about the key to its success.

The comment he received most often that initial year was that the show's midseason episodes were considered superior to the first few segments. He said:

I think about halfway into the season the actors began to know the characters they were playing. They began to know what line didn't sound right. And the audience too became more familiar with the characters. I think that's when the show began to pick up popularity.

It was still Newhart's steady-as-she-goes performance and demeanor that balanced out the various eccentricities of the various characters on the show, much like his subtle interpretation of Dr. Hartley helped to hold together the sanity of his band of clients who met mostly in group therapy.

In comparing Dr. Hartley to Ted Knight's heightened portrayal of the egocentric TV anchorman Ted Baxter on *The Mary Tyler Moore Show*, Newhart went on to explain how the audience was initially unfamiliar with Baxter. "Then," he said, "as they got to know him, they'd laugh in anticipation of what he was going to say—then they'd laugh again when he actually said it." Newhart believed the same thing transpired about halfway through the first season of *The Bob Newhart Show*, when, "people got to know us."

Bob Newhart, the person, however, has always been easy to know. He was born in Chicago (in which *The Bob Newhart Show* was set), the second of four children to Julia Pauline Newhart and George David Newhart. His father was a salesman for a plumbing and heating firm and, as Newhart once explained, his parents "didn't have all that much money," but they paid for his education, which included attending Loyola University, where he received a degree in commerce. He worked after school, so he did not have time to participate in drama in high school. After serving in the army for two years, he entered and dropped out of law school. Before, during, and after, he had a number of jobs, including a position for an insurance company, a meat market delivery boy, a copywriter, a clerk, even a pin-spotter in a bowling alley, and finally, an accountant. He was so dedicated to the latter position he would make certain the petty cash accounts would even out by digging into his own pocket.

Was he the class comedian?

"I was somewhat caustic in high school," he told Herz. "But I was never the life-of-the-party type. I was never the lampshade-on-the-head or the buffoon-type."

That said, he was performing with a stock company of actors in a theater in Oak Park. To keep themselves busy, he and a friend began making lengthy and antic phone calls, which they eventually recorded and utilized as audition pieces. Warner Bros. ultimately heard the tapes and, in 1960, released "The Button Down Mind of Bob Newhart," which dealt with a press agent, and what he called "Madison Avenue types." This led to nightclub acts and eventually television appearances before and after *The Bob Newhart Show* (including his other popular CBS sitcom, *Newhart*, which originally aired from 1982 to 1990).

The all-hands performer has also enjoyed an extensive film career, in movies like *Elf* (2003).

As he concluded to Herz: "I'm proudest of being considered a professional in my work. [Legendary comedian] Ed Wynn once described a comic as a person who says funny things—and a comedian as a person who says things funny. In that sense, I guess you would say I'm a comedian."

PART III

THE JOHNNY ANGELS

Before Justin Bieber was in his baby bib, and New Direction turned the corner of success, male teen idols were rampant on television, sometimes propelled to stardom because of the likes of Dick Clark and Pat Boone, both of whom hosted music variety shows geared toward young viewers.

Clark's status as "TV's oldest teenager" spoke volumes to his legendary presence on television as the voice of *American Bandstand*, which introduced American audiences to teen sensations like Paul Anka, Frankie Avalon, the Platters, the Jackson 5, the Osmond Brothers, and on and on. As the 50s turned into the 60s and on into the 70s, young TV viewers fawned over Billy Gray and Paul Petersen, Ricky and David Nelson, Don Grady, Barry Williams and Christopher Knight, Bobby Sherman, David Cassidy, and more.

An optimum example of the young male teen TV craze is *The Monkees*, the "Prefab Four" (short for "prefabricated") musical band that was granted its own 1966–1968 half-hour NBC-TV sitcom (with music) following the British musical invasion in the early 60s. Four young actors were selected from among more than four hundred who auditioned for the show that would ultimately become the small-screen edition of what The Beatles were delivering with groundbreaking feature films like *Help* and *A Hard Day's Night*.

Manic camera angles and uplifting music were the mainstay of those Beatle flicks, and such traits soon became replicated by *The Monkees*, aka Davy Jones, Peter Tork, Micky Dolenz, and Mike Nesmith on their show.

Tommy Boyce and Bobby Hart, writers of many of The Monkees' songs, observed quickly that when brought in to the studio together, the four actors would try to make each other laugh. As a result, an on-screen chemistry was born—along with lots of hit records, such as "Last Train to Clarksville" (a Boyce and Hart composition) and "I'm a Believer" (penned by Neil Diamond).

The Monkees was a unique media experience that almost singlehandedly defined the male TV idol experience. Not until the syndicated TV show *Solid Gold*, or certainly not before Music Television (MTV) was introduced to the mainstream in 1981, did young male music performers on TV reach the Monkees' level of fame.

Young non-musical male performers, pre- and post-Monkees, certainly made their TV mark, including Willie Aames, who before being cast as Scott Baio's sidekick Buddy Lembeck on the 1980s TV sitcom, *Charles in Charge* (which first aired on CBS, then in syndication), was the all-American boy of 70s television.

After making six periodic appearances as boyfriend to Kristy McNichol's Buddy Lawrence on ABC's *Family*, Aames graduated to regular series status as Tommy Bradford for four seasons on *Eight Is Enough*, which ultimately might be defined as a one-hour combination of *The Waltons* and *The Brady Bunch*. Whereas *The Waltons* was set in the Depression era with seven children, and whereas the Bradys added together six siblings in the late 60s and early 70s, *Enough* had eight kids, counting Aames's Tommy as the second oldest son (behind Grant Goodeve, who replaced a certain then-unknown young actor named Mark Hamill who went on to ignite and conquer the galaxy "far, far away" in the *Star Wars* feature film franchise).

Although Willie's Tommy character started on *Enough* as only fourteen years old, Aames was in reality seventeen. As he told Peggy Herz in 1978, he enjoyed playing younger. In one episode, Tommy went on his first date and got stood up. That actually happened to Aames in real life. "I went to the girl's house and she wasn't there," he laughed.

Aames remains a slight 5'6", but those stats never stunted his success, on screen or off. "My height has never really been a problem," he relayed to Herz. "I haven't really wished I was taller."

"I didn't become an actor because I wanted to act," he decided. "I wanted to become a marine biologist. But most of all, I wanted to be accepted."

Along with many other young male icons of television in the 50s, 60s, and 70s, Aames certainly became exactly that. A closer look at a few more such idols offers some insight into exactly how that particular road to stardom is paved (with a few bumps along the way).

23

Ricky Nelson
The Adventures of Ozzie and Harriet

You can't please everyone, so you gotta' please yourself.

—Ricky Nelson

Ricky and David Nelson were America's children in the 50s and into the 60s. They literally grew up before our eyes and ears on *The Adventures of Ozzie and Harriet*, which began as a family radio show in 1944, and was later transmitted, with pictures, on ABC-TV from 1952 to 1966. With the Nelsons essentially playing themselves (sort of), Ricky stood out as an actor and musical artist, in the process moved from being the brash young comic Greek chorus to his father Ozzie's laid back shenanigans to one of the biggest rock-and-roll music stars of the pre-Beatles era. If Elvis Presley was the King, Ricky Nelson was the one America's parents most heartily approved of; and with those soul-searching eyes of his, America's sister wasn't going to argue the point.

Born Eric Hilliard Nelson on May 8, 1940, in Teaneck, New Jersey, Ricky attended Gardner Street Public School, Bancroft Junior High, and Hollywood High School, all in Los Angeles. He had an older brother David, who also appeared on their radio and TV show, along with their parents, Ozzie and Harriet (Hillard, nee Peggy Louise Snyder). Ricky, who died in a tragic small plane crash on New Year's Eve 1985, was married to Sharon Kristin Harmon (older sister to Mark) from 1963 to 1982, a union that produced children Tracy, who went on to follow in her father's acting footsteps, twins Gunnar and Matthew (who formed the musical band called "Nelson"), and Sam. He also had another son, Eric, by girlfriend Georgeann Crew.

Ricky's performing career began when his father decided that he and David should play themselves on their parents' radio program, where the boys had already been

Globe Photos

characters but voiced by other actors. Ricky often stole the show with his wisecracks and charm, appearing in 432 episodes of the series. In the meantime he became a pop singer, introducing songs on the show (including his first #1 single, "Poor Little Fool"), and became the first TV personality to do so. From 1957 to 1962 he had thirty Top 40 hits, more than any other vocalist except Elvis (who had fifty-three) and Pat Boone (who had thirty-eight). By 1960 his fan club had nine thousand chapters, and his career further expanded into feature films, including the 1959 Howard Hawks western classic *Rio Bravo* with John Wayne, Dean Martin, and Walter Brennan. Musically, he reached the Top 40 one last time with 1972's "Garden Party," and made periodic guest-star appearances on TV shows like *The Streets of San Francisco* (which featured fellow male icon and future big-screen legend Michael Douglas, son of Kirk).

On *Saturday Night Live* in 1979, Ricky spoofed his sitcom image, finding himself *Twilight Zone*–style among characters from vintage sitcoms such as *I Love Lucy*, *Father Knows Best*, and *Leave It to Beaver* (a concept that was later utilized to some extent for the 1998 motion picture *Pleasantville*).

On December 31, 1985, the small plane he was flying in on his way to a New Year's Eve gig in Dallas, Texas, ran into trouble. He and his band crash-landed two miles from De Kalb, Texas. The severely burned pilots survived by escaping through cockpit windows, but all seven other occupants, including Ricky, did not.

He was posthumously inducted in the Rock and Roll Hall of Fame (1987) and the Rockabilly Hall of Fame (2004), and was ranked #91 on the *Rolling Stone* list of the 100 Greatest Artists of All Time.

In "Ricky the Dreamer," a classic episode of *The Adventures of Ozzie & Harriet* that first aired April 10, 1957, the TV-Ricky once told his TV-mother, "I think teenagers like to feel that they're just people with normal, average reactions, and rhythm and blues records usually tell a story or express an emotion."

However, Ricky might just as well have been speaking to his mom in real life, as the emotional loss expressed by the family, friends, and millions of fans who were devastated by his demise decades later remains immeasurable.

24

Billy Gray
Father Knows Best

Paul Petersen
The Donna Reed Show

Gosh!

—Bud Anderson, as played by Billy Gray on *Father Knows Best*, and Jeff
Stone, as played by Paul Petersen on *The Donna Reed Show*

In the 50s, 60s, and 70s, children respected their parents on sitcoms like *Father Knows Best* and *The Donna Reed Show*. Shelley Fabares's teenage Mary Stone had a great deal of admiration for her father, pediatrician Dr. Alex Stone, as portrayed by Carl Betz on *Reed*, and Elinor Donahue as Princess Anderson and Lauren Chapin as her younger daughter Kitten Anderson held in high regard their TV dad, Jim Anderson, as portrayed by Robert Young.

It was the male bonding between fathers and sons on both these series that holds specific interest. On *Best*, Billy Gray played with introspective aplomb the daring but relatively reserved Jim "Bud" Anderson Jr., while Paul Petersen's energetic performance as Jeff Stone on *Reed* always remained likable and never off-putting. While *Best* was the more realistic of the two shows, offering a more solid balance of both comedy and drama, with relatively superior scripts to *Reed*, each program made it a point to convey just how important the father-son relationship was to the core of the family.

In the process, Bud and Jeff were, on both a subliminal and conscious level, presenting TV viewers with the ideal model of how to be a proper young man—within and outside the family unit. Gray and Petersen stepped up to the plate to help convey that message and interpret their given characters with theatrical talents seemingly beyond their years.

Paul Petersen
Globe Photos

Both actors were articulate, animated, athletic, and sincere in each of their interpretations. Gray's diction, in particular, remains notable. In several episodes of *Father Knows Best*, he can be heard delivering the phrase "at all," with precise annunciation. While both his Bud and Petersen's Jeff characters would of course argue and tease their television sisters, they still remained loyal if either of their siblings were somehow challenged or in trouble, in or outside the family unit.

Upon close inspection of any segment of *Best* featuring Gray, or of any episode of *Reed* focusing on Petersen, it becomes abundantly clear just how perfectly cast each actor was as his character. During the course of both long-running series (*Best* originally aired for six seasons, and *Reed* for nine years), they grew into and with their roles from boyhood to manhood with impressive thespian bravado—and a fine balance of comedic and physical agility to boot.

Gray explains how his life and career commenced as an actor:

My mother was an actress, Beatrice Gray. She appeared in movies with Western stars, Johnny McBrown, Bob Steele, Gibson, that type of thing. One day my brother was in a play, my older brother, a school play I think it was or something, and I was running up and down the aisle. A lady said, "Take me to your mother."

It turned out that it was my mother's agent. The agent said, "I think I can get this kid some work." I was about five at the time. So I started going on interviews for bit parts and got them. I got almost every interview I went on for years. It was kind of peculiar. But I was kind of a smart-ass kid. I guess that's what they were looking for.

As to his original interview/audition for *Father Knows Best*, Gray says, it was "simply a regular interview; nothing out of the ordinary," after which he "probably" received a call-back, followed by a screen test. "We did a little scene around the kitchen table for a test," he adds. "I got the part. There was nothing unusual about it. It was a normal job interview. It turned out to be something long-lived. There was one incident:

I had also done a pilot for a show called *Annie Oakley*. They wanted to go ahead with that. The decision was made to opt for *Father Knows Best* as opposed to the *Annie Oakley* show; that was the only memorable incident regarding getting the show."

Gray was born January 13, 1938. He married twice; first to Donna Wilkes, then to Helena Kallianiotes.

Petersen was born September 23, 1945, in Glendale, California, and wed three times: Brenda Benet (1967–1970), Hallie Litman (1974–1988), and Rana Jo Platz (1992 to the present).

Following the cancellations of *Father Knows Best* and *The Donna Reed Show*, it was a challenge for both Billy Gray and Paul Petersen to find work. They each

Billy Gray
CBS/PhotoFest

made periodic guest appearances on various shows beyond their famous sitcoms, but the roles were few and far between. And while Gray appeared in two *Best* TV-reunion movies with his cast-mates (including TV mom Jane Wyatt, who contributed instruction to his fine on-screen diction), Petersen and his costars from *The Donna Reed Show* never had the opportunity to reunite in full for any such nostalgic production.

While both Gray and Petersen experienced several personal setbacks, they remained strong over the years. According to imdb.com, Peterson in particular went through practically the worst that could transpire in the life of a former child star upon experiencing Hollywood's severe rejection. Unlike others, however, such as Anissa Jones (*Family Affair*), Rusty Hamer (*Make Room for Daddy*), and Dana Plato and Gary Coleman (*Diff'rent Strokes*), he survived. Consequently, Petersen today is considered the most dedicated and loyal advocate in protecting both present-day child stars and one-time celebrities. In 1990, he formed A Minor Consideration, a nonprofit child-actor support organization that has had a significantly positive effect on hundreds of members of the entertainment industry—of all ages.

25

Tony Dow and Jerry Mathers
Leave It to Beaver

I don't think a lot of people realize the influence TV has on our kids. Kids take a lot of their cues from it in their dress and conduct.

—Jerry Mathers

Jerry Mathers and Tony Dow were natural performers, particularly when it came to interpreting their characters on *Leave It to Beaver*, which first aired on ABC and CBS from 1958 to 1963. With Tony as older brother Wally Cleaver, playing opposite Theodore Cleaver, aka the Beaver, the two actors truly seemed like the kids next door.

One key to their appeal was the huge assist they got from the writers. The writers would script out the kids' lines and then let their own kids rewrite them as kids from that era would actually say them. That gave Wally and the Beaver a freshness and naturalness not found anywhere else on television. Anyone doing research on 50s slang as used by teenagers should forget watching the darker images and edgier precepts presented in movies like *West Side Story*, *Rebel Without a Cause*, or *The Blackboard Jungle*. Instead, watch *Leave It to Beaver*, and take a quick course in how kids really talked in the late 50s and early 60s.

As the time, young viewers at home instantly identified with Wally and the Beaver, while parents perceived the show through their children's eyes. Mom and Dad may have wished to have offspring as ideal as those portrayed on *The Donna Reed Show* (the almost too-perfect Mary Stone as played by Shelley Fabares, and her sassy, younger but ultimately wiser brother Jeff Stone, as performed with precision by Paul Petersen). But such was not the case on *Beaver*.

Mathers and Dow were the Real Deal—keeping baby alligators in the toilet tank and hiding their latest misadventures from the prying eyes of Ward and June Cleaver (Hugh Beaumont and Barbara Billingsley).

Today, Dow explains the events that led to his casting on *Beaver*:

Tony Dow, left; Jerry Mathers, right
Globe Photos

I was a diver and I had a coach named Johnny Reily, who was a nine-times-national diving champion. And we worked out at the Hollywood Athletic Club and there was a lifeguard there named Bill Bryant who was an actor. And one day, he asked my Mom if I'd be interested in auditioning a TV series pilot [*Johnny Wildlife*]. She said "Ok," and I put on my blue suit and went over to Columbia Studios and he proceeded to go in and meet with [studio executive] Harry Ackerman and I got the part . . . but I never acted, nor had any aspirations to act.

Ackerman made sure that Dow would find his way to playing opposite Jerry Mathers in *Leave It to Beaver*.

As media historians Will Jacobs and Gerard Jones explained in *TV Gold* magazine, July 1986:

Leave It To Beaver was a monument to an America that we always wanted and never quite reached. The founder of the family, father Ward Cleaver [as played by Hugh Beaumont], was the American of his generation. He had grown up in the poverty-stricken farms of the Depression, had been hardened by that but had been instilled with an unshakable set of values ("Why, when I was a boy, Beaver, we understood the value of a dollar"). He came out of his youth with one dream, which was The Dream of America in those years: to build a materially better life for his children.

Wally and the Beaver were played to perfection by Dow and Mathers. As the *TV Gold* writers went on to assess, "Wally was the perfect teenager: a letterman in sports, popular with the girls, his eyes on his future."

"And Beaver himself . . . there's never been a cuter kid."

26

Tim Considine, Don Grady, Stanley Livingston, Barry Livingston
My Three Sons

I loved *My Three Sons.*

—Don Grady

Whenever Don Grady played Robbie Douglas on *My Three Sons* (CBS, 1960–1972), he always looked concerned, as if worried that dad Steve Douglas (Fred MacMurray) would see that new scratch on the car. It was a testament to the good heart and soul of Grady, who left us much too soon—on June 27, 2012—from cancer at age sixty-eight. On *Sons*, Don's Robbie wasn't cocky like older brother Mike (Tim Considine, who left the series in 1965). Robbie could sometimes be feisty, as in an early episode of the series when he and Mike got into somewhat of a scrap. As Grady explained in 2010, it wasn't a difficult scene to play. "Tim and I weren't getting along while filming the fight scenes and the director encouraged us to grapple with our real-life issues as creative expression."

Don's Robbie and Tim's Mike were not as playful as their two younger TV siblings, as played by real-life brothers Stanley Livingston and Barry Livingston (the latter of whom joined the series in 1963). Robbie was sensitive, tender, and easily bruised, just like the actor who brought him to life. Grady gained more confidence and wisdom as a performer when he moved into the role of the elder brother as Mike's character was written out of the show. And he was most believable taking Tina Cole (of the musical King Family) as his TV bride and becoming the father of three sons of his own.

Each of the *Sons* stars were and remain extremely popular with classic television followers.

Born December 31, 1940, Considine went on to become an author, photographer, and automotive and motor sports historian. His books include *The Language of Sport* and *American Grand Prix Racing*.

Stanley Livingston, born November 24, 1950, is one of the most respected and prolifically talented former child stars in the industry. He continues acting today, as well as directing, and founded the acclaimed Actor's Journey Project, which helps aspiring actors hone and succeed at their craft.

Barry Livingston, born December 17, 1953, has performed in countless TV and feature film roles since appearing on

From left: Barry Livingston, Tim Considine, Stanley Livingston
Globe Photos

Sons and has authored the best-selling memoir, *The Importance of Being Ernie: From My Three Sons To Mad Men—A Hollywood Survivor Tells All*.

Yet it was Don Grady who became the *Sons* central heartthrob.

Born Don Louis Agrati on June 8, 1944, in San Diego, Grady attended Burbank High School in Burbank, California. His parents were Lou Anthony Agrati and Mary B. Castellino. He was married to Julie Boonisar from 1976 to 1979, and in 1985 wed Virginia Lewsader, to whom he remained wed until his untimely demise, but not before being blessed with two children: Joey Grady and Tessa Grady (from his second marriage).

Before *My Three Sons*, Don appeared as one of the original Mouseketeers in *The Mickey Mouse Club* beginning in 1955. Between 1957 and 1960 he made guest appearances on numerous other TV shows, including *The Ann Sothern Show*, *Buckskin*, *Alcoa Theatre*, *The Restless Gun*, *Colt .45*, *Wichita Town*, *Zane Grey Theater*, *Law of the Plainsman*, *Death Valley Days*, *The Betty Hutton Show*, *The Rifleman*, *Startime*, *Wagon Train*, *Have Gun—Will Travel*, and *The Detectives*. He played Robbie

Douglas for twelve seasons on *My Three Sons* (from 1960 to 1972), and composed music for the 1964 episode "First, You're a Tadpole."

Although never attaining the pop-star status of Ricky Nelson, as a solo artist, Don had a hit song at #132 on the Billboard Singles Charts in 1966 with "The Children of St. Monica." He was also a drummer and vocalist for the band Yellow Balloon, which also had a hit tune, also titled "Yellow Balloon," which reached #25 on the Billboard Pop Charts in April 1967.

Between 1971 and 1984, Don made TV guest appearances on shows like *Love, American Style*, *The Wild McCullochs*, and *Simon & Simon*. He later composed the theme music for *The Phil Donahue Show*, and in 1990, appeared on *The All New Mickey Mouse Club* syndicated TV show. Between 1996 and 2004, Don composed music for television documentaries and specials, including *The Revolutionary War*, *When Animals Attack 3*, *Intimate Portrait*, *Why Dogs Smile & Chimpanzees Cry*, *The Burning Sands*, *Passages*, *Truth or Scare*, *Good Neighbor*, *Gilda Radner's Greatest Moments*, *Weird Travels*, *Innovation: Life, Inspired*, and *The AFI Life Achievement Award: A Tribute to Meryl Streep*.

Don Grady
ABC/PhotoFest

On playing Robbie Douglas on *My Three Sons*, he once said, "My acting abilities probably helped, but I still believe the reason I got the part was because the cleft in my chin looked like Fred [MacMurray]'s."

Stanley Livingston, alongside his TV brothers Considine, Grady, and real-life brother Barry, performed on *My Three Sons* instinctively, displaying a natural talent that some adult actors, even with significant years of training, never accomplish. How is that?

"For some child actors, there is a natural ability to perform. . . to know how to act in a fictional situation, how you would act in a real situation. . . without any awareness of the camera. They're just in their own little world, and the dialogue comes out as real.

You're not acting. You're *being*, which is what many adult actors are always striving to do. 'I want to become an actor to act,' they say. But acting is really not acting. . . it's being a particular character and discovering all the attributes of that character and becoming that character, as opposed to emoting or hamming it up. Children, in general, have a natural propensity to not be impressed. . .and so do child actors."

"For example," Stanley goes on to explain, "I didn't know who Fred MacMurray was. He was just some big tall guy on the set that I heard of. The only thing I knew about at the time was that he was the dad in *The Shaggy Dog* and he was the guy in *The Absent-Minded Professor*."

Stanley concludes of his time on *Sons*, with Considine, Grady, and Barry:

We really lucked out because the people involved with the show were really good at working with kids [including Peter Tewksbury, who had helmed several episodes of *Father Knows Best*]. He was one of the first directors on our show, and he really set the tone and characters for the show. He was the one director who really cared enough about the characters to take the time to work with the actors to make work whatever scene we did.

27

David Hedison
Voyage to the Bottom of the Sea

In your career, you must be so careful; otherwise, you get caught in a particular image, and it's hard to break.

—David Hedison

From classic motion pictures like *The Fly* (1958) and *Live and Let Die* (1973, in which he played CIA pal Felix Leiter to Roger Moore's James Bond), to producer/director Irwin Allen's TV edition of his 1961 feature *Voyage to the Bottom of the Sea*, to back on the small screen with daytime TV serials such as *Another World*, David Hedison's star power is across the board, says Professor Jeff Thompson. On television in particular, his espionage series *Five Fingers* (NBC, 1959-1960, costarring Luciana Paluzzi) should have made Hedison a prominent TV lead but, as Thompson observes, that show "came and went [just prior to *The Avengers/Man from U.N.C.L.E.*] spy wave that would have made it a success."

Hedison found more solidified TV fame for four years with *Voyage to the Bottom of the Sea* and, as Thompson observes, "stood out among the guest stars, gadgetry, and gimmicks" that defined that series. "Hedison's earnest, heroic performance as Commander Lee Crane was central to the show and its cohesion—not to mention its 'believability.'" Just as Hedison had accomplished on *The Fly,* Thompson says playing Crane on *Voyage* granted the actor a platform to perform that was "grounded in reality in the midst of the unreality of the events around him."

Born Albert David Hedison Jr. on May 20, 1927, in Providence, Rhode Island, Hedison graduated from Brown University. His parents were Albert David Hedison

(Heditisian) Sr. and Rose Boghosian. In 1968 he married Bridget Mori, to whom he remains wed, and they have two children: Alexandra (who is married to actress/director Jodie Foster) and Serena.

Hedison decided to become an actor after seeing *Blood and Sand*, the 1941 motion picture about bullfighting starring Tyrone Power. He had his first role at age sixteen, appearing in the high school play, *What A Life*, in which he portrayed the school principal, Mr. Bradley. "It was a terrific experience," he said, "and I just knew that I had found the profession I wanted to be involved in for the rest of my life . . . At the time I was inspired by James Cagney and many of the contract players at Warner Bros. Today, unfortunately, no one inspires me."

Hedison formally commenced his career with the Sock and Buskin Players at Brown University before moving to New York to study with Sanford Meisner and Martha Graham at the Neighborhood Playhouse and with Lee Strasberg at the Actors Studio. He also studied drama at HB Studio in Greenwich Village in New York City. He received a Theatre World Award for the most promising newcomer after appearing in the play, *A Month in the Country*.

Billed as "Al Hedison" in his early film work, he was cast in 1959 as double agent Victor Sebastian in *Five Fingers*, for which NBC insisted he change his name. From

there on in, he's been known as David Hedison, utilizing his middle moniker as his first. A few years later, he was nominated for an Emmy Award for an episode of ABC's *Bus Stop* (1961-1962), during which he was also chosen to play Captain Crane in the original, big-screen edition of Allen's *Voyage to the Bottom of the Sea*, but was unable to take the part due to scheduling conflicts. After appearing in the 1950 feature *The Lost World*, also helmed by Allen, Hedison was uncertain about working again with the director, but ultimately signed to do the TV edition of *Voyage* once he learned that Richard Basehart was cast as his costar (portraying Admiral Harriman Nelson).

PhotoFest

Hedison's other headlining roles include runs on another daytime TV soap opera, *The Young and the Restless*, and once more playing Felix Leiter in a second Bond film, *License to Kill* (1989, this time opposite Timothy Dalton as 007). In 2008, Hedison celebrated the thirty-fifth anniversary of *Live and Let Die* in England, with autograph signings and memorabilia shows, and by composing the introduction to the Bond comic book *The Paradise Plot*.

Hedison's first love is acting live on stage. As he once said, "When I go back to theater I feel good about myself. When I do films or TV, it's to make a little bread to pay my mortgage or whatever and when I've made the money I do theater again. And when I get a part I like, a part I can work on, that satisfies me. I feel good about myself. Most of the time, I don't even watch what I do on TV. I go in, get the job done, and just know it's nothing. It's a job. Sometimes, I try something different and I'll watch out of curiosity. Generally, I don't watch too much of what I do. Movies are basically the same, except it's more money spent on sets."

His experience on *Voyage to the Bottom of the Sea*, in particular, was less than sea-worthy: "Irwin Allen would yell at us every time we tried [to inject humor], so we quit trying. He even made us re-shoot scenes, if they were too 'light-hearted.' Irwin decreed [the series] would be grim. So we were grim, and the show was grim.

"Of course," he added, "there are pictures you never want to see again—most of the films I've made like *The Fly*, *The Lost World*, *Marines, Let's Go* [1961]. There's a whole slew of shit I avoid like the plague and when I know they'll be on TV I have a dinner party and invite my friends over so they can't see them."

A few years after his TV *Voyage* ended, Hedison rejected the chance to play dad Mike Brady on *The Brady Bunch* because, as he decided, "after four years of subs and monsters, who needs kids and dogs?"

28

Desi Arnaz Jr.

Here's Lucy

I've lived over 200 years in 60!

—Desi Arnaz Jr.

Some people are born to be stars. Others are born the children of a star. Rarely is the case when a star is born the child of two stars. Such was the case with Desi Arnaz Jr., who, along with his talented sister Lucie Arnaz, was born to and raised by the famous Lucille Ball and Desi Arnaz. That's an awful lot of talent to go around. But it was all meant to be—from the minute young Desi appeared on the cover of *TV Guide*, shortly after his legendary mother brought him into the world.

He would go on to make guest appearances on the various editions of his mother's TV sitcoms, and for a time, he was part of a young rock band called Dino, Desi & Billy, which also featured the son of another famous star, Dean Martin. But it was his costarring role on *Here's Lucy*, his mom's second-to-last sitcom, that made him a household name.

Some children of stars are just that: fortunate enough to be born into financial stability, and finding work because of their family connections. But in the case of Desi Arnaz Jr., he backed up his gifted status in life with talent. And it didn't hurt to have a whole lot of good looks thrown into the fold. Like his father, Desi Jr. was trim, charismatic, and loved to perform the Latin beat. While his father became famous for playing the conga drums, Desi Jr. was content to play the core drum set for Dino, Desi & Billy. When he and his sister started their weekly regular acting appearances on *Here's Lucy*,

Globe Photos

his father could not have been more proud. Both Desi Jr. and little Lucie could act—and they proved it with their precise ability to deliver a comedic line. Any actor in a dramatic role can make an audience member cry. But make 'em laugh? That takes a whole other measure of talent—and Desi Jr. delivered it.

Unfortunately, Desi did not stay with *Here's Lucy* for its entire six-year run, and he was missed by legions of fans. But whenever the series is discussed, his costarring status on the show does not go unmentioned.

Desi Jr.'s birth, on January 19, 1953, in Los Angeles, was one of the most celebrated and publicized events of his generation, as the entire world followed Lucille Ball's real-life pregnancy in tandem with Lucy Ricardo's on *I Love Lucy*, the first sitcom produced and starring his famously multitalented parents, Lucille Ball and Desi Arnaz (Sr.).

Here's how it all began: Desi Jr.'s photo with his world-famous mother graced the very first cover of *TV Guide* and, because of financial tie-ins the cover was subtitled: "Lucy's $50,000,000 Baby!"

All of this because his mother and father opted to make Ball's real-life expectancy a part of her sitcom's storylines for a portion of the second season (while the word "pregnancy" was never allowed to be spoken or heard). On the show itself, however, little Desi did not portray "Little Ricky." However, he did appear on the final half-hour episode of *I Love Lucy* as an extra in 1957 and, after his parents divorced in 1960, made four appearances as Billie Simmons on *The Lucy Show* between 1962 and 1965.

In 1965, at the age of twelve, Desi Jr. had a Top 40 hit with the song "I'm a Fool," for which he performed on the drums with Dino, Desi & Billy (Dean Martin's son Dino died tragically in a small plane accident on March 21, 1987).

After the sixth season of *The Lucy Show*, the actress, having sold Desilu and all its shows to Gulf & Western Industries, decided to create a new series for her new production company. She saw this as an opportunity to bring her teenage children into the act during those formative years that required closer parental supervision. Thus Desi Jr. and his sister Lucie Arnaz played her children, Craig and Kim Carter. Desi played a teenage Craig Carter in fifty-three episodes of the series titled *Here's Lucy*. He then left the series after three seasons for a film career that unfortunately never fully materialized.

While Desi's career may have been slightly hampered because he resembled his iconic dad so strongly and had the same name, he still managed to achieve a significant measure of stardom on his own. He has sustained an air of charisma and manners throughout his entire life and career up until today. He loved his parents dearly, and respected his stepfather, Gary Morton (married to Ball from 1961 until her passing in 1989). He wed twice: first to actress Linda Purl (from 1980 to 1981), and since 1987, to Amy Bargiel Arnaz. They have two daughters, Julia and Haley.

Beyond *Here's Lucy*, Desi's other television appearances include *The Mod Squad*, *Love, American Style*, *Streets of San Francisco*, *Love Boat*, *Fantasy Island*, and *Matlock*. His notable film roles were *Red Sky at Morning* (1971), the titled leading role in the unsuccessful family musical *Marco* (1973), Robert Altman's *A Wedding* (1978), and *The Mambo Kings* (1992) wherein he portrayed his real-life father. Since 1986 Desi has lived in Boulder City, Nevada, where he directs the Boulder City Ballet Company and owns the historic Boulder Theatre, where he has produced many shows including tributes to Lucille Ball and Dean Martin as well as ballets and dance recitals. In 2010 he and his sister starred in *Babalu*, a tribute to Desi Sr. that played in New York City, Miami, and Washington, DC.

As he told the *Miami Herald* in 2010, the *Babalu* tribute was "the most fun you can have as a percussionist to play Big Band and American Swing, which Dad combined with Latin rhythms. It's just extraordinary fun . . . powerful and challenging at the same time."

As to Desi Jr.'s overall appeal, the former teen idol, with his big brown eyes and warm heart, remains one of the most beloved male icons not only from the 50s, 60s, and 70s, but of all time.

29

Bobby Sherman
Here Come the Brides/Getting Together

As far as advice to potential teenage idols, there is no formula.

—Bobby Sherman

No discussion of young male TV icons would be complete without including Bobby Sherman. With a sparkle in his eye, a few songs in his heart, and a dazzling smile, Sherman became a TV star first via his appearances on the musical TV show, *Shindig!*— followed by a costarring role with Robert Brown and David Soul (later of *Starsky & Hutch*) on the unique one-hour family show, *Here Come the Brides*. Loosely based on Broadway-play-turned-feature-film *Seven Brides for Seven Brothers*, *Brides* debuted on ABC in 1967 and lasted only two seasons. But classic TV lovers have long remembered its charming theme song ("the bluest skies you'll ever see are in Seattle"), as well as Sherman, who during the time, had several hit songs including "Julie, Do You Love Me."

Television writer Larry Brody worked on *Brides* with Sherman, and as he recalls:

I wrote my first paid television scripts for *Here Come the Brides*. Ostensibly, the hero of the series was the oldest brother, played by Robert Brown, but it became clear in a hurry that Bobby Sherman was the one people were tuning in for, so the scripts began emphasizing his character more and more, and along with that, David Soul's because the characters were close in age and played off each other well.

At the time, a lot of people didn't understand Bobby's appeal, but to me it was obvious. He was terrific at playing sweet, shy (his character was written as stuttering for the first season but that was omitted after he scored as a pop star), and sincere . . . because that's really how he was. I don't know if male viewers liked him, but every man who knew him did, and every woman TV viewer I knew at the time, whether old or young, thought he was "so cute." And "so cute" is a key to stardom.

With regard to Sherman's on-screen interaction with one particular *Brides* costar, Brody adds:

Globe Photos

David Soul had a reputation for eccentricity among the staff of *Here Come the Brides*. [But] as a writer, I found David the perfect foil for Bobby Sherman. They worked well off each other and it was fun to put them in scenes together. He was a very good straight man, as was proven later in *Starsky & Hutch* [in which Soul played opposite Paul Michael Glaser].

Born Robert Cabot Sherman Jr. on July 22, 1943, in Santa Monica, California, Bobby Sherman had the kind of music idol appeal that drove his fans wild, long before the Justins—Bieber and Timberlake—had a similar effect on teenage girls.

Best known for his role as Jeremy Bolt on *Brides*, Sherman graduated from Birmingham High School in Van Nuys, California, in 1961, and later attended Pierce College in Woodland Hills, California.

His parents, Robert Cabot Sherman Sr. and Juanita "Nita" Freeman, also delivered a sister for Bobby named Darlene. His interest in music began at age eleven when he learned to play the trumpet. He eventually was able to play sixteen musical instruments.

In 1962 Sal Mineo composed two songs and arranged for Sherman to record them. In 1964, Sherman sang at Mineo's Hollywood party, where he made such an impression, he landed an agent and a regular gig on *Shindig!* Sherman later appeared on an episode of *The Monkees* (NBC, 1966–1968) playing a pompous surfer/singer named Frankie Catalina in the vein of singer Frankie Avalon. He also entertained TV audiences for a brief time as the costar of the short-lived sitcom, *Getting Together*, a 1972 ABC spin-off from *The Partridge Family*.

From 1971 to 1978, Bobby was married to Patti Carnel and, years later, in 2011, wed Brigitte Poublon. He has two sons, Christopher and Tyler, and is a grandfather of six.

Sherman's recording career earned him seven gold singles, one platinum single, and five gold albums. He also had a total of seven Top 40 hits.

From the late 60s to the mid-70s, Sherman toured the country and the world giving concerts to sellout crowds of mostly wailing young females. The screaming was so boisterous that Sherman experienced hearing loss.

In 1986, the still-dashing performer was cast on the TV show *Sanchez of Bel Air*. In 1998, after a twenty-five-year absence, fans flocked to see him in concert as part of *The Teen Idol Tour* with Peter Noone, and former *Monkees* TV costars Davy Jones and Micky Dolenz.

Sherman did his last concert as a solo performer in Lincoln, Rhode Island, on August 25, 2001. He ranked #8 in *TV Guide*'s list of "TV's 25 Greatest Teen Idols" (from the January 23, 2005 issue). When he guest-starred on television's *Emergency!*, he found a new calling and became an emergency medical technician (EMT) in real life. He has subsequently worked with the Los Angeles Police Department which, in 1999, named him the Reserve Officer of the Year.

Along with wife Brigitte, Sherman founded the Bobby Sherman Volunteer EMT Foundation, an organization that coordinates medical services at many community and charity events in Southern California. Although he is mentioned, Sherman did not participate in Jonathan Etter's 2009 nostalgic paperback *Gangway, Lord: The Here Come the Brides Book*.

As he told the *Los Angeles Times* on two separate occasions, first in 1993 and 1998, "I've had a couple of instances where my patients would look up and say, 'Hey, you're Bobby Sherman.' It turns into a kind of placebo effect. It works every time. On one call in Northridge we were working on a hemorrhaging woman who had passed out. Her husband kept staring at me. Finally he said, 'Look, honey, it's Bobby Sherman!' She said, 'Oh great, I must look a mess!' I told her not to worry, she looked fine.

"I made a decision to give myself a break and do stuff I wanted to do," Sherman concluded. "Being a teen idol afforded me so many different things in my life. God bless the fans. They made me a teen idol, and I wouldn't change a thing."

Christopher Knight and Barry Williams
The Brady Bunch

Far out!

—Greg Brady, as played by Barry Williams on *The Brady Bunch*

For many male fans of *The Brady Bunch* (ABC, 1969–1974), it's been *Marcia, Marcia, Marcia* for decades, with regard to central female sensation Maureen McCormick, who played the eldest daughter of that name on the long-running sitcom (and a few of its sequels).

For the majority of female *Brady* followers (and most likely a few male admirers, too), it's been *Peter, Peter, Peter* and *Greg, Greg, Greg*, the oldest screen brothers on the list of *Brady* shows, specials, movies, etc., as portrayed by Christopher Knight and Barry Williams, respectively—both of whom have later found success on reality TV shows.

Starting with the younger of the two, Knight was born Christopher Anton Knight on November 7, 1957, in New York City. When he was just three years old, the family, including father Edward and brother Mark, along with siblings Lisa and David, moved to Los Angeles, where Chris and Mark began auditioning for roles to help supplement the household income. Chris soon started performing in TV commercials (for Toyota, Tide, Cheerios, and more), and then came his iconic role as Peter Brady. In between it all, and after, he attended El Camino Real High School in Woodland Hills, California, and later, UCLA, and made guest appearances on an *ABC After-School Special*, *One Day At A Time*, "The Bionic Boy" two-part episode of *The Six Million Dollar Man*, *Happy Days*, and *CHiPs*.

In 1988 Knight cofounded several successful technology and software companies and excelled in high-tech marketing and sales. In late 1995 he and his friend Frank Paniagua founded Kidwise Learningware—a company that designed, produced, and published interactive edutainment products for children.

In 2003 Knight hosted the series *TV Road Trip* for the Travel Channel and was involved with the celebrity version of Discovery Health Channel's *Body Challenge*, which debuted in the fall of 2004. He also starred in the VH-1 reality show *The Surreal Life* in 2003. It was on that show that Knight met his third wife, *America's Next Top Model* star Adrianne Curry. In 2005 Knight and then-wife Adrianne were featured in their own reality show called *My Fair Brady*, which lasted three seasons.

Married twice before (to Julie Schulman, 1989–1992, and Toni Erickson, 1995–2000), Knight once observed of his monumental and unending *Brady* affiliation: "It's an honor to have been part of something so core to so many lives. The show has evolved beyond its original intent and form and has transcended . . . itself!"

Knight's TV brother, Barry Williams (married twice: Diane Martin, 1990–1992; Eila Mary Matt, 1999–2005; and with one son: Brandon Eric Williams) had previously said this about his pop-culture place in Brady-mania: "I don't think of myself as a role model. I do try to live in a compassionate, considerate, and positive way. The only advice I can offer is to find what you love to do, find the joy in it, and express yourself through your passion."

Born Barry William Blenkhorn on September 30, 1954, in Santa Monica, California, Williams attended Palisades High School in Pacific Palisades, California, and Pepperdine University in Malibu. His parents were Doris May Moore and Frank Miller Blenkhorn; he has two siblings, Craig and Scott Blenkhorn.

Williams decided he wanted to be an actor at the age of four and, by the age of eleven, was already taking acting classes

Christopher Knight
Globe Photos

and courses in film and television techniques. Williams made his acting debut
on television in 1967 on *Dragnet*. Before
landing his role on *The Brady Bunch*,
Williams also had guest roles on *Adam-
12*, *The Invaders*, *That Girl*, *Mission:
Impossible*, *The Mod Squad*, *Here Come
the Brides*, and *Bartleby, the Scrivener*.
After *The Brady Bunch*, he toured as
a solo singer and became involved in
musical theater.

Barry performed on Broadway in
the musical *Romance/Romance* and
was awarded the Former Child Star
"Lifetime Achievement" Award by the
Young Artist Foundation in 1989. He
wrote the *New York Times* bestseller
*Growing Up Brady: I Was a Teenage
Greg* (which was adapted for television
in 2000).

In 2011 Barry appeared in the Playboy
Channel show *Camp Playboy* and cur-

Barry Williams
Globe Photos

rently hosts the satellite radio trivia show, *The Real Greg Brady's Totally '70s Pop
Quiz Starring Barry Williams* (broadcast Saturday on Sirius Satellite Radio's "Totally
'70s" channel).

Both Knight and Williams appeared in the various *Brady* TV incarnations like *The
Brady Bunch Variety Hour*, *A Very Brady Christmas*, and *The Bradys*, the latter two
of which also featured actress Caryn Richman (*The New Gidget*), Nora Brady, who
wed Greg. As she recalls, "It was wonderful fun to get to 'marry' into the Brady
family and play Greg Brady's wife. . . . The Brady cast shared such a long history
together, so I was especially grateful for his generosity in making me feel at home
with them."

Richman reaches back to the original incarnation of *The Brady Bunch* when
addressing the core and continued appeal of Williams as Greg: "He was so likable
and relatable in his efforts to be the wisest. . .and sometimes bossiest. . .older brother.
He was earnest and charming and we rooted for him as he made his way through his

teenage years. It didn't hurt that he was so so very handsome and had the most beautiful blue eyes ever! Who didn't have a crush on Greg Brady?!"

Before Richman joined the matured Brady brood, she says Williams had already incorporated other attractive qualities to the adult Greg, who became a pediatrician. "Barry is smart and grounded and funny and extremely charming . . . all of which he brought to his role as a doctor." She remembers filming one particularly romantic scene with Williams in front of the fireplace for an episode of *The Bradys*, the short-lived dramedy edition of the *Bunch* franchise (which was nicknamed bradysomething, in reference to the then-popular hour-long yuppie dramedy, *thirtysomething*; ABC, 1987–1991). "I was struck by how tender and sweet the scene was," Richman says. "It was more simple and intimate than what we had gotten to play before and a real treat. Barry is. . .and always has been. . .the consummate pro."

Richman reconnected with Williams at a recent *Brady Bunch* Convention, and was overwhelmed with his talent and showmanship. "Whether it's live on stage or on the TV screen," she says, "audiences love him. And then there's always those [blue] eyes!"

Richman didn't have many on-screen moments with Christopher Knight, but she also singles out the same facial feature, and more, as a key component in describing the long-lasting appeal of Barry's younger TV brother. "Chris was also so much fun to work with, and had his own brand of sparkle in his [brown] eyes. He's playful, a little mischievous, adorable and spirited, with the best smile ever! It lights up his whole face! All the Brady boys were charming, but Chris had a certain impish quality—and still does!"

31

David Cassidy
The Partridge Family

Everything in my life was about performance when I was doing *The Partridge Family.*

—David Cassidy

There is no prettier example of a classic male teen icon in TV history than David Cassidy, who played oldest sibling Keith Partridge on ABC's *The Partridge Family* (1970–1974). The son of Jack Cassidy and stepson to his *Partridge* costar Shirley Jones (married from 1956 to 1974 to Jack who died in a fire December 12, 1976), David once shared his thoughts on his relationship with these two very special people in his life:

[Shirley] was a great help to me in my difficult relationship with my Dad and served as a great buffer. In the end he found it more and more difficult to cope with my fame and success and he was very tortured by her fame and success . . . and that he had not achieved a higher level. I loved him and admired him but I just couldn't find a way to have it be okay for him. It was a rough one for us. I forgive him for all of it. We are all flawed. Somehow or another, we all get through it. I worshipped him and loved him and I loved all of the things he gave me in my life as a human being.

Born David Bruce Cassidy to actor Jack and actress Evelyn Ward on April 12, 1950, in New York City, David attended Rexford High School, in Beverly Hills, California. His stepbrothers, born to father Jack and the Oscar-winning Jones, are fellow male TV icon Shaun, and the younger Patrick and Ryan. David was married to actress Kay

Lenz from 1977 to 1983, later wedded to Meryl Ann Tanz from 1984 to 1986, and, in 1991, married Sue Shiffrin (from whom he filed for divorce in 2014). His children include actress Katie Cassidy (with model Sherry Williams Benedon), and Beau Devin Cassidy.

Because his actor parents were often touring, David, in his early years, was raised by his maternal grandparents in a middle-class neighborhood in West Orange, New Jersey. In 1956, he found out from the neighbors' children that his parents had been divorced for over two years. They hadn't told him because they were gone so much they thought he was better off not knowing. He made his acting debut in the Broadway musical *The Fig Leaves Are Falling*.

Globe Photos

David moved with his father and Jones when they came to Hollywood, and Jones, more than Jack, became his mentor. Beginning in 1969, David had featured roles in *Ironside*, *Marcus Welby, M.D.*, *Adam-12*, and *Bonanza*. The producers *of The Partridge Family* cast him because of his good looks, and at first, weren't interested in his singing. He lobbied to be the lead singer and convinced the producers to give him the chance.

The first Partridge Family single, "I Think I Love You," went on to be a #1 hit in 1970—the first season of the series. Playing solo, Cassidy sold out arenas in the United States and all over the world. In 1974, a gate stampede at a show in London's White City Stadium injured 650, thirty were taken to the hospital, and one girl, fourteen-year-old Bernadette Whelan, died from her injuries. In 1978, Cassidy received an Emmy nomination for an episode of *Police Story* titled "A Chance to Live."

In the January 23, 2005, issue of *TV Guide*, David was ranked #1 in "TV's 25 Greatest Teen Idols." In 2011, he was one of the contestants on *Celebrity Apprentice*, on which his daughter Katie made a brief appearance.

Besides *The Partridge Family*, David starred in a short-lived, very well made, if oddly titled, one-hour crime-drama called *David Cassidy: Man Undercover*, which aired on NBC from 1978 to 1979. The show was nowhere near as popular as *The Partridge Family* and camouflaged Cassidy's key appeal, which Cassidy family friend Roger Hyman succinctly now sums up as follows:

The Partridge Family was a very fresh and welcomed face for TV in the early 1970s, and the face of David Cassidy helped to secure a place for the show in classic television history. The show had an eternally appealing ensemble cast, masterfully written and impeccably acted. . .and sung, producing nine hit albums in just three years' time. The smart and forward-thinking decision to cast David as Keith Partridge was tremendous and impactful. The character was mostly played as a straight man and fall guy for the antics of his TV kid brother Danny. . .played by Danny Bonaduce, and band manager Reuben Kincaid portrayed by Dave Madden. The comedic timing was second to none and David's Keith fell for everything. Where David stole the show, and the hearts of every teen girl in America at the time, was the lead singer for the Family. This helped launch him to become one of pop-culture's most sensationalized teen idols and pop-singers of the '70s. David was every girl's dream man with a voice to swoon into the sunset. He had an energy, wit, and charisma that put *The Partridge Family* and him not only on TV's most watched list—but at the top of the pop charts.

32

Donny Osmond
The Donny & Marie Show

I'm still wearing purple socks.

—Donny Osmond

He was a little bit rock and roll, and born into a family of music. His legendary hit songs include "Go Away Little Girl" and "Puppy Love," and with his sister Marie, he had one of the most popular musical variety shows on television. As he assessed back in 1971, at the peak of his musical career, which began with his four older brothers on NBC's *The Andy Williams Show*:

Andy's father saw [my brothers Alan, Wayne, Merrill and Jay] on television from Disneyland one night. They reminded him of the Williams Brothers when they got started, and he thought it would be a novelty to have them on . . . Andy's show. He called us in Utah and asked us to come in and audition. [My brothers] sang as a quartet for quite a while before I got interested. My first public appearance was in Chicago when I was five years old . . . We all got started, really, by entertaining our family at home. We've always had Family Night on Friday night [with dinner by candlelight]. After our meal, we'd take turns putting on a program.

In the summer of 1978, entertainment reporter Martin A. Grove was "privileged" to have spent a partial afternoon talking with a few members of the Osmond musical family for a publication titled *TV Stars Today Special*. He used the word "privileged" because, as he explained in the article, "A Candid Conversation with the Osmonds," he considered the legendary showbiz brood to be "some of the very nicest people [he] had the pleasure of interviewing. . . . They are in real life every bit as natural and human as they appear on TV."

At the time, that was a reference to ABC's then–super hit variety series, *The Donny & Marie Show*, which was head-lined by two of the family's most popular and closest members, siblings Donny and his younger sister Marie. As Grove went on to assess, these two ageless perform-ers, then in their late teens/early twenties, were "probably the youngest celebri-ties" to host their own variety show. Marie was only sixteen when the pro-gram began as a midseason replacement series in January 1976 on ABC, and her older brother Donny was only eighteen. "Despite their youth," Grove clarified, "they are seasoned performers."

Donny and his entire Osmond fam-ily (including children and countless cousins) are as wholesome as American apple pie, and they never denied it. Why

Globe Photos

would they? It's one of the "secrets" to their everlasting appeal. As Donny explained to Grove in 1978, "If I didn't have my family in this business, I'd get out of it right quick because it's a very shaky business and it's a hard business. If I couldn't have my family with me I would definitely think about quitting. Because they've helped me so much . . . when we travel we always travel together as a family.

"We don't go to [Hollywood] parties," Donny continued. "We have our friends in the business. But we're very busy working and traveling. But when we go home, we're home people . . . We're down-to-earth."

Home, for the Osmonds, is Provo, Utah, where Donny and all of his siblings were raised by their parents George and Olive May Osmond.

Linda Burton, a friend of the Osmonds, summarizes how the multitalented, mul-timember family's life and values shaped Donny's humanity and subsequent appeal:

Donny comes from an amazing family. His parents showed [him], and Marie and all of his brothers so much love. They taught each of them right from wrong and, in doing so, they did something right! The family always stuck together, through any and all challenges . . . including early financial hardship . . . The entire country loved *The Donny and Marie Show* back in the 70s. Decades later when Donny and Marie went to Vegas for a six-week show, their managers realized that it would be a good place to let fans come from around the world to see them. And they ended up performing for years at the Flamingo, where they're still going strong . . .

Another thing about Donny and all the family is that they *give back*. The Children's Miracle Network Hospitals nonprofit was started by their mom Olive, along with co-founders Marie and [male TV icon] John Schneider, and the entire family has for years been entertaining at Disneyland and Disney World, raising over two billion dollars for Children's hospitals in the United States and Canada.

Donny and all the Osmonds have been entertaining people for over fifty years. Donny, alone, has sixty albums to his name. He's come a long way since the teen idol days with "Puppy Love." . . . He has a very loyal following because he's so nice to all of his fans! He shares with them his struggles as well as his accomplishments. He keeps them up to date on his personal life . . . when his sons graduate high school, go on a mission, when he was expecting his first grandchild. All of it. And not all entertainers do that. You always come away from his concerts with a smile. He's down-to-earth. He's a family man and a religious man. He follows his beliefs and isn't ashamed to say so . . . He's always stuck by his morals and that is one of the reasons his fans are there for him.

33

Shaun Cassidy and Parker Stevenson
The Hardy Boys

One of the major reasons that I went into this business is that there are so many roads you can take. I can go into the producing end of it. The writing I can always do, whether it be for myself or other people. Directing. Acting. I'll always be doing something somewhere.

—Shaun Cassidy

So do blondes really have more fun, even if they are guys?

That's clearly been the case for countless male TV icons through the decades, everyone from Edd Byrnes (*77 Sunset Strip*) and Martin Milner (*Route 66* and *Adam-12*), to Willie Aames (*Eight Is Enough*) to Shaun Cassidy and Parker Stevenson (*The Hardy Boys*). Also fitting this blond bill are Vince Van Patten and Leif Garrett, who made guest appearances on many legendary shows before costarring as brothers on the beloved, if short-lived CBS one-hour family dramedy *Three for the Road* (1975-1976).

TV icons Shaun Cassidy and Parker Stevenson, stars of *The Hardy Boys* (brought to the small screen by the prolific Glen A. Larson), embraced their measure of teen idol status years before Cassidy would go behind the scenes as a producer for hit TV shows (like *Picket Fences*, CBS, 1992–1996), and a decade or so prior to Stevenson's appearance on the original NBC edition of *Baywatch* (the syndicated mid-1990s edition of which transformed Pamela Anderson into the Farrah Fawcett of her generation).

Writer and voiceover artist Roger Hyman, who grew up with Shaun, offers his thoughts on how the *Hardy Boys* series (which shared its airtime with *The Nancy*

Drew Mysteries, first featuring Pamela Sue Martin, and then Janet Louise Johnson) reached beyond the regular teen idol status of a TV show, and made a positive impact on young viewers, potentially inspiring them to do more reading of both the original "Hardy Boys" (and "Nancy Drew") novels, as many such contemporary cross-media literary and TV and film adaptations do today:

> Both Shaun and Parker were clean-cut, stunning to look at and demographically perfect for the show. They had no "issues" that would speak otherwise. They were an aspirational pair that got teens glued to TV. There was no talk of drugs or violence—just a real all-American family show. The books were hugely popular and this made sense on many levels to do. The stories portrayed on screen were paint by numbers perfect, so it engaged the viewers to read. It's very much akin to the "Harry Potter" series to pre-teens of today. My niece was reading the books at age 7 or 8 because she fell in love with the movies and characters. It was the same thing with *The Hardy Boys*. The imagery and involvement on the screen brings everything to life, and the result is wholeheartedly engaging.

Shaun Cassidy
Gene Trindl/Globe Photos

Whereas a show such as *Murder, She Wrote* later provided a "thinking-hero" for the senior set of mystery story lovers in the 1980s and 1990s, *The Hardy Boys/ Nancy Drew Mysteries* did the same for the teen set of the 70s. Or as Hyman states it, "anything positive that can bring print to life is a good thing. But it has to be done right, of course."

The Hardy Boys did get it right, even though Hyman believes it wasn't the show per se that was popular, but rather a combination of factors. For example, it was the show-runners who contacted Cassidy's managers who subsequently convinced him to do the series. As a result, Cassidy's involvement became a significant reason for the show's success. "At the time, Shaun was the biggest singing teen sensation and filled arenas worldwide with screaming teen girls. And this was a 'synergy' move to get him to branch out and see how much money could be made from his talents. Shaun could have hated acting and wanted out, although he did do many TV movies. Eventually, he gravitated to working behind the camera."

Hardy Boys heartthrob Parker Stevenson offers his insight into the show's success, and how it increased and encouraged the readership of its young viewers, many of whom began to devour the original novels—a development that might not have transpired had the show not made its way to ABC:

Parker Stevenson
Globe Photos

> *The Hardy Boys* had a successful 3-year run because it was FUN. Yes, there was a built in audience because of the long publishing history of the original books but the TV series . . . had a lighthearted charm. [The TV show] benefited from the audience's interest in solving each episode's mystery, the phenomena of Shaun's successful musical career, and Universal Television/Pro Art's successful Merchandising Campaign that drove viewership back to the show and back to the original book series. ABC succeeded in turning a charmingly innocent American classic into a ratings success and in the process revitalized the publishing success of the original book series.

PART IV

COWBOYS, LITTLE JOES, JOHN-BOYS, AND JETHROS

They were the country boys, the cowboys, and the good ol' boys who ran television throughout the 50s and 60s and on into the 70s. The homespun charm of this special breed of male TV icon was personified by countless talented actors, one of whom was Michael Landon, who as producer and director, could easily be categorized as a jack of all trades. But because of his starring status on family westerns like *Bonanza* and *Little House on the Prairie*, his life and career is explored here among the likes of Richard Thomas from *The Waltons*, James Arness from *Gunsmoke*, and Hugh O'Brien of *Wyatt Earp*.

Ann Hodges remembers O'Brien "very well" as Wyatt Earp. "He played the brave lawmaker, and he was perfect for that role . . . because he was appealing to women. I think you have to appeal to women when you're on television, almost first, above any other demographic, and then they kind of lead their husbands or their boyfriends or other male viewers to what they watch, outside of sports and other types of traditionally male-dominated or geared programming. Women," from Hodges perspective, "sort of rule[d] the TV roost. And I think they still do."

Chuck Connors, star of ABC's *The Rifleman* (1958–1963) was another favorite of Hodges, who resides in Houston, Texas. "I was at my doctor's office the other day and in the lobby," she recalled recently, "and *The Rifleman* was airing on the TV at the Texas Medical Center. And everyone was looking at that show . . . all ages. And two of the older patrons in the lobby said, 'Isn't it great to see a show like this again. We had forgotten how good it was.'"

What struck Hodges most about Connors's performance on *The Rifleman* was that this character, Lucas McCain, was such a devoted father to his son Mark, as played by Johnny Crawford. That aspect of Connor's portrayal, says Hodges, "only endeared him more so to the audience." Ultimately, he was a positive father figure. He was stern, and yet he was tender. "He was a single father and parent, and there weren't many of those on television at the time." As such, Connors was, as Hodges puts it, "ahead of the game."

Two other classic TV cowboys that made an impression upon Hodges were Doug McClure and James Drury, who costarred on *The Virginian* (NBC, 1962–1971). "They were both extremely good on that show," she says, "and James Drury in particular created a wonderful character as cowboy, a lawman and a straight shooter." From Ann's point of view, Drury was so good on *The Virginian* that she felt he was "underappreciated as an actor, and kind of disappeared" after that series ended its original run.

Rick Lertzman adds and concludes of the *Virginian* duo:

James Drury played the leading role of *The Virginian* who never was given a name and remained a mysterious figure. Doug McClure played his top hand, Trampas. Lee J. Cobb was also in the additional cast as Judge Garth. James Drury had a distinct resemblance to Gary Cooper who originated the role in a 1929 film. His character, who was the foreman of the Shiloh Ranch, was a rather laconic and tough minded cowboy. In contrast to [McClure's] serious minded [character] Trampas was a fun-loving, rowdy cowboy who added a lighter touch to the action. Their Ying and Yang distinct personalities gave the program a unique balance. Both actors appeared in a variety of roles in several subsequent series, which never reached the popularity of *The Virginian*.

However, many other television westerns and their male leads equaled the popularity of *The Virginian* stars.

34

James Arness
Gunsmoke/How the West Was Won

Fess Parker
Davy Crockett/Daniel Boone

Matt Dillon was the kind of guy who's low-key, but stands for what is right.

—James Arness

Gunsmoke star James Arness was a hulking giant of an actor, not unlike his good friend, mentor, and infrequent costar John Wayne. In fact, it was Wayne who recommended the 6'7" Arness to CBS for the role of US marshal on *Gunsmoke*, the black-and-white half-hour pilot that Wayne hosted and introduced.

The equally towering Fess Parker made his TV mark on and as *Davy Crockett* and then *Daniel Boone*. According to a report in 2012, Walt Disney, proprietor of the Davy Crockett franchise, prevented Parker from accepting additional acting roles that would have transformed him into a significant big-screen presence following his TV catapult to stardom.

The ABC show *Disneyland* (which held various titles over the years, including *The Wonderful World of Disney*) presented three core *Crockett* segments in 1955, which Walt then transformed into a motion picture. But when the motion picture producers of, for example, *The Searchers* (1956) wanted to cast Parker, Walt refused to let him be anything but Crockett.

After his days as Davy finally came to a close, Parker fortunately found additional and similar TV fame as Daniel Boone, and later became a multimillionaire real estate mogul. Through it all, and decades of marriage, and until his demise at eighty-five in 2010, his wife, Marcella, remained right by his side.

Fess Parker, left; Buddy Ebsen, right
Globe Photos

Arness possessed a quiet authority that made his role as Matt Dillon an iconic legend of television's golden era for two decades. Shortly before he died (at eighty-eight on June 3, 2011, at his Brentwood, California, home), Arness shared his insight on playing his part so well:

"If Matt Dillon had to shoot somebody, you'd cut around to him. You could see that he just hated to have to do that and he felt a sort of revulsion over it. That's something that hadn't really been done much up to that point.

"With *Gunsmoke*," he went on to say, "we had an outstanding quality of writing. The show had been on radio for three years, so they were able to fine-tune the characters. What made us different from other westerns was the fact that *Gunsmoke* wasn't just action and a lot of shooting; they were character-study shows. They're interesting to watch all these years later."

Older brother to fellow male TV icon Peter Graves (*Mission: Impossible*, CBS, 1966 to 1973), Arness entered the world as James King Aurness on May 26, 1923, in Minneapolis, Minnesota. He attended West High School in Minneapolis and Beloit College in Wisconsin (from 1942 to 1943). His parents were Rolf Cirkler Aurness and Ruth Duesler. He was married to Virginia Chapman from 1948 to 1963, and Janet Surtees from 1978 to his death. He had three children: Craig (adopted from his first wife's previous marriage), Rolf, and Jenny (both from his first marriage).

Arness served in the US Army during World War II and was severely wounded in the leg at Anzio. He enjoyed a brief career as a radio announcer before giving acting a shot, with a supportive role in his first motion picture, *The Farmer's Daughter* (1947). He soon played larger parts in features like *Stars in My Crown* (1950, which also starred Amanda Blake, his Miss Kitty costar from *Gunsmoke*), director John Ford's

Wagon Master (1950), *The Thing From Another World* (1951), and the sci-fi classic *Them!* (1954).

Arness performed alongside John Wayne in *Big Jim McLain* (1952), *Hondo* (1953), *Island in the Sky* (1953), and *The Sea Chase* (1955).

Beyond *Gunsmoke*, Arness also took a TV western lead in the small-screen rendition of *How the West Was Won*, a hit series that aired on ABC from 1976 to 1979, in which he portrayed Zeb Macahan. Taking a nod from John Wayne, Arness also starred as Detective Jim McLain in an NBC-TV show revisiting Wayne's motion picture character called *McLain's Law* (which aired for only one season, 1981-1982).

James Arness
PhotoFest

His other performances included Jim Bowie in *The Alamo: Thirteen Days to Glory* (1987) and Thomas Dunson (the John Wayne role) in a remake of *Red River* (1988). He returned to the role of Matt Dillon in five *Gunsmoke* TV-films, made between 1987 and 1993.

Ann Hodges concludes:

James Arness was the typical Western-type actor, and certainly the Westerns made him. I don't think he would have done as well in any other role other than Marshal Matt Dillon. But his image was so strong as that character, that everyone had in their mind at that time . . . so many who were stereotypes like Roy Rogers and Gene Autry (the singing cowboys) were almost caricatures of the cowboys. But such was not the case with Arness.

35

Michael Landon
Bonanza/Little House on the Prairie

"The one thing I need to leave behind is good memories."

—Michael Landon

Michael Landon enjoyed an astonishing career as an actor, writer, director, and producer. His thespian success, in particular, was all the more impressive given that he was relatively small in stature (5'9"), and retained a boyishness that would have robbed a lesser man of the aura of authority needed to attain his career heights. He became popular on television not only in the 50s, 60s, and 70s, but throughout the 80s until July 1, 1991, when he succumbed to liver and pancreatic cancer at only age fifty-four. But he will forever be remembered as Joseph "Little Joe" Cartwright on *Bonanza*, caring father Charles Ingalls on *Little House on the Prairie*, and Jonathan, the Angel, on *Highway to Heaven* (which aired on NBC from 1984 to 1989).

Actor Radames Pera played "Young Grasshopper" on *Kung Fu* (ABC, 1974–1976), after which he was cast as John Jr. on *Little House* (which also featured heartthrob Dean Butler as Almando James Wilder). Pera recalls Landon as "a consummate pro and real 'actor's director,'" but also someone who had ambivalence about the fame he found, both embracing and suffering from it. Despite a nagging inferiority, he created an empire by planting a worthy flag in America's (and France's) heart that continues waving to this day. But at what price? At the very least a workaholic, he created a paid family around him while his actual families often suffered from his absence. Though he also died before his time, he chose to leave an enduring legacy of mod-

ern fables and demonstrations of spiritual strength during hard times." Born
Eugene Maurice Orowitz on October
31, 1936, in Forest Hills, Queens,
New York, Landon was the son of Eli
Maurice Orowitz, a movie theater manager, and Peggy O'Neill, an actress. He
became a champion javelin thrower in
high school, and won a track scholarship
to the University of Southern California
but dropped out after a year. He studied
at Warner Bros. acting school, changed
his billing to "Michael Landon" (which
he lifted from a Los Angeles telephone
book), and made his acting debut on
the big screen in 1957 in *I Was a Teen-
Age Werewolf.* He went on to portray
a headstrong farm boy in 1958's *God's
Little Acre* and a Confederate hero in
1959's *The Legend of Tom Dooley.*

NBC/PhotoFest

Landon received his big break at age twenty-two when he was hired to play Little
Joe Cartwright on *Bonanza,* which was, among other things, television's second-lon-
gest-running western (fourteen years next to CBS's two-decade-old *Gunsmoke*),
and the first hour-long western filmed in color. Toward the end of his days on the
Ponderosa (which for a time was not only the title of the Cartwright's on-screen
homestead, but also the syndicated edition of the show), Landon started directing episodes, which later led to his full-time acting, producing, and directing duties on *Little
House on the Prairie* (the 1982-1983 ninth and final season of which aired without his
on-screen presence), and *Highway to Heaven.*

Landon married Dodie Levy-Fraser (1956–1962), Lynn Noe (1963–1982), and
Cindy Clerico (1983–1991), and divorced twice. His children include Mark Fraser
Landon (adopted from first wife's earlier marriage), Josh Fraser Landon (adopted as
an infant), Cheryl Lynn Landon (stepdaughter from second wife's earlier marriage),
Leslie Ann Landon, Michael Landon Jr. (a successful TV director in his own right),
Shawna Leigh Landon, Christopher Beau Landon (from second marriage), Cindy
Clerico, Jennifer Rachel Landon, and Sean Matthew Landon (from third marriage).

Michael Sr.'s striking good looks, accented by his deep blue eyes, razor-sharp cheekbones, full mane of tasseled locks, and wide, illuminating smile, won over tons of female audience members of every age. His behind-the-scenes theatrical abilities, intellect, creative vision, and sense of humor earned him accolades among his peers of every gender, and further added to his charismatic persona. The extensive amount of time, money, and effort he donated for years to the televised *Easter Seal Telethon* (which he had periodically hosted) showed his generosity as a human being.

On July 1, 2011, the twentieth anniversary of Landon's passing, journalist Peter Manseau published the article, "Touched by a Michael Landon: America's Jewish Angel," for the *Religion Dispatches* section of the website for the University of Southern California. As Manseau observed, "While no secret, it was not very well known at the time that Landon had endured anti-Semitic taunts and bullying in his youth."

A measure of it all played out on *Little House on the Prairie*, when Landon met with a young writer named Paul Wolff, who penned the episode, "The Craftsman." Helmed by Landon, airing on January 8, 1979, and set at the end of one summer within the show's nineteenth-century setting, this segment dealt with Albert Quinn Ingalls (Landon's on-screen son as played by Matthew Labyorteaux), who becomes an apprentice for Isaac Singerman (John Bleifer), a craftsman who happened to be Jewish. As an unfortunate consequence, Albert's classmates berate him for his association with Singerman, and Laura (Melissa Gilbert) is also verbally abused when she defends Albert. In the end, Singerman dies, and Albert learns to take pride in his work, signified by planting an acorn to grow into a tree to repay the earth for the one he utilized in his carpentry.

According to Manseau, "The Craftsman" was the first television job for Wolff, now a professor of screenwriting at the University of Southern California, and he credited Landon and the actor's integrity for granting him his first big break. "He was serious about who he was, about being Jewish," Wolff explained. "He had been looking for a way to announce it to the world."

Manseau later said Landon was so convincing an angelic presence on all three shows that many in Christian America thought they had lost one of their own when the iconic actor died. "After all," Manseau wrote, "this was the man responsible for *Highway to Heaven* [which the *Los Angeles Times* once pegged *Jesus of Malibu*, an endearing term which stuck with a few NBC staffers], the weekly extrusion of spiritual melodrama that first convinced network executives that American viewers would enjoy being touched by an angel."

"If further proof were needed," Manseau continued, Landon appeared on the Christian-geared TV talk show *The 700 Club* describing feeling "electric" when portraying the "God-fearing icons of family values."

Bonanza displayed a measure of that mindset, as certainly did the faith-geared *Highway to Heaven*. But *Little House on the Prairie* remains his most popular series in the morale-based realm of classic television. As Landon once surmised about the show, "The main values of *Little House on the Prairie* are the little things that nobody seems to care about anymore: the simple needs of people and how difficult it was in those days out West to supply them."

Manseau later assessed, "Leaving for another time the question of whether or not *Little House on the Prairie* was pure schmaltz, it's worth remembering on the anniversary of Michael Landon's death that the man otherwise known as Little Joe Cartwright, Charles Ingalls, and the angel Jonathan Smith had a *yiddishe kop* under that nice head of hair."

In 2014 Ann Hodges decided:

The key to Michael Landon's success was his sweetness. And I say that because he started out playing the sweet son, Little Joe, on Bonanza, then later as the sweet angel Jonathan on *Highway to Heaven*. But in between those shows, he was the sweet father on *Little House on the Prairie*, which really made him a main-stay of television. And people still love *Little House*, including my 12-year-old grandchild who watches that show today, religiously.

36

James Garner

Maverick/Nichols/The Rockford Files

> The characters I've played, especially Bret Maverick and Jim Rockford, almost never use a gun, and they always try to use their wits instead of their fists.
>
> —James Garner

One of the most easygoing actors of his generation, James Garner exuded a star quality of relaxed competence and composure. As cowboy Bret Maverick on the popular western *Maverick* (ABC, 1957–1962) or private eye Jim Rockford on *The Rockford Files* (NBC, 1974–1980), he could solve whatever crisis was at hand if someone could hold his drink while he did so. He made it all look like he wasn't acting at all—which is the best kind of acting there is. He and Clint Eastwood, who starred on TV's *Rawhide* a few years before he became a big-screen legend, were two of the first actors to successfully make the transition from television star to full-fledged movie star.

Garner was born James Scott Bumgarner April 7, 1928, in Norman, Oklahoma, the youngest of three sons to Weldon Warren Bumgarner and Mildred Scott (Meek). His mother died when he was only five, and his father remarried. But little James and his new step-mom did not get along, which significantly contributed to the failure of the marriage. By the close of World War II, his father had moved to Los Angeles, while Garner, now sixteen, joined the US Merchant Marine. After challenged by a severe bout of seasickness, Garner followed his dad to LA, where he attended Hollywood High School and was named most popular student. His physical education teacher suggested he try modeling, which he did for a while, then returned to Norman, where he excelled at sports but dropped out before graduating. After serving in the National Guard for his first seven months in California, he was stationed as a rifleman for a little over a year in Korea, where he received a Purple Heart for one of his two injuries.

In 1956, he married Lois Clark, with whom he had two daughters: Gigi and Kimberly.

Two years before, Paul Gregory, a former schoolmate from Hollywood High, convinced Jim to accept a nonspeaking role in the Broadway production of *The Caine Mutiny Court-Martial*, starring Henry Fonda. From that moment on, Garner had the acting bug and went on to enjoy a successful show business career, which included many fine TV-movies, such as 1999's *One Special Night* with Julie Andrews, his costar from two of his most successful motion pictures: Paddy Chayefsky's *The Americanization of Emily* (1964) and Blake Edwards's *Victor Victoria* (1982). His other movies include *The Great Escape* (1963), *Murphy's Romance* (1985, for which he received an Oscar), *Space Cowboys* (2000), *The Notebook* (2004), and more than forty others. While his role on *Maverick* created his early measure of success on television, it was by way of *Rockford* that Garner solidified his status as a male television icon. Writer Will Murray addressed the transition in the July 1986 issue of *TV Gold* magazine, describing *Files* as "delightfully eccentric." Jim Rockford first appeared in an episode of Stephen Cannell's short-lived TV series, *Toma*, the quick-change-artist/detective and precursor to Robert Blake on *Baretta*. Seeing the character's promise, Cannell brought *Rockford* to Garner, who was intrigued. As Murray went on to explain, when the two-hour pilot for *Files* debuted in 1974, the Rockford character wasn't the latter-day Maverick who captured America's attention but, as Murray put it, "a rock-jawed, cynical and down-at-heels private eye. An ex-con, he did five years at San Quentin for a truck hijacking others had pulled off. During his confinement, he boned up on the law and studied all the closed cases—like his—that no one ever bothered to reopen."

Globe Photos

Years later, a mere three months into what was becoming what some consider to be the best season of *The Rockford Files*, production stopped when Garner complained of exhaustion. He claimed that numerous injuries he had suffered over the entire six-year run of the series had taken a toll on his health to such a degree that he could no longer continue working in episodic television. He would return to playing the character in a series of TV reunion movies, and he'd step into the father-figure role on ABC's *8 Simple Rules for Dating My Teenage Daughter* following John Ritter's tragic death in 2003. But other than that, Garner never returned to television in any weekly capacity.

A dedicated family man, Garner was married to Lois Clarke from 1956 until he died of a heart attack at 86 (on July 19, 2014). Kind and compassionate, professional and dependable, and progressive and talented in thought and acting style, he also stood firm by his personal convictions. He admittedly could at times become confrontational and rarely walked away from an argument—especially if he felt his actions or cross words were justified. Into this mix, he struggled with legal woes, namely for decades against Universal Studios, proprietor of *The Rockford Files*, feeling financially slighted with regard to royalties, mixed in with the physical challenges that resulted from years of the show's action-adventure sequences. He ultimately was pleased with a settlement between all parties concerned, and in the process copped to campaigning for and utilizing certain natural and unorthodox remedies to ease his various developing disabilities. As he relayed in his best-selling book, *The Garner Files: A Memoir* (published in 2011), "I smoked marijuana for 50 years . . . It opened my mind to a lot of things . . . its active ingredient, THC, relaxes me and eases my arthritis pain. I've concluded that marijuana should be legal."

Garner's appeal as a male icon, on television or otherwise, remained as steady and strong as the man himself. Ann Hodges concludes: "James Garner was what every woman loved. He was virile. He was beautiful and he was fun. And [as an actor] he could do anything. He was definitely a *ladies' man*." In comparing the actor to Maverick and Rockford, Hodges adds, "I think he often played the same character, but of course, in different settings. But he was off-screen who he was on-screen . . . completely likable."

37

Clint Eastwood
Rawhide

Clint Walker
Cheyenne

The TV box has a tremendous capacity to reach people.

—Clint Walker

Clint Eastwood starred on *Rawhide*, a western that initially aired on CBS from 1959 to 1965. Clint Walker took the western lead in *Cheyenne*, which was first broadcast on ABC from 1955 to 1963. As a youngster, Walker worked the riverboats going down the Mississippi and Illinois Rivers, pushing barges to Chicago, then all the way down to New Orleans. The actor ultimately arrived in Hollywood, and made a screen test. As he once recalled, "As luck would have it, Warner Bros. saw my screen test, put me under contract, and I wound up making *Cheyenne*."

Both Clints were big, brawny presences on the small screen and entertained TV audiences for years. Eastwood went on to translate his western success to the big screen with a series of what were termed spaghetti westerns, and in the *Dirty Harry* franchise. His talents were then further transferred into becoming an Oscar-winning feature film director of new classics like *Unforgiven* (1992), *Million Dollar Baby* (2004), *Gran Torino* (2008), and countless others.

According to media historian Rob Ray, the key to Eastwood's appeal is "Quiet determination. He's a latter-day Gary Cooper. . . . a man of few words and few unnecessary actions. Clint was and is a star. Like Ron Howard and Robert Redford, he's also [an actor who is] one of the finest directors in the business." In comparison to Walker, who went on to star in the short-lived ABC TV series, *Kodiak*, Ray says:

Clint Eastwood
Globe Photos

Clint Walker is a hulking giant of a man. Like Clint Eastwood, he was very quiet, but without Clint Eastwood's intensity. To me Clint Walker was more of a teddy bear. Eminently fair, honest and forthright and ever the gentleman. Clint Eastwood was more brooding, as if his quietness was his way of keeping a lid on some sort of powder keg. Eastwood's way of gritting his teeth when he spoke indicated a suppression of violent emotions. Clint Walker's speech evoked tranquility and peace.

TV writer Larry Brody never watched *Rawhide*, but he did know Eastwood in the 80s and 90s, through actor Doug McClure (*The Virginians*), who was a close mutual friend of both. "Great guy," Brody says of Eastwood. "Cool and open and generous. And I both admire and respect him as a man who gives credit where credit is due."

Brody explains the history behind one of Eastwood's most recognizable on-screen signature lines:

A friend of mine wrote a script based on his own life. He was a friend of Clint's also, and showed the script to him. As soon as Clint read it, he bought it. Not for the story or the characters but because of one line of dialog, said by the abusive father to his son when, in the script, the son had been so badly treated that for just a second it looked like he was about to hit him back. "Go ahead," the father said eagerly, "make my day." Clint paid a substantial sum for the script just so he could use that line in *Sudden Impact* [aka *Dirty Harry*]. I mean a very substantial sum. And my friend got a writing credit on the film as well.

Both Clint Eastwood and Clint Walker are still going strong.

Born May 30, 1927, Walker, according to Wikipedia, has a net worth of four million dollars. He married three times: Verna Garver (1948–1968), Giselle Hennessy (1974–1994), and Susan Cavallari (since 1997). He has one daughter (Valerie Walker) and one sister (Neoma L. Westbrook).

Born May 31, 1930, Eastwood was married twice: Maggie Johnson (1953 to 1984) and Dina Eastwood (1996 to 2014). Eastwood also had several loving partners (including actresses Sondra Locke and Frances Fisher) and several children (Scott, Francesca, Kyle, Alison, Morgan, Kimber, and Kathryn Eastwood).

Clint Walker
Globe Photos

The key to both actors' long life and good health may be found in Walker's personal philosophy. As he once said, "End your day with a smile, a happy thought, and a grateful heart."

38

Max Baer Jr.
The Beverly Hillbillies

Yee-hah!

— Jethro Bodine, as played by Max Baer Jr. on *The Beverly Hillbillies*

There must be something to being super-dim and mega-handsome. Just ask Jethro Bodine, the monumental TV character so enthusiastically portrayed by Max Baer Jr. (who today prefers to be known as just Max Baer) on CBS's *The Beverly Hillbillies* from 1962 to 1971. Jethro may have been born as "mountain folk," but because his Uncle Jed Clampett (Buddy Ebsen) struck gold ("Texas tea"), he was fortunate enough to have "loaded up the truck and moved to Beverly . . . Hills, that is"—with the entire Clampett family, including Elly May (Donna Douglas) and Granny (Irene Ryan).

Not exactly the brightest bulb in the bulb box ("If brains was lard, Jethro couldn't grease a pan"), the young Mr. Bodine still very much had a way with the ladies, especially Miss Jane Hathaway (Nancy Culp). Miss Jane, secretary to banker Millburn Drysdale (Raymond Bailey), who guarded Jed's millions, always had a thing for Jethro—and she wasn't shy about expressing those feelings. Ultimately, Miss Jane became the voice of "Everywoman" . . . meaning, every woman viewer at home who was attracted to Baer's brawny and likable performance as Jethro.

Born Maximilian Adalbert Baer Jr. on December 4, 1937, in Oakland, California, Baer's parents were champion boxer Max Baer and Mary Ellen Sullivan. He was married to Joanne Kathleen Hill from 1966 to 1971.

Baer's first acting role was in a stage production of *Goldilocks and the Three Bears* at the Blackpool Pavilion in England in 1949. He earned a bachelor's degree in 1959 in business administration from Santa Clara University (minored in philosophy). He began working in television in 1960, making guest appearances on shows like *Maverick*, *Surfside 6*, *Bronco*, *The Roaring 20's*, *Sugarfoot*, *Cheyenne*, *Hawaiian Eye*, *77 Sunset Strip*, and *Follow the Sun*.

In 1962 he was cast as Jethro on *Hillbillies*, which CBS initially aired until the network opted to cancel as one executive put it "every show with a tree in it," purging all country-geared programming for what was considered the more sophisticated shows that were surfacing at the time (e.g., Norman Lear's *All in the Family*).

Between 1972 and 1991, Max made guest appearances on shows like *Love, American Style*, *Fantasy Island*, *Matt Houston* (on which Buddy Ebsen had a recurring role), and *Murder, She Wrote*. He wrote, produced, and acted in the 1974 hit film *Macon County Line*. He also produced, directed, and acted in *The Wild McCullochs* (1975) and produced and directed *Ode to Billy Joe* (1976).

In 1991 he purchased the rights to the *Beverly Hillbillies* name from CBS and has used the show's theme and its characters for casinos, theme parks, restaurants, cosmetics, and consumables. With International Game Technology he has licensed *Beverly Hillbillies*–themed slot machines including "Clampett's Cash,"

Globe Photos

"The Bubblin' Crude," and "Moonshine Money." He's also working to launch *Beverly Hillbillies*–themed casinos in Nevada.

Much wiser than his most famous TV male alter ego, Baer today offers this exclusive insight into the extremely likable interpretation of Jethro Bodine, and how important a role the audience plays in the scheme of things with regard to an actor's performance; especially a television audience:

> When you play a role like Jethro, it's for other people to judge, because it's pretty
> hard to be subjective or objective about yourself. You just do the best you can with

the material that you're given, and then you try to add to it [with your performance] as much as you possibly can. But in the end, it's the audience who has the final say. "Well, we liked what you did" or "We don't like what you did." And you really don't have any other way of evaluating it.

As long as you give 100 percent, even if you're sick. Don't bullshit, and say, "Oh, I can't show up." You show up! You do your job—and you do it as if you aren't sick . . . because it's going to be on film in perpetuity. You're not going to be able to put a little quote at the bottom of the screen saying, "Well, he wasn't as good today because he was sick . . . or emotionally disturbed or had a headache." You have to give a good performance. You have to perform well. And, in my case [with Jethro], if I have made the people laugh—and even if they can laugh at my expense—it's okay. I don't care. They can laugh with me or at me. It doesn't matter . . . just as long as they laugh. Because if I can make them laugh, then I believe that my performance was a successful one. I can't evaluate it as to what degree of success it was. But I can say it did what it was supposed to do.

Baer did just that, winning over millions of Jethro fans for decades, including his *Hillbillies* costars, including fellow male costar Buddy Ebsen, about whom Baer once said, "To me, Buddy was the star of *The Beverly Hillbillies*."

The majority of the main *Hillbillies* stars are now gone, including Ebsen and Donna Douglas, who passed away in 2015, leaving Baer as the sole surviving cast member from the series. In 2013 Douglas spoke highly of both Ebsen and Baer:

Buddy . . . he was the best! I had most of my scenes with him, he reminded me so much of my own dad. Once at the beginning of the show's run, my dad went to town and someone yelled, "Hey Jed Clampett" to him. It was so precious, as my parents were so proud of my success! And then Max and I were with Buddy the night before he died at the hospital.

Max Baer did well as Jethro because he didn't come across as so dumb that you didn't like him. He gave me a hard time then and still does. But we all were like a family. Max could complain about any one of us (for whatever reason), but do not let someone else say something about one of us. Boy—would Max really let that person have it. He'd defend us just like with a real family member.

TV historian Jeffrey D. Dalrymple, who was good friends with Douglas, and who remains so with Baer, concludes of Max's maximum portrayal of his beloved Bodine character:

Max Baer as Jethro was perfect casting. The goofy ear to ear grin. . .his laugh. . .his ability to make you laugh along with him [or at him, as Baer himself has assessed], you believed episode after episode, that he truly was a country bumpkin with only a sixth grade education. When he held his fingers up to cypher 2 + 2 = 4, he made the character of Jethro Bodine his own, and we all delighted in his plans to be a brain surgeon, a movie director, or a double naught spy. You believed Uncle Jed, Granny, and cousin Elly May were his family because they played it so well. And Max had the ability to blend in with the other cast members, without overplaying or under playing Jethro. He was a good actor and a good guy, and he still is. . .along with a talented writer, and a successful businessman.

39

Richard Thomas
The Waltons

Goodnight, John-Boy!

—As spoken by countless members of *The Waltons*
to the iconic male TV character portrayed by Richard Thomas

An acclaimed and diverse performer, Richard Thomas is best known in the world of classic television for his Emmy-winning performance as John-Boy Walton on *The Waltons*, which began as a 1971 Christmas TV-movie titled *The Homecoming*. Before that, Thomas delivered early riveting performances on notable series such as *Marcus Welby, M.D.*

A decade or so after the original *Waltons* program ended in 1981, Thomas returned to playing John-Boy in a series of TV-reunion movies, and later hosted the heartwarming weekly docu-show, *It's a Miracle*. *Miracle* deftly utilized his affable charms to introduce true tales of inspiration and courage from the files of real people who have experienced or required otherworldly assistance to overcome various life challenges; never had a host been more suited to a role.

But it was on *The Waltons* that Thomas really shined (along with the Emmy-winning Michael Learned, Ralph Waite, Will Geer, and Ellen Corby, and that show's entire cast of young actors). He rode that country-geared show into becoming one of the best-acted weekly family dramas in the history of television (*The Carol Burnett Show* once did a take-off titled *The Walnuts*, thus confirming that satire and imitation are the sincerest forms of flattery).

Since playing John-Boy, Thomas starred in several hit TV-movies, notably 1990's *It* (based on a Stephen King novel, and starring Thomas's good friend and former *Waltons* semi-regular John Ritter), and *The Christmas Box* (which aired in 1995, and was based on the book of the same name).

Globe Photos

With each performance or appearance, the viewer trusts Thomas to deliver the goods. He's got it all down: the perfect pauses between lines of delivery; the ideal level of emotional display. He's never overtly melodramatic or shallow in any of his portrayals, but always just *right*. His theatrical generosity on screen has been appreciated by his various costars through the years.

Thomas was only six years old when he made his live-stage debut, and a mere seven years of age when he premiered on television. His parents were professional ballet dancers, who performed with the National Ballet of Cuba and with the New York City Ballet and, for a time, operated a ballet school in New York City.

Besides the various Broadway and TV shows in which he has appeared, Thomas has appeared in feature films like *The Last Summer* (1969) and *Red Sky at Morning* (1971). He has always loved to work and as entertainment journalist Peggy Herz once pointed out, he "settled into the role of John-Boy Walton with the ease of a farm boy donning his coveralls."

The initial six years of *The Waltons* are superior to the remaining three seasons of the show for one main reason: Richard Thomas as John-Boy Walton. The actor as the character was literally the narrative driving voice of the series. Although the opening and closing voiceover was provided by show creator and resident genius Earl Hamner, it was Thomas's earthy performance in the lead that linked the other characters together.

As John-Boy, Thomas interpreted some of Hamner's real-life adventures growing up in the blue mountain country of the Depression era, with his expansive brood of brothers and sisters. They were originally presented in Earl Hamner's novel and subsequent

1963 movie, *Spencer's Mountain* (starring Henry Fonda and James MacArthur in the John-Boy role, then called Clay-Boy). Hodges says, "Hamner was brilliant in capturing that time period [the 30s-40s]," and Richard Thomas was the inter-connecting element that "sealed the show's success."

On the significance of *The Waltons* series in general, Hodges adds, "It was a wonderful show, and I really think it did an awful lot for the country. I thought it showed a family that really cared about each other; and a family who didn't necessarily have a lot of stuff. But you just knew that all of those kids were being brought up right . . . they were going to make something of themselves. It was just inspiring because it reminded people so much of their childhood, particularly those who grew up in the Depression Era, in which the show was based."

Says Ann Hodges of Richard: "He was wonderful as John-Boy. Very talented, so much that I think he could have done even a lot more than he's done. As far as being an actor is concerned, he just 'had it' and still has it. But he was wonderful for John-Boy and he was just the right age for it, and everything just fit him to a 'T' in that role."

Born June 13, 1951, Thomas married Alma Gonzales on February 14, 1975. They had one son, Richard Francisco, born in 1976, and triplet daughters Barbara Ayala, Gweneth Gonzales, and Pilar Alma, born August 26, 1981. They divorced in 1993. Thomas married Georgiana Bischoff on November 20, 1994. They have one son, Montana James Thomas, born July 28, 1996. At the time she married Thomas, Bischoff had two daughters from previous marriages, Brooke Murphy and Kendra Kneifel. Daughter Kendra Kneifel has since changed her name to Kendra Thomas.

Thomas has worked and continues to perform consistently as varied characters in countless TV, film, and stage productions since *The Waltons*, including contemporary shows like the FX series *The Americans* (in which he's played Frank Gad in more than thirty-nine episodes since 2013).

But it's the perfect packaging of his down-home charm as John-Boy that will remain forever embedded in the psyche of the classic TV viewer.

40

John Schneider and Tom Wopat
The Dukes of Hazzard

> I believe you should be a gentleman, and that's old-fashioned.
>
> —John Schneider

They brought fun, adventure, and the carefree spirit back to television. After CBS purged its schedule of all country-geared shows in the early 70s (for more realistic comedies and dramas like *Maude* and *Kojak*), the network returned trees to its screens with programming like *The Dukes of Hazzard*.

Originally starring John Schneider, Tom Wopat, and Catherine Bach as cousins Bo, Luke, and Daisy Duke of Hazzard County, Georgia, *The Dukes of Hazzard* became a Friday night staple for years.

The series, which also starred Denver Pyle, Rick Hurst, Sorrell Booke, James Best, and countless other likable actors, was created by Rod Amateau and Gy Waldron—and was similar in fun and feel to the *Smokey and the Bandit* feature films of the era. According to Wikipedia, the series was more specifically inspired by the 1975 movie *Moonrunners*, which was also created by Waldron, and had many identical or similar character names and concepts.

At the center of the show were Schneider and Wopat. One blond, one dark-haired; both masculine and tough; and yet charming and free-wheeling, driving around in their customized 1969 Dodge Charger stock car (which they nicknamed the General Lee).

The series still remains popular today, as proven by the sales of the Christmas musical CD released by Schneider in 2014 featuring eighteen tunes, including what *Rolling*

Tom Wopat, left; John Schneider, right

CBS/PhotoFest

Stone magazine described as "a bromantic reinterpretation of 'Baby, It's Cold Outside.'" And according to *People* magazine, in a live performance from December 2, 2014, Wopat called his pal Schneider "dude" somewhere in the middle and name-checked the *Hazzard* brothers' bright-orange vehicle.

Born April 8, 1960, in Mount Kisco, New York, Schneider has married twice: Tawny Little (1983–1986) and Elly Castle (1993–2014). He has three children: Chasen Joseph, Karis, and Leah Schneider.

Born September 9, 1951, in Lodi, Wisconsin, Wopat married twice: first to Kathy Wopat and, since 1984, to Vickie Allen. Both actors continued to work after the original *Dukes* ended. Schneider has enjoyed a lengthy run as Clark Kent's father on the CW series *Smallville*, and is one of the featured stars of *The Haves and the Have Nots*, now in its hit fourth season on the Oprah Winfrey Network (OWN), while he and Wopat also have successful musical careers.

For a recent online profile in *Digital Journal*, Schneider summarized the core ingredients to *Dukes'* appeal:

It has something for everyone. I think for many people who grew up watching it, their fondest memories of their grandparents were watching it on a Friday night. Now those grandparents are gone. So when they think of *The Dukes of Hazzard*, they think of Grandma and Grandpa and the wonderful time they spent with them.

But, I do meet three- or four-year-olds who are just as crazy about the Dukes as their parents were almost forty years ago, who seem to have discovered it on their own. It's a bit of an enigma. It is good clean fun about [what the show's theme] song says, 'two–modern-day Robin Hoods,' but I believe it's unfair not to include [Bach's] Daisy in that.

PART V

THE BAD BOYS AND HEAVIES

They looked like trouble, made trouble, and, most of the time, they were trouble. But without question the "bad boys" of television have their legions of fans—and their own brand of allure. By mimicking the James Dean types of the big screen, but adding a kinder, gentler presence more fitting and strangely welcoming for the small screen, the more serious gents of TV, though rough around the edges, bared their big hearts to and were welcomed by the viewing audience.

Some showed up in the more obvious bad boy image, as with a young Ryan O'Neal as Rodney Harrington on ABC's *Peyton Place*, and Michael Parks on NBC's *Then Came Bronson*.

As entertainment journalist David Dacks explained in his *Pop/Rock Question and Answer Book*, Michael Parks rose to fame as a "sensitive man on a motorcycle," as the star of *Bronson*, which aired for only one season in 1970. He was described as "young, restless, bright, strong, impatient, soft-spoken, and out-spoken." Some said he was difficult to work with, that he was definitely not "the boy next door." On *Bronson*, he "portrayed a character who roamed the highways and dusty sideroads on his motorcycle, fearless and unafraid."

In real life, Dacks said, Parks was apparently "afraid of some things." Namely, he was reluctant to fly. For a guest shot on *The Ed Sullivan Show* he insisted on taking a three-day cross-country railroad trip rather than a six-hour flight.

Parks was born April 24 in Corona, California, during a time of what Dacks called "uncertainty and rootlessness." "Home" for the family of two boys and three girls was often an empty warehouse, a garage, or a temporary campsite. When his father wasn't working as a truck driver, his family sifted and stacked oak leaf mold for sale to nurseries. At only fourteen years of age, Parks was on his own. He attended twenty-one schools, never graduating from high school, but somehow attended junior college.

Parks's career as an actor began in San Francisco and Sacramento, California. In Hermosa Beach, a few miles south of Los Angeles, he auditioned for and landed one of the lead roles in a local production of a play titled *Compulsion*. Talent agent Jack Fields saw him in the play, and the rest became history. But the "bad boy" image he presented on *Then Came Bronson* certainly stemmed to some extent from his real life. For a time he also had a brief recording career with MGM Records. His album of country songs, *The Long Lonesome Highway*, only added to a certain "wild one" persona.

Other TV performers followed more fully in the musical and sweaty dance shoes of Elvis Presley's initial musical TV appearances, some even playing out the bad-boy image to the fullest extent with musical variety programs of their own. The prime example of this would be Tom Jones, a British import who might best be described as a cross between Presley and Engelbert Humperdinck.

The variety series, *This Is Tom Jones*, debuted on ABC in 1969, and aired until 1971. While Elvis ignited the swivel-hips-musical-sensation of the small screen with his first appearance on CBS's *The Ed Sullivan Show* (September 9, 1956), Jones played the dance card with the entire physical-kit-and-kaboodle on a weekly basis with his energizing weekly seductions.

While his name suggested danger, perhaps only subliminally (it matched the title of Henry Fielding's most famous novel about a "bastard" from birth), Jones's live act taped for TV produced a lot a sweat—and tears from more than a few of his female fans in the studio audience (and most probably thousands more at home). Whereas most variety programs of the era concentrated on comedy skits with a few song and dance numbers (such as *The Carol Burnett Show* and *The Dean Martin Show*), *This Is Tom Jones* focused on the vocal and very visual and physical, theatrical gymnastics of its leading musical "moving" man.

While Pat Boone, Dick Clark, Ron Howard, among other performers showcased the good boy persona next door, John Travolta's Vinnie Barbarino played out the teen-hood up the street, or in the case of Henry Winkler's "Fonz" on *Happy Days*, the high school dropout hood in the room over the garage. Both eventually graduated high school, with Fonzie finally passing his GED (General Education Development) test, and leaving the TV space wide open for future bad boys in the 80s, 90s, and beyond (such as Luke Perry on *Beverly Hills, 90210*, as Dylan—another subliminal reference to a "bad boy," groundbreaking musical legend Bob Dylan).

Television "bad boys" of an older set were defined by their serious issues with social interaction (such as the bigot Archie Bunker, as played by Carroll O'Connor on *All in the Family*, or the rarely smiling Lou Grant, as played by Ed Asner on *The Mary Tyler Moore Show*, or the private eye Frank Cannon, portrayed by William Conrad on *Cannon*). The fact that they carried around a few extra pounds conveniently allowed them to be ambiguously defined as heavies.

Despite their less admirable traits, each of these characters still somehow managed to strike a chord with the TV audience, mostly due to the core talents, dedication, and energetic performances of the actors who brought them to life.

41

George Maharis and Martin Milner
Route 66/Adam-12

Having covered some half a hundred cities, towns, villages and wide spots in the road . . . George and I fairly wallowed in the comfort of our own home base.

—Martin Milner

Driving down the TV byways of *Route 66* (CBS, 1960–1964), George Maharis as Buz Murdock and Martin Milner as Todd Stiles were an interesting combination of street smarts and artistic aspirations. Maharis could get into a fistfight at a moment's notice and recite poetry to the thug he had just pummeled into submission. His dark, Greek good looks coupled with his wrong-side-of-the-tracks accent made him an audience favorite. It was the perfect marriage of actor and role that he never managed to duplicate once he left the series (due to a serious bout with pneumonia, when he was replaced by Todd's new driving partner, Lincoln Case, as played by Glenn Corbett).

Maharis's portrayal of Buz made him the show's heartthrob. Buz was inner-city-wise and tough, while Milner's Todd was refined, rich enough and off-center enough to own that Corvette that he drove into one adventure after the next. *Route 66* was never the same after Maharis left, but when it was good—it was great—and the original duo were dynamite with their own individual take on the bad boy image.

In the summer of 1990, Maharis and Milner were interviewed by *Corvette Quarterly* magazine. They talked about what it was like to work on the series, what made it unique, and how giving the home viewer a front-row seat to the country's panorama contributed to the television landscape. When asked about the show's controversial topics, Milner credited show writer Stirling Silliphant and *66* producer Bert Leonard for having the courage to push the envelope:

> Stirling always had a finger on the pulse of what was happening before the general public seemed to know about it. We did [an episode] on LSD called "The Thin White Line," when nobody really knew what LSD was. I had certainly never heard of it, but Stirling had. I think he was kind of in the vanguard on things like that. And Bert Leonard had the good sense to go along with him on those [decisions] . . . I thought it was wonderful. I thought we were breaking new ground. I was always very happy with the storylines on the show . . . The fact that we were pioneering a very innovative way to make television—to do it on the road, in the actual locations. We were doing something nobody else had ever done, and nobody really has done it since [by 1990], either. But one of the sad things is that we weren't in color, because we were in so many beautiful spots [around the country], like being in Vermont in the fall when the leaves were changing.

Over a lengthy TV series, the actor's personality often merges with that of his character. Maharis said that playing Buz allowed him to express his personal beliefs from Buz's point of view, "a philosophy of the way . . . this particular person lived his life." This was important for the actor to convey, as opposed to what he felt was "going on in other shows."

Maharis's personal best episodes of the show include "Even Stones Have Eyes," in which Buz is blinded, which allowed the actor to utilize his theatrical muscles more than his physical stamina. As a result, he says, this episode "was always really a nice one for me." One of his other favorite segments was titled "The Mud Nest," and that's because his two brothers, Bob and Paul, performed in a story in which they played siblings in search of their mother.

Another aspect of the series that he said remains embedded in his memory

Martin Milner, left; George Maharis, right
CBS/PhotoFest

was how with every subsequent season on the series Buz and Todd, aka Maharis and Milner, would get to drive a different shiny-new high-end vehicle. "We never would explain how these poor kids had a brand-new Corvette every year," he mused, "but it was called 'dramatic license' and we left it at that."

Larry Brody has been involved with several classic shows, including *Police Story*, an anthology that aired on NBC in the 70s. He chatted a little bit about *Route 66*, which aired while he was still in high school:

> I watched a few episodes but never got into it because, contrary to my family's fears, I had too much to do outside in the real world. My particular peer group—I was the drummer-leader of a very popular band that played all the school dances and such— did talk about the series quite a bit, but 99% of that conversation was about what a sensationally beautiful and fast car the heroes' Corvette was. I fell in love with it as well, and the first car I ever considered my own was a 59 Corvette that I bought for $1500 used when I was a sophomore in college. Unfortunately, it was white instead of red like the *Route 66* 'Vette, so it didn't give my shallow self the full satisfaction I'd hoped for.
>
> At the time, I was an audience member just turning on the TV in order to see an interesting story and relax. I never noticed whether the stories featured the heroes and their problems or the guest cast and its particular tribulations, and neither did anyone else I knew. A TV show was a TV show, and as good as *Route 66* may have been, at the time it [showcased] the ultra-tough/ultra-cool kickass heroes I really wanted to see . . . and, I suppose . . . be.

After fellow male TV icon Burt Reynolds paved the way for male nudity in print with his visual spread in *Cosmopolitan* in 1972, Maharis followed with a similar layout in the newly formed *Playgirl* magazine. He was hoping to revive a career that had somewhat stalled since exiting *Route 66*. And to some extent, he was successful. He made guest appearances on TV shows like *McMillan & Wife*, and in TV-movies including ABC's *The Victim* (1972).

Milner's career proved to be significantly more successful with a costarring spot opposite Kent McCord on Jack Webb's *Adam-12*, on ABC's short-lived but critically acclaimed *Swiss Family Robinson*, and a season of that network's groundbreaking family drama, *Life Goes On*.

42

Jonathan Frid and David Selby
Dark Shadows

I thought the role on *Dark Shadows* would go on for about three or four weeks. And then, the phenomenon began, the role caught on, the mail started to flood in.

—Jonathan Frid

Every weekday afternoon, from 1966 to 1971, devoted TV viewers of every age flocked to watch *Dark Shadows*, the unique ABC daytime gothic serial that spawned two of the most popular soap stars of all time: Jonathan Frid and David Selby.

Frid portrayed Barnabas Collins, the tortured, lovelorn vampire with heart. Selby was Quentin Collins, initially a menacing ghost and later revealed to be an alcoholic womanizer turned into a werewolf with compassion. Both characters were repentant of their unfortunate lot in life, and Frid and Selby brought to their roles what remains an everlasting appeal unlike any other in television male icon history, daytime, prime-time, or otherwise.

Dark Shadows was created by visionary producer Dan Curtis, director and/or producer of some of TV's finest and favorite films and mini-series, including *The Night Stalker* (1972), *Trilogy of Terror* (1975, starring Karen Black), *The Winds of War* (1983), *War and Remembrance* (1988-1989), a 1991 *Shadows* remake for NBC, and so much more. Due to *Dark's* invention, Frid and Selby introduced scary new American sex symbols and canonized untraditional saints in the church of classic TV. The show became the first *alternative* daytime serial, focusing on the lives of a bizarre troupe, instead of relatively *regular* ones (ages before NBC let loose its supernatural daytime

Jonathan Frid
Dan Curtis Productions

persuasion with *Passions* in 1999). A significant portion of its audience was rare among soaps—legions of counterculture pre-teens and teens who rushed home from school and replaced their stereos with TVs. (The show was fully covered by *16 Magazine* and *Tiger Beat*, the teen titan periodicals of the day!) The series became the first non-primetime soap to be syndicated (eons before the onset of the all-soap channels). It premiered in a time littered with assassinations, illicit drug use, a sexual revolution, and a misbegotten war; many fans, with somewhat lost souls of their own, pined to find themselves in another realm—a mystical realm.

Born Jonathan Herbert Frid December 2, 1924, in Hamilton, Ontario, Canada, Frid's career highlights include the live stage tour of his one-man show and countless other theater performances, such as his role as Jonathan Brewster in *Arsenic and Old Lace* presented at Chicago's Schubert Theatre. Beyond *Dark Shadows*, his TV appearances include acclaimed TV-movies like *The Devil's Daughter* (ABC, 1973) and rare talk show guest-spots on *The Mike Douglas Show* and *The Merv Griffin Show*, as well as the game show, *The Generation Gap* (as did *Shadows* costar David Henesy). He never married nor had children.

Born February 5, 1941, in Morgantown, West Virginia, David Selby married Claudius Newman in 1963. They have one son, Jamison (named after David Henesy's young Jamison Collins, who looked up to his Uncle Quentin on *Dark Shadows*).

Frid's Barnabas wound up featured in upscale magazines like *Time* and *The Saturday Evening Post*, and *Shadows* spawned two successful feature films (1970's *House of Dark Shadows* and 1971's *Night of Dark Shadows*), while the TV series moved forward, then finally succumbed to a stake in the hard core of its appeal. Still, the show did not die. NBC's updated primetime addition resurrected the franchise in the early 90s and childhood devotee Johnny Depp took on the role of Barnabas in a 2012 feature film adaptation. Massive amounts of memorabilia and countless followers refused to gather cobwebs and instead gathered for regular *Dark Shadows* Festival cast reunion/fan conventions (one in June 2016—for the fiftieth anniversary of *Dark's* debut).

Years after the show ended, Frid tried to make sense of it all. "I suppose women see Barnabas as a romantic figure," he said, "because I played him as a lonely, tormented man rather than a Bela Lugosi villain. I bite girls in the neck, but only when my uncontrollable need for blood drove me to it. And I always felt remorseful later." As to his appeal with the younger crowd, he said, "Youngsters . . . are looking for a new morality. And he is Barnabas. He goes around telling people to be good, then suddenly sets out and bites somebody's neck. He hates what he is and he's in terrible agony. Just like kids today, he's confused—lost and screwed up and searching for something. I'm a lovable and pitiable vampire. All the girls want to mother me."

Producer/writer Jim Pierson has composed and/or compiled several *DS* books with and without *Shadows* star Kathryn Leigh Scott (who played Maggie Evans and Josette Collins, the love of Barnabas's life—and death) and has for decades remained the keeper of the flame for the show's legacy. A trusted colleague and confidant to Curtis (who passed away March 27, 2006), Pierson served as a producer and marketing director at Dan Curtis Productions from 1990 until Dan's passing in 2006; Pierson is now the official representative for the Curtis estate. He offers his unparalleled insight into the immortal appeal of *Shadows'* two top male leads, beginning with Frid, a classically trained actor who attended the Yale School of Drama, as well as the Royal Academy of Dramatic Art in London:

> Jonathan Frid had a commanding presence. He knew how to utilize his voice in a compelling, dramatic manner with a certain eloquence, especially when speaking as Barnabas. There was a specific formality to his voice as well as a hesitation at times which, he readily admitted, had a great deal to do with his inability to learn an exuberant amount of lines on a daily basis [which is par for the course for daytime soap stars]. He was not a quick-study, particularly early on in the series before he became acclimated in the role of Barnabas. But that really worked toward the development of the character, as Barnabas was somewhat preoccupied and basically felt out of place.

Both Frid and Barnabas retained what Pierson terms "a charming but suspenseful quality" that stood apart for all of those different reasons. "Jonathan was nervous, and he really didn't know what he was getting into," Pierson says of Frid's initial involvement in the series. Expanding on how Frid himself once described his most famous TV persona, Pierson says Barnabas was "a romantic character that women in particular loved," despite the fact that he was not "a classically handsome young soap star," which, too, "wasn't necessarily the case at that time on daytime soaps in general, when middle aged and older actors were more heavily featured."

Indeed. It wasn't until after *Shadows* ended its original run and into the the mid-to-late 70s with afternoon soaps like *All My Children* and *The Young and The Restless* when, as Pierson says, the networks started "youth-in-izing" the daytime soaps with a focus on teen, twenty-something, and thirty-something actors, which are now so frequently emphasized. Pierson is also quick to point out that *Shadows* was the first daytime soap to appeal to a young demographic as well as the housewives:

> Jonathan was in his 40s, and had a very mature appearance but women of all ages just loved him. Yes, Barnabas was a vampire to the kids, who got into the spooky stuff, but the young women, teenagers on up, just admired him too in their own way. Barnabas loved Josette Collins, and he had this wistful quality that was very appealing to the women who wanted that type of devoted love in their life.

Frid, who had initially signed on to do the series for only thirteen weeks, became the star of the show. But Curtis and ABC learned by way of countless fan letters that his presence as Barnabas was, as Pierson recalls, "something that needed to be maximized . . . and that's when the Barnabas storyline was extended." At first he was to be killed by the medical Dr. Julia Hoffman (as flamboyantly played by Academy Award–nominated actress Grayson Hall). Instead, Julia fell in love with Barnabas and literally changed his life by special blood injections that help to free him for a time from the vampire curse that was placed upon him by the witch Angelique (Lara Parker), after he spurned her love for Scott's Josette.

Selby was cast as Quentin in December of 1968 because Frid had told Curtis that he was simply unable to carry the brunt of the show. Usually, soap actors were only scheduled maybe three days a week, and some of them less than that. Frid was often pushed to four or even five days. "Jonathan was overwhelmed. He also often made publicity appearances on weekends throughout the country. It wasn't easy for him," Pierson says.

Thereupon, Selby's Quentin came to serve as what Pierson calls the "second in command. He was younger and went from playing mute [as the silent ghost of Quentin in the 1969 storyline] to a matinee idol, and the big star of the show when they went back into the past [to the 1897 storyline, which was extended because *Shadows* had received its highest ratings since Frid's debut]."

"It became kind of like the Quentin/ Barnabas show," Pierson adds, and during the peak period of 1969 reached up to twenty million viewers and enjoyed a top-selling soundtrack album and hit single ("Quentin's Theme," also titled "Shadows of the Night," was composed by Robert Cobert with lyrics by Charles Green).

A gracious and humble David Selby credits those behind-the-*Shadows*-scenes for his Quentin success including writers like Sam Hall (husband to Grayson Hall), directors Lela Swift and Henry Kaplan, and creator/producer Curtis, who also helmed episodes of the series.

"We had a good team," he intones.

Like Frid, Selby was initially apprehensive about working on the series, but for different reasons. With regard to his debut as the silent ghost of Quentin in the 1969 storyline, Selby recalls being told, "Well, you won't be speaking for a while."

David Selby
Dan Curtis Productions

"I didn't know that at all," he says today with a smile.

But while taping *Dark*, he was littered with trepidation.

Some decades before, more than a few silent film stars (with a lack of voice control and talent) lost their jobs once talking-pictures came into the fray. Selby feared a similar fate, and thought, "Oh, no . . . once the audience hears me talk, that'll be the end of it."

His worries proved unwarranted. The audience fell in love, not only with his vocal and theatrical prowess, but with his 6'2" frame, his handsome face, accented by his crystal-blue eyes, and every tasseled hair on his head, including the long side-burns that graced his chiseled high-cheek bones. While Frid's Barnabas had his own unique hairstyle (his tresses were combed like little stalactites across his forehead), Selby's Quentin had his distinctive look, which also included a long blue frock.

"I loved that coat!" Selby says today. "It was Quentin's staple, and I used to call it my uniform," which, like all the show's costumes, were designed "on the spot" (by the wardrobe department, supervised by Ramsey Mostoller), as opposed to contemporary farming-out methods.

As to the sideburns, they were first created by the makeup department (supervised by Vincent Loscalzo, then Selby grew his own.

Such exterior adornments, combined with the audio mystique presented with "Quentin's Theme" (which, along with all the show's haunting background music, was performed by the Robert Colbert Orchestra), resulted in Selby's iconic status in TV history.

"It was all so wonderful," Selby recalls.

None of it, however, he adds, would have transpired without the vision of famed casting director Marion Dougherty, who literally sent Selby to the New York offices of Dan Curtis for the initial audition. The actor relives how it all happened:

> I met with Marion. We talked for a while and she said, "Come with me." She then put me in a cab with her, paid for the fare, and I soon found myself in Dan's office, which was on Park Avenue at the time. A few days later, I auditioned with a little scene for Dan, and Marion was there again, too. Dan was an avid golfer, and I remember having to move a few golf balls off the floor to make some room to stand. And from there, I did the scene with Kathy Mann, my scene partner at that time. Dan looked at me on camera the very next day in the studio on 53rd Street and that was it.

Once signed on as Quentin, Selby's initial core scenes were performed with then-child actor David Henesy as young David Collins, who was the first to interact with Quention's ghost (via telephone).

Besides *Dark Shadows*, Selby went on to find success with starring roles in two other series, this time, in primetime. First, as Michael Tyrone on *Flamingo Road* (NBC, 1980–1982), which was followed by his portrayal of Richard Manning on *Falcon Crest* (CBS, 1982–1990), as well as many other TV shows and films.

He continues to act on television and film, as well as write. Along with Kathryn Leigh Scott and Lara Parker, he is the author of several *Shadows* and non-*Shadows* related books, and novels, while he also writes plays and performs in live theater productions around the world. One of his more unique publications is a photographic history of his stage, TV, and movie career, titled *In and Out of the Shadows*, which features his original poetry for each section. He's also authored *My Shadows Past*, a text-driven remembrance of the entire political and social period of change that was concurrent with the original run of *Dark Shadows*, while his newest book, *Live in Shadows*, is actually poetry and song lyrics.

Of his time on *Dark Shadows*, Selby is nothing less than grateful—and modest. In explaining his appeal on the show, he suggests:

> Maybe it was a mesh of my performance and the character. Maybe it had to do with all my hopes and dreams, and maybe I personalized all of that into Quentin, even from the standpoint of growing my hair a little longer. Maybe it all harkened back to the swashbuckling performances of actors like Errol Fynn, when acting was all just sheer make-believe and pretend.

With regard to his colleague Jonathan Frid, Selby says, "He was so very talented. No other actor could have brought to that role what Jonathan did. He was such a gentlemen and loyal friend. I miss him dearly."

Frid died April 14, 2012—only months before Johnny Depp resurrected Barnabas Collins in the *Dark Shadows* feature film in which he and Selby (along with Kathryn Leigh Scott and Lara Parker) appeared in cameo performances.

43

Henry Winkler
Happy Days

I don't know how to ride a motorcycle, actually.

—Henry Winkler

Henry Winkler was surprised when he won the role of Arthur "The Fonz"/"Fonzie" Fonzarelli on *Happy Days*. As he revealed to Peggy Herz in 1974, "They wanted a big guy with greasy hair. When I walked in, I said, 'Excuse me. I don't think I'm the guy you want.'" But then the show's producers sat him on a motorcycle, gave him lines, and Winkler "made up the character" as he went along.

"Fonzie is a tough guy who acts cool," the actor said, but he wanted the character to "be a human being." He wanted Fonzie to be someone who made mistakes. "I refused to have him combing his hair all the time. Fonzie may have a soul of leather but he has a big heart."

Television scribe Marty Nadler worked with Winkler on *Happy Days*, and other shows produced by Garry Marshall. Nadler believes Winkler's success was interconnected with Ron Howard's portrayal of Richie Cunningham on *Days*:

What made them appealing was that they were opposite each other. Richie was like the nerdish guy that really wasn't sophisticated around women and stuff like that and Fonzie was the tough guy. But Fonzie had a heart and he also recognized that Richie was a good guy. At one point, I don't know if you know this story, but the network got all kinds of mail on Fonzie. He only had three lines in an episode and all the kids were writing in saying "Who is this guy in the leather jacket, we like this guy."

So the network called Garry [Marshall] in and said that "We want to change this to *Fonzie's Happy Days* and we want most of the stories to be about Fonzie. And Garry said, "They don't understand that Amos doesn't work without Andy and basically you need both to make the show work." And when they said they were going to call it *Fonzie's Happy Days*, Garry said, "Well, who's going to produce the show, 'cause I'm taking Ronnie over to NBC and do a show." And right away ABC said "Oh no . . . *Happy Days* is a good title. And it works because Richie and his family became Fonzie's family."

Globe Photos

Happy Days was set in the 50s and, as Winkler recalled in 1974, "It seemed to be a time when many people lived comfortably. But it also seemed to be a boring, uninformed time. Our show is a romantic look at the past. Young people like it because they can see how their parents lived. They also like the music of the 50s. It was much less driven than the music today [of the 70s]."

"Young people also seem to like the character of Fonzie," added Winkler, who calculated he then signed about "50 autographs a day." In 1975, at the height of *Happy*'s popularity, the actor traveled to New York, and was "stopped about every 20 seconds" by fans on the street wanting his signature.

Born in New York City, on October 30, 1945, and as the only son of Ilse and Harry Winkler (a former president of an international lumber corporation), Henry desired to be a thespian since the age of seven, when he made his acting debut at the Hilltop Nursery School, portraying a tube of toothpaste and "recreated the part in first grade." He later played Billy Budd in the eighth grade and appeared in his first musical, "Of Thee I Sing," while a junior in high school. Originally, his parents were very much against his theatrical aspirations. "They kept me out of everything they could," he said. "I was a terrible student in high school." Winkler was told he was smart, but he was a rebel—and did "much better" in college, where he studied drama. "I did better because I was working for myself," he relayed, "not for anyone else."

Throughout high school and college, Winkler studied in Switzerland for four-month intervals and worked in a lumber mill in a small German town. Yet, he was not sidetracked from his theatrical aspirations. He graduated from McBurney School for Boys in New York City, and later attended Emerson College, where he studied both drama and psychology. He went on to Yale for eighteen months as a professional member of the university theater group, with which he performed in more than thirty live stage productions. While he would one day play Fonzie, the world's most popular high school dropout, Winkler in real life was hardly that. He trained nine years to become an actor and attained a master's degree in theater arts. "One thing I learned in drama school," he confided to Herz. "Don't live in the middle. Be committed to your life and to yourself. Be in a situation because you *want* to be there."

Winkler had many productive performances over the years before hitting it big as Fonzie on *Happy Days*. He appeared in several radio and TV commercials, as well as live stage productions, on and off Broadway. Upon advice from his agent, Winkler moved to California, arriving on September 30, 1973. On October 5, he delivered his lines with comedic precision in a bit role on CBS's *The Mary Tyler Moore Show*, followed by another appearance on that network's *The Bob Newhart Show*, and in a CBS TV-movie titled *Menace*, starring Patty Duke. His iconic role on *Happy Days* soon followed and the rest, as they "aayyye," is history.

44

John Travolta
Welcome Back, Kotter

> I never knock Vinnie [Barbarino].
> He broke me through the sound barrier.
>
> —John Travolta

"What? . . . When?? . . . Where???"

Such was the monosyllabic, singular word sequence that was verbalized with lyrical hoodlum aplomb by "sweathog" Vinne Barbarino as played by the legendary John Travolta on the classic TV sitcom *Welcome Back, Kotter*, which aired on ABC from 1975 to 1979. Originally envisioned as a star vehicle for stand-up comedian Gabe Kaplan, and based on his real-life experiences attending a Brooklyn high school, *Welcome Back* (with its catchy tranquil theme song by John Sebastian) instead became a breakout platform for Travolta.

Today, Travolta is a superstar of the big screen, best known for countless popular motion pictures, including his first big hits *Saturday Night Fever* (1977) and *Grease* (1978), both of which were filmed while he was taping his second to last season of *Kotter* (and which earned a combined box office gross of over 610 million dollars). It was *Saturday/Grease* producer Alan Carr who had noticed Travolta's *Fever*-pitch-perfect charisma on *Kotter*, and the rest became history. While Farrah Fawcett brought glamour, grace, and glitz back to Hollywood for the female set via ABC's *Charlie's Angels*, Travolta nearly singlehandedly reignited both the feature film musical and music industry in general. When he delivered his personal best two-step in *Urban*

Cowboy (1980), he then also helped to reinvigorate and mainstream country music for the masses.

The provocative dance moves and unique screen presence that he displayed in *Fever*, *Grease*, and *Cowboy*, and to some extent on *Kotter* (as well as in later movies such as 1995's *Get Shorty* which, like the *Look Who's Talking* trilogy [1989, 1990, 1993] was one of his many "comeback" films), were heralded by everyone from Fred Astaire to New York critic Pauline Kael. According to the publication, *Celebrate the '70s*, Kael reveled in John's "thick and raw sensuality . . . Travolta gets so far inside [his roles] he seems incapable of a false note."

It all started with Travolta's sizzling performance as Ba-Ba-Ba-Ba-Ba-Barino on *Welcome Back, Kotter*. As author Peggy Herz explains in her book, *TV's Fabulous Faces*, ABC from the start took notice of Travolta's potential, even though the network was uncertain about the *Kotter* series. But once on the air, both Travolta and the series exceeded expectations. *Kotter* became a massive success in the ratings and, as Herz observed, Travolta as Barbarino "became a teen idol."

ABC/PhotoFest

Born February 18, 1954, as one of six children to Salvatore and Helen Travolta of Englewood, New Jersey, Travolta was inspired to become an actor by his mother, who had worked as a teacher, director, and actress for two decades. His father once presided over a business in Hillsdale, New Jersey, and before that, was a semi-pro basketball player. Travolta's brothers, including Joey Travolta, who enjoyed a brief acting and singing career shortly after his brother's rise to mega-stardom, were also athletes. "My father enjoyed all of our careers," Travolta told Herz. "Both my parents were interested in everything we did."

Travolta quit high school in his junior year at just sixteen years old to become a full-time actor. He was performing in summer stock productions in Pennsylvania, and then played in an off-Broadway revival of the play *Raine*. From there he performed in the national touring company of *Grease*, playing second male lead Kenickie, years before he played top dog Danny Zuko in the film version. "We traveled all over the country," he said in 1977. "I also did *Grease* on Broadway and was in [the stage play] 'Over There' with The Andrew Sisters for nine months." He was "working too much to go to school at the same time." But he enjoyed working, and his mother understood that. As did his three older sisters, who were also actresses, including Ellen Travolta. "I saw a lot of shows and plays," he explained. "Acting was all around me."

By 1972, he was eighteen, and moved west—to Los Angeles; then came *Welcome Back, Kotter*, which, on some level, granted him the opportunity to complete his education, if within the somewhat realistic if fictional confines of a TV show. According to what he told Herz in 1977, the young sweathogs of *Kotter*, who also included Ron Palillo (as Horshack), Robert Hedges (as Juan Epstein), and Laurence Hilton Jacobs (as Freddie "Boom-Boom" Washington, and for a while, Stephen Shortridge as Beau De Labarr), were fairly true to life. "They harass the teacher and so on. That's all part of school. I was an excellent ranker in school. I wasn't the champion, but I got a lot of laughs. I was something of a practical joker throughout school."

Travolta even admitted to having a teacher like Mr. Kotter, who was "very funny. He communicated with us. He handled us, but with a sense of humor. We laughed, but we learned. Kotter is that kind of teacher."

"Some of the things we say on the show aren't quite what real kids would say," Travolta concluded. "But the *Kotter* kids are more believable than any other teenagers you see on TV."

John Travolta's unique combination of believability, likability, talent, and appeal will most likely not be repeated by any new up-and-comer anytime soon.

45

Ed Asner
The Mary Tyler Moore Show/Lou Grant

Carroll O'Connor
All in the Family

William Conrad
Cannon

> I regard myself as a beautiful musical instrument, and my role is to contribute that instrument to scripts worthy of it.
>
> —Ed Asner

Jackie Gleason was the first major heavy-set superstar of the television age. He would be followed to some extent by Fred Flintstone in animated form on *The Flintstones*, the popular cartoon series that landed in primetime eons before *The Simpsons*. In fact, *The Flintstones* had been loosely based on *The Honeymooners* segment on *The Jackie Gleason Show*.

But around the time that *The Jackie Gleason Show* was winding down in 1971, CBS premiered *The Mary Tyler Moore Show*, which introduced TV audiences to what would become several male icons: One was Ted Knight, a strikingly handsome actor who had worked for years in supporting roles on shows like *The Twilight Zone*. Years after his *Moore* stint as the egotistical TV anchorman Ted Baxter (who was outmatched in self-absorption only by his even more strikingly handsome younger brother played by Jack Cassidy [father to stepbrothers David and Shaun Cassidy], Knight would find fame in the 80s as the harried husband to Nancy Dussault and father to Lydia Cornell and Deborah Van Valkenburgh on *Too Close for Comfort* (which later transmuted into *The Ted Knight Show*). Gavin MacLeod, once known as merely a co-worker to Moore's Mary Richards, would later lead the cast of *The Love Boat* on Saturday nights at 10:00 p.m., and John Amos was weatherman Gordy Howard, a role he would leave for the popular Norman Lear sitcom, *Good Times*, which he would also leave in a contract dispute (amid the ever-increasing popularity of his on-screen son Jimmie Walker as J. J. "Dynomite" Evans).

But the most popular male icon on *The Mary Tyler Moore Show* was none other than Ed Asner, who played the gruff Lou Grant, Mary's boss, good friend, and almost-lover (at least in one episode that toyed with the idea). Like Gleason, Asner had a little extra weight on his frame, which was slightly smaller than Jackie's. But also like Gleason, Asner's slight paunch did not derail his popularity or success as an actor. A working thespian on the stage and screen for decades before being cast as Lou Grant, Asner appeared in countless plays and TV shows, including *Route 66* and *Hawaii Five-0* (the original and recent updated edition).

Over the years, on the big screen or small, he's portrayed his fair share of Santas in Christmas feature films and TV-movies. After leaving *The Mary Tyler Moore Show*, he suited up once more as Lou Grant for a spin-off series of the same name, which became the first one-hour weekly drama to to spawn a half-hour sitcom. Because he was now the lead in his own series, network executives and producers thought it might benefit his Grant persona (as well as potentially his own real-life health) if he slimmed down for the role. He did so, but the shift in body weight was not fully embraced by his fans. So he packed the pounds back on, and once more he became a feast for the eyes of his fans. Unfortunately, Asner's personal politics got in the way of Grant's success, and the show was cancelled. But the actor

Ed Asner
Globe Photos

has not stopped working since, delivering his usual top-level performance, even if only lending his voice to animated feature film classics like *UP!* from 2009.

Asner describes his most famous character: "He wasn't sappy. He was a straight-shooter. He was tough, but kind. He had his limits—and I would say that's always the defining mark in the creation or development of a character . . . finding balance."

Like so many of his male TV icon colleagues, such as Robert Wagner and David Selby, Asner credits the writers with giving him good material to work with. "It all starts with the scripts," he says. "Good writing has to come first, before an actor can properly interpret a role, a story, or a situation."

On the *Moore Show*, that would be series creators James L. Brooks and Allan Burns. Before, during, and after *Moore*, Asner has made hundreds of appearances on stage, film, and TV, including classic performances alongside Martin Milner and George Maharis on TV's *Route 66*, created by Stirling Silliphant, who also wrote most of the show's compelling episodes. "He was a genius," says Asner.

Other great performances of Asner's were in TV-movies like *The Gathering* (ABC, 1977), or the groundbreaking mini-series, *Rich Man, Poor Man* (ABC, 1976), based on the novel by Irwin Shaw. Here, Asner played the hardened Axel Jordache, father to the

Carroll O'Connor
Globe Photos

show's two main leads: Peter Strauss, who played Rudy, the "rich man," and Nick Nolte, who played Tom, the "poor man." Asner's Axel could be described as Lou Grant on steroids, or as the actor puts it, "an example of a tortured individual who slapped around his sons, but at the same time offered subtle implications of his deep kindness."

Asner says his acting "benefited greatly from the story's translation from book to screen" because the character of Axel was given more texture in the TV adaptation.

Into this mix of slightly overweight actors personified by Asner come Carroll O'Connor and William Conrad.

While O'Connor didn't exactly play the most heroic of roles with Archie

Bunker on *All in the Family*, this loudmouth bigot of a character hit a chord with viewers of the transitional 70s, when war, peace, drugs, rock and roll, and any other controversial topic could hit the airwaves. If something needed to be debated, rest assured O'Connor's Archie would take his stand on his own little Bunker hill, confronting issues in opposition to Rob Reiner's Michael "Meathead" Stivic, Archie's liberal son-in-law, married to daughter Gloria (as played by Sally Struthers).

Debuting on CBS in the summer of 1971, *All in the Family* also featured the Emmy-winning Jean Stapleton, who played Archie's seemingly dim-witted, but ultimately fully functional housewife and independent woman of every means. After Stapleton decided to leave the series (insisting that Edith die to do so), O'Connor continued playing Archie in the spin-off series, *Archie Bunker's Place*, which originally aired from 1979 to 1983. *Place* found a measure of success, but with Edith now gone, and Mike and Gloria now divorced and nowhere to be seen (beyond a periodic guest appearance), it just wasn't the same.

But O'Connor made his mark as Archie Bunker, only to turn the audience on their heads when he resurfaced on a regular series role in the late 80s and early 90s as William O. "Bill" Gillespie, in the TV edition of *In the Heat of the Night* (the 1967 film version of which featured Rod Steiger). It was an exact opposite role to Archie, and O'Connor reveled in the opportunity not just to distance himself from the Bunker part, but to prove his diversity as an actor. Of course, he had already done that before starring in *All in the Family*, with guest-shot appearances on TV shows like *That Girl* (in which he played a self-absorbed Italian opera singer), and in motion pictures (like 1963's *Cleopatra*). But for the TV audience, the switch from bigot Archie to the compassionate police officer in *Heat* (with a mostly all-black cast of characters) was a triumphant career move for the actor.

Before and after O'Connor played Archie, his fellow weight-challenged acting colleague William Conrad was heating up the entertainment industry with voiceover work on the radio. Entertainment historian and author Randy Skretvedt, aka Randy Brian, host of the popular classic radio show *Forward into the Past* (www.kspc.com), hails Conrad as "one of the most prolific and prominent radio actors of the late 40s and early 50s." Cannon was particularly prominent on CBS's long-running series *Suspense!* and *Escape*. Radio listeners would recognize his distinctive, deep voice on *The Adventures of Sam Spade*, *The Lux Radio Theatre*, *Mister President*, *The Whistler*, and many other series.

He finally got the chance to star when producer Norman Macdonnell tested him for the leading role of Sheriff Matt Dillon on *Gunsmoke*. Originally Macdonnell didn't

William Conrad
PhotoFest

want Conrad for the part, because he seemed to be everywhere on radio. After testing many other actors, Macdonnell conceded that Conrad was the perfect voice for the part. Indeed he was, and *Gunsmoke* became one of the greatest of all radio series, despite the fact that it made its debut after television was eroding the medium's audience. It ran from 1952 to 1961. Conrad and his radio co-stars wanted to appear in the television version in 1955, but the perennially overweight Conrad was vetoed in favor of handsome James Arness.

Conrad was also an imposing presence in movies, appearing as a hit man who dispatches Burt Lancaster in *The Killers* (1946). In the late 50s and early 60s, he concentrated on directing for television, although he returned to vocal acting as the intense and tongue-in-cheek narrator of the *Rocky and Bullwinkle* cartoons for Jay Ward. He did a great deal of narration for television in the 60s and 70s as well (notably on *The Fugitive*), but the success of the series *Cannon* (CBS, 1971–1976) and *Jake and the Fatman* (CBS, 1987–1992) revived his on-camera career.

Conrad retained such fond memories of his fellow radio performers that he couldn't bear to speak about them later in his life after so many had died. When Leonard Maltin wanted to interview Conrad about his radio work, the actor replied that he would consent only if Maltin got him a VHS copy of the 1939 film *Of Mice and Men*. Maltin quickly found a copy, and Conrad reluctantly consented. He was a vintage movie buff with a large collection of films; studio head Jack L. Warner gave him the title prop from *The Maltese Falcon* as a token of gratitude for his work at Warner Bros. The prop sat on a bookshelf in Conrad's home from the 1960s until he died in February 1994. It was auctioned and brought $398,500.

Through it all, Asner, O'Connor, and William Conrad redefined the word "heavy" when it came to character descriptions in television.

PART VI

THE SUPERSLEUTHS

William Conrad on *Cannon* was merely a big fish in the big pond of TV detectives, police officers, and other crimefighters.

Cannon, originally airing on CBS from 1971 to 1976, was one of the manifold police and detective shows that ran rampant throughout the 50s, 60s, and 70s on television. Second only to the western, the crime (and many times punishment) shows told stories of intrigue, personal and sweeping tales, all entertaining, from *The M Squad* to *The Mod Squad*, from *The Rookies* to *SWAT*, from *Longstreet* to *Ironside*; they were all there in fine form, from head to toe. Dressed either in uniform, casual wear, or to the nines, the male crimefighters took on their evil opponents with panache. Every so often, a comedic edition would be thrown into the fray, such as on *Car 54, Where Are You?* and *Barney Miller*, both of which, ironically, were considered by some to have been the most realistic police television shows in history.

Car 54 featured Fred Gwynne, Joe E. Ross, and Al Lewis (who would later re-team with Gwynne for *The Munsters* on CBS, 1964–1966). The squad room featured on *54* also included African-American actor/comedian Nipsey Russell who, along with Dom DeLuise and Bob Newhart, became a semi-regular on *The Dean Martin Show* over the course of that show's 1965–1974 run on NBC. While both Newhart and DeLuise would find a larger more personal fame in other areas of television and film, in retrospect, Russell's portrayal of Officer Dave Anderson on the first season of *Car 54* became one of his most notable early performances. Unlike stereotypical characters of color that appeared on shows such as *The Jack Benny Show* and *Bachelor Father*,

Nipsey was not so much defined as an African American, but rather a police officer who just happened to be an African American. It was a groundbreaking role, and the first of its kind, even years before Diahann Carroll become TV's first African-American woman to play a non-stereotypical female role on the NBC sitcom *Julia* (1968–1971). Even while Desi Arnaz was making the grade as the first Latin star of a TV show, sitcom or otherwise, via *I Love Lucy*, his role of Ricky Ricardo still played off stereotypes.

Russell, meanwhile, broke the mold for crimefighters: before Bill Cosby made strides when he paired with Robert Culp on NBC's *I Spy*; before Clarence Williams III paired with Michael Cole (and Peggy Lipton) on *The Mod Squad*; before George Stanford Brown's historic appearance with Sam Melville, Michael Ontkean, and later, Bruce Fairbairn on *The Rookies*; and before the monumental minority casting of Latin heartthrob Erik Estrada when he partnered with Larry Wilcox on NBC's *CHiPs*.

Morever, there most likely might not have been any future *Mod Squad* cross-teaming of Cole and Williams, had first there not been the *I Spy* duo of Cosby and Culp. Rick Lertzman explains:

I Spy was the television program that helped change the segregationist approach of the television industry in the mid-1960s. The brainchild of master producer/actor Sheldon Leonard, it brought one of the most unique and controversial pairings on television screens. It featured Robert Culp as "international tennis player" Kelly Robinson and Bill Cosby as his "trainer" Alexander Scott. While both portrayed tennis "bums" they were in actuality top "secret" agents for the Pentagon. The series broke new ground by starring an African-American actor in a leading role. Culp and Cosby were partners in their adventures that had them globetrotting throughout the world. While Culp brought his sophisticated, dry, witty charm, it sharply contrasted with the flippant and sardonic Cosby. The ratings soared even though there were several southern television stations that refused to air the show. However, both Cosby and Culp agreed that "Our statement is a non-statement" and never discussed any racial issue on the program.

Richard Roundtree carried the diverse baton from Cosby and Williams, by transplanting his thirteen million dollar feature film success with 1971's *Shaft* into a TV series edition for ABC. In 2009 director Gordon Parks, who helmed the theatrical *Shaft*, described Roundtree's big-screen character as "a ballsy guy," who thought, "to hell with everybody . . . he goes out and does his thing." Slightly more mild than the "blaxploitation" motion picture from which it sprang, the small-screen *Shaft* became the first weekly one-hour police detective series to star an African American in the single lead—and while the series did not match the success of the movie, Roundtree's male iconic status remains unmatched in classic TV show history.

The following pages present a slightly closer look at some other popular and groundbreaking supersleuths of the small screen.

46

Efrem Zimbalist Jr.
77 Sunset Strip/The FBI

I ended up with my life slanted towards television, and I just accept that.
I think you play the hand the way it's dealt. That's all.

—Efrem Zimbalist Jr.

Not only was he dashing, daring, and debonair, but Efrem Zimbalist Jr., who passed away at age ninety-five on May 2, 2014, was also distinguished. He first reached iconic TV status as private detective Stu Bailey on the hit TV series *77 Sunset Strip*, then two years later he was cast as Inspector Lewis Erskine on that same network's weekly crime drama, *The FBI*.

The father to actress Stephanie Zimbalist (*Remington Steele*, NBC, 1982–1987), Efrem had steel blue eyes, an everlasting tan that put George Hamilton to shame, and a generous, spiritual heart. According to media historian Rob Ray, the key word in describing Zimbalist is integrity. "He was handsome, but not in a particularly noteworthy way, but had an authority that was not overpowering. If Jack Webb was the clichéd caricature of his time, law enforcement officer Efrem Zimbalist Jr. was the real deal. With his ever-present suit and tie, he personified what the FBI stood for, protecting our American Way of Life from those who would abuse it or take it down."

Although Larry Brody never worked with Zimbalist on either the *FBI* or *Strip* shows, as it turns out the legendary scribe watched *Sunset* when it first aired. "The show had three alternating detectives, but the only one I wanted to see during those early teen years was Zimbalist. His character was mature, adult, and steady. You knew just looking at him that he could handle everything thrown his way, and that he'd protect you, period. I think he was the most perfect father figure on TV until Patrick Stewart's Picard took the crown away from him (on the syndicated sci-fi series, *Star Trek: The Next Generation*, which debuted in 1986).

It's hardly surprising that the son of renowned Russian-born concert violinist Efrem Zimbalist Sr. (1889–1985) and Romanian-born opera singer Alma Gluck (1884–1938) would desire a performing career of some kind. According to imdb.com, Zimbalist was born in New York City on November 30, 1918. Surrounded by people of wealth and privilege throughout his childhood, Efrem Zimbalist Jr. received a boarding school education. Acting in school plays, he later trained briefly at the Yale School of Drama but didn't apply himself enough and quit. As an NBC network radio page, he auditioned when he could and found minor TV and stock theater parts while joining up with the Neighborhood Playhouse.

Warner Bros./PhotoFest

Zimbalist was wounded as part of the Army infantry in World War II and received the Purple Heart. After he recovered, a director and friend of the family, Garson Kanin, gave the aspiring actor his first professional role in his Broadway production of *The Rugged Path* (1945), which starred Spencer Tracy. With his dark, friendly, clean-scrubbed good looks and a deep, rich voice that could cut butter, Zimbalist found little trouble finding work. He continued with the American Repertory Theatre performing in such classics as *Henry VIII* and *Androcles and the Lion* while appearing opposite the legendary Eva Le Gallienne in *Hedda Gabler*.

Zimbalist then tried his hand as a stage producer, successfully bringing opera to Broadway audiences for the first time with memorable presentations of *The Medium* and *The Telephone*. As producer of Gian Carlo Menotti's *The Consul*, he won the New York Drama Critics' Award and the Pulitzer Prize for best musical in 1950. A subtle motion picture debut opposite Edward G. Robinson in *House of Strangers*

(1949) did little for his career due to the untimely death of his wife Emily (a onetime actress who appeared with him in *Hedda Gabler* and bore him two children, Nancy and Efrem III) to cancer in 1950. Abruptly abandoning acting, he served as assistant director/researcher at the Curtis School of Music for his father and buried himself with studies and music composition.

In 1954 Efrem returned to his acting roots with a daytime television soap lead (*Concerning Miss Marlowe*). It was famed director Joshua Logan who proved instrumental in helping Zimbalist secure a Warner Bros. contract. Despite forthright second leads in respectable movies like *Band of Angels* (1957), *A Fever in the Blood* (1961), and *Wait Until Dark* (1967), it was television that best utilized his elegant, modest acting style. His roles as sophisticated private investigator Stu Bailey on *77 Sunset Strip* (1958) and the dedicated inspector Lewis Erskine on *The FBI* (1965) would be his ultimate claims to fame.

In 1991 he satirized his image in the big-screen comedy *Hot Shots!* In addition to theater projects over the years, Efrem utilized his deep voice with narrations and cartoon voiceovers, including that of Alfred the butler on a Batman animated series.

In 2003 he completed his memoir, titled *My Dinner of Herbs*. Father of three, grandfather of four, and great-grandfather of three, he settled in Santa Barbara and later in Solvang, California, with longtime second wife Stephanie until her death in 2007 of cancer. He and daughter Stephanie also performed on stage together in his later years, their first play together being *The Night of the Iguana*. His eldest daughter Nancy died in 2012.

Zimbalist once said:

> If I would characterize my life, I would say that I was a very lucky actor who came into very lucky times, and got to Hollywood, and was put under contract by Warners [Bros. Studios] in the very last days of the studio contract era, and was privileged to go through that time which is gone now. When you learned that you inspired someone, it's a huge honor.

47

Peter Graves, Martin Landau, Greg Morris, and Peter Lupus

Mission: Impossible

> Good morning, Mr. Phelps.
>
> —A taped voice greeting from Peter Graves's character on *Mission: Impossible*

The TV men of *Mission: Impossible* were the perfect representatives of the ideal male presence on the classic small screen. Strong silent types . . . intelligent . . . heroic . . . even tempered . . . they had it all.

Martin Landau, who played Rollin Hand, was born June 20, 1928, in Brooklyn, New York. He was educated at James Madison High School and the Pratt Institute. In 1957, he married future *Impossible* costar Barbara Bain, and they had two daughters: Susan and Juliet.

At age seventeen, Landau joined the *New York Daily News* as a cartoonist, but his heart belonged to acting. Accepted into the prestigious Lee Strasberg Actors Studio from among two thousand applicants, Landau had classmates such as Steve McQueen and James Dean. He debuted on Broadway in *Middle of the Night* in 1957 and made his first major film appearance in Alfred Hitchcock's *North By Northwest* (1959), but his big break came playing Rollin on *Impossible*.

Initially credited as "special guest" for fear the show might interfere with his film career, by the second season he was the star, though still contracted on an annual basis. For playing a spy of many disguises and accents and sometimes dual roles, Martin was nominated for three consecutive Emmys. Landau was with the show from 1966 to 1969. Ironically, his replacement was Leonard Nimoy. (Landau had been

Gene Roddenberry's first choice for the Nimoy role of Mr. Spock on *Star Trek*.) For thirty-three years he was married to Bain, with whom he returned to TV on the UK-produced and syndicated sci-fi show, *Space: 1999* (which aired from 1975 to 1977).

Landau then became a highly regarded character actor on film, garnering Oscar nominations for Francis Ford Coppola's *Tucker* (1988) and Woody Allen's *Crimes and Misdemeanors* (1989) and winning the Best Supporting Actor Oscar for Tim Burton's *Ed Wood* (1994).

Peter Lupus, who played Willy Armitage, was born June 17, 1932, in Indianapolis, Indiana. He attended Jordan College of Fine Arts, at Butler University in Indianapolis. In 1960, he married Sharon M. Hildebrand (1960–present), and they had one son, Peter Lupus III.

Lupus was a bodybuilder who held the titles Mr. Indianapolis (1954) and Mr. Indiana (1960). Like strongman Steve Reeves, he became a film star in titles such as *Muscle Beach Party* (1964), *Hercules and the Tyrants of Bayblon* (1964), *Goliath at the Conquest of Damascus* (1965), *Challenge of the Gladiator* (1965), and *Giant of the Evil Island* (1965). His big break, which enabled him to move away from "sword and sandal" B-pictures and the former stage name of "Rock Stevens," was as the muscle man, Willy Armitage, on *Mission: Impossible*.

Left to right, top: Barbara Bain, Peter Graves; bottom, Peter Lupus, Greg Morris, Martin Landau

CBS/PhotoFest

Although he had very little dialogue, his strong, silent character was featured in 161 episodes. During the fifth season when the producers decreased his appearances there was a fan outcry and his appearances grew and improved in quality. His later television work included some typecasting as Antar the Caveman on *Fantasy Island* (1980) and the short-lived (but cult favorite) *Police Squad* (1984) in the recurring role of Detective Norberg. On July 19, 2007, a month after his seventy-fifth birthday, he broke his own Guinness World Record as the oldest person to bench-press over three hundred pounds. At age seventy he had lifted 76,280 pounds in twenty-seven minutes. He later surpassed this by lifting 77,560 pounds in twenty-four minutes and fifty seconds.

As he told *Muscle Training Illustrated* magazine in July 1968, "The studio got quite a bit of fan mail about me, so they have worked to beef up my part. It's more of a 'straight' role now with less emphasis on the pure muscle end of it. I enjoy the image change . . ."

Peter Graves, who played James Phelps on *Mission*, was born Peter Duesler Aurness on March 18, 1926, in Minneapolis, Minnesota. He attended the University of Minnesota. His parents were Rolf Cirkler Aurness and Ruth Duesler, and his older brother was James Arness (*Gunsmoke*). He was married to Joan Endress from 1950 to his death in 2010. They had three children: Kelly, Claudia, and Amanda.

Graves followed his sibling Arness into show business, avoiding confusion with the *Gunsmoke* star by using his mother's family's name. Stardom eluded him for some time despite work in notable film roles like Billy Wilder's *Stalag 17* (1953) and Charles Laughton's *Night of the Hunter* (1955). Though he played on 116 episodes of the television series *Fury* (1955–1960), thirty-four episodes of *Whiplash* (1961), and twenty-six episodes of *Court Martial* (1965-1966), his big break came when he joined *Mission: Imposssible* in its second season.

After Steven Hill as Daniel Briggs left the series, Graves came on as James Phelps, the new IMF (Impossible Missions Force) leader. Graves stayed with the show until the end of its initial run (143 episodes), reprising the role of Phelps thirty-five more times on a second *Mission: Impossible* series (1988–1990). Life between impossible missions included the 1983 miniseries *The Winds of War* and the 1988 sequel *War and Remembrance*. He leant his distinctive narrative voice to A&E's *Biography* (1994–2001). His career took a comical turn, playing Captain Oveur in the blockbuster movie spoof *Airplane* (1980). Graves almost turned down the role, thinking it "the worst piece of junk," but changed his mind after meeting with the movie's writers David and Jerry Zucker. The film grossed more than eighty-four million dollars and Graves's lines in the parody almost eclipsed the famous phrase his Jim Phelps was greeted with: "Good luck, Jim. This tape will self-destruct in five seconds."

In 2011, Graves was interviewed for the PBS series, *Pioneers of Television: Crime Dramas*. "I remember the very first *Mission* I did," he said, "as we conquered the villains, I let the slightest smile just crease one side of my face. The next day Bruce Geller is down on the set saying 'Don't editorialize!'"

Graves succumbed to a heart attack on March 14, 2010, four days before his eighty-fourth birthday.

Born in Cleveland, Ohio, Greg Morris began his acting career in the 60s with television guest spots on many series like *The Twilight Zone, Ben Casey*, and, in a historic "diverse" episode of *The Dick Van Dyke Show*. In 1966, he was cast in his most recognizable role as the electronics expert Barney Collier on *Mission: Impossible*, where, along with Peter Lupus and Bob Johnson, he became the only actor to remain with the series throughout its entire run.

While in college, Morris was active in theater and hosted the late afternoon jazz radio show, "Tea-Time," on the University of Iowa station, WSUI. He co-produced concerts at the university with a student friend.

After Iowa, Greg's first professional stage role was in *The Death of Bessie Smith*. One of his earliest television roles was a cameo appearance on *The Dick Van Dyke Show*, when Rob and Laura think they've gotten the wrong baby from the hospital. In the 1963-1964 season, he appeared on ABC's college-geared drama, *Channing*, starring Jason Evers and Henry Jones.

Following the cancellation of *Mission: Impossible*, Greg appeared in a few films and TV shows (including *The Six Million Dollar Man*) before he was cast as Lt. David Nelson during the second season of the TV series *Vegas*.

After that series ended in 1981, Morris made guest TV appearances, and returned to his most famous *Mission* role for a remake of the *Impossible* series in the early 90s (which also featured his son Phil Morris, who was cast as Grant Collier, Barney's offspring).

Greg also performed in two episodes of TV's *What's Happening!!* as Lawrence Nelson (father of Dwayne) and in three segments of *The Jeffersons*, in which he reprised his role of an electronics expert (although not as Barney Collier). Morris was also a frequent guest-star on *Password* and *Password Plus* in the 60s and 70s.

He died on August 27, 1996, of brain cancer in Las Vegas, Nevada. He was sixty-two years old.

48

Robert Vaughn and David McCallum
The Man from U.N.C.L.E.

Patrick McGoohan
Secret Agent/The Prisoner

> I didn't want to be famous. I just wanted to earn enough money to have a nice life and enjoy acting.
>
> —David McCallum

Sean Connery as James Bond was big on the big screen.

Robert Vaughn and David McCallum duplicated such super-spy success on the small screen with *The Man from U.N.C.L.E.*, which originally aired on NBC. Patrick McGoohan, of TV's lesser-known series, *Secret Agent*, was also relatively popular.

Documentary filmmaker and classic TV fan John Scheinfeld, perhaps best known for the theatrical documentaries *The U.S. vs. John Lennon* (2006) and *Who Is Harry Nilsson?* (2010) as well as the hit 2004 TV miniseries, *The 100 Greatest TV Characters*, had this insight as to why classic shows like *The Man from U.N.C.L.E.* and *Secret Agent* were and remain standouts of the genre:

There is nothing secret about how famous Robert Vaughn and David McCallum became playing Napoleon Solo and Illya Kuryakin—an American and a Russian, working together as secret agents, proving that humanity could overcome politics. This working relationship really captures the hopeful, optimistic spirit of the 1960s and engages viewers in a unique way. While other series were played strictly for laughs

Robert Vaughn, left; David McCallum, right

NBC/PhotoFest

(*Get Smart*) or drama (*Secret Agent*), or drama with jaunty good humor (*I Spy*), *The Man from U.N.C.L.E.* had tongue firmly planted in cheek. This made it not only fun, but seriously cool. One cannot underestimate the cool factor—every week there were cool gadgets, cool villains, seriously cool and curvy femme fatales, not to mention Kuryakin's very cool black turtleneck. It was when tongue-in-cheek drifted into camp that the ratings started to go downhill. But what would-be-recruits for The United Command for Law and Enforcement will always remember is the extraordinary chemistry between Vaughn and McCallum. Even today, viewers still enjoy the fun they're having every week working with each other and battling nefarious scoundrels to save the world.

What makes *Secret Agent* such a classic is its star, Patrick McGoohan. One of the most charismatic actors in the history of television, viewers absolutely cannot take their eyes off him. Every gesture, every turn of the head, a hint of a smile, his uncompromising nature and silent sense of control carries such weight and intensity that the audience is left perpetually on the edge of their seats. That the scripts are smart and the plots and characters complex (not to mention the hero, John Drake, uncharacteristically does not carry a gun or kiss a girl), makes it that much more compelling.

Born Robert Francis Vaughn on November 22, 1932, the dark-haired American actor has amassed a long list of stage, film, and television work. His best-known TV roles include the suave spy Napoleon Solo in the 1960s series *The Man from U.N.C.L.E.* and the wealthy detective Harry Rule in the 1970s series *The Protectors*. In film, he portrayed one of the title characters in *The Magnificent Seven* and Major Paul Krueger in *The Bridge at Remagen*, while he also provided the voice of Proteus IV, the computer villain of *Demon Seed*.

Vaughn was also popular in British television. He depicted grifter and card sharp Albert Stroller in the drama series *Hustle* (2004–2012), then he turned to perennial favorite soap opera *Coronation Street* where he portrayed Milton Fanshaw, a romantic counterpoint to Sylvia Goodwin, played by veteran English actress Stephanie Cole.

David Keith McCallum Jr. (born September 19, 1933) is a Scottish actor and musician. He is best known for his roles as Illya Kuryakin, a Russian secret agent, in *The Man from U.N.C.L.E.* (1964–1968), as inter-dimensional operative Steel in *Sapphire & Steel*, and for his current role as NCIS medical examiner Dr. Donald "Ducky" Mallard in the series *NCIS*.

Patrick McGoohan
Globe Photos

Patrick Joseph McGoohan (March 19, 1928–January 13, 2009) was an American-born actor who was brought up in Ireland and Britain, where he established an extensive stage and film career. His most notable roles were in the 1960s television series *Danger Man* (renamed *Secret Agent* when exported to the US), and *The Prisoner*, which he co-created. McGoohan wrote and directed several episodes of *The Prisoner* himself, occasionally using the pseudonyms Joseph Serf and Paddy Fitz. Later in his career, he moved back to the United States and subsequently appeared as murderers in four *Columbo* episodes, twice winning an Emmy. He was featured in John Sturges's *Ice Station Zebra* (1968), David Cronenberg's *Scanners* (1981), and played King Edward "The Longshanks" in Mel Gibson's *Braveheart* (1995).

49

Michael Cole and Clarence Williams III
The Mod Squad

One of the staggering things is that if you work in TV, and particularly in a series, that first season you're at the studio all day long, working 14 and 15 hours a day. But when you hit the hiatus period and you go off to wherever you decide to go for relaxation, all of a sudden everybody knows you.

—Clarence Williams III

The dynamic dual casting of *The Mod Squad*'s leading men Michael Cole (as Pete Cochran) and Clarence Williams III (Lincoln "Linc" Hayes), alongside Peggy Lipton (Julie Barnes) with a supporting performance by Tige Andrews (Captain Adam Greer), helped make the series (first run on ABC from 1968 to 1973, and executive produced by Aaron Spelling) into one of TV's most popular police/detective shows. The show's featured trio of hip, young, hot police officers ("one white, one black, one blonde," as so designated by the famous promotional tag) stands out as the stuff of legends. The charismatic combination of these actors was "solid" (as Linc might have coined it). Beyond the general groundbreaking draw of a racially integrated cast, the teaming of this particular troupe of actors made the series a hit. Their unique performance style, individually and as a group, delivered the goods, sometimes with just a subtle glance. Each had the ability to convey much, sometimes without saying a word. Their silent moments spoke volumes. Michael Cole explains, first by giving credit to *Squad*'s producer:

There *was* an amazing chemistry between us, even if we didn't speak any lines. I don't know how that happens across the board, but with *The Mod Squad* it was due to Aaron Spelling's astuteness for casting. And when you have the kind of working relationship that we all had on our show . . . the kind of mutual respect that myself, Clarence, Peggy, and Tige shared . . . with the rest of the cast and the writers and producers, directors, all the way up to and including Aaron. . .sometimes character dialogue gets in the way. If a show is written well . . . and *Mod Squad* was . . . if it's clear that the characters do love one another . . . which Pete, Linc, Julie and the Captain did . . . you don't need a lot of words.

Born Michael Charles Cole on July 3, 1945, in Madison, Wisconsin, Cole attended East High School in Madison and later the Estelle Harman Actors Workshop. His mother was Kathleen Hyland, who also gave birth to his siblings Ted, Colleen, and Debbie. He married Shelley Funes in 1996, and he has one daughter, Jennifer Holly Cole (from a previous marriage).

Michael grew up in a working class neighborhood and was raised by a single mother. He quit school in the ninth grade and tended bar in Las Vegas for a while before turning his people skills to acting. When Cole was first cast in *The Mod Squad*, he couldn't afford an apartment and was sleeping under the freeway near the corner of Sunset and Gower in Hollywood. Later on he took a bed in Lee Strasberg's Actors' Studio, where he learned, worked, and literally lived the famous theatrical technique of "method acting" (originated by Constantin Stanislavski, by which the student mystically transforms into or attempts to become his or her fictional character). Cole also later lived for a time in Spelling's home.

Cole had a "tough" upbringing, as did his character, Pete Cochran. As the actor assesses, "That's essentially what my life was. It's like I was born to play Pete. Everything about his life was mine, except that he grew up in Beverly Hills, and I did not. But everything that

Clockwise from left: Peggy Lipton, Clarence Williams III, Michael Cole, Tige Andrews
Globe Photos

transpired in my life seemed to prepare me to play him on *The Mod Squad*, as if it was destined to happen."

Cole had always admired two opening credit sequences from episodic television series: one from *The Fugitive*, during which the train crashes and from which David Jansen (as Dr. Richard Kimble) escapes; and the trademark opening of *The Mod Squad*. Giving credit once more to Spelling, Cole addresses the latter, which was stylishly accented with riveting background music, as Pete, Linc and Julie run separately and desperately down an abandoned dark pathway until they finally connect in the end:

> When we needed an opening for *The Mod Squad*, Aaron hopped on his studio golf cart for weeks, running around the Paramount lot [where the show was filmed]. Finally he saw this area where different sets were storaged. Out of the creative blue, one particular set caught his eye, and he told his set team, "That's it! Clear this area out. Water it down, and light it real dark." Although I don't know how you light something dark. . .but they did. And that became the set we used for [the] opening credit sequence. Combined with the music, it was magic.

Cole's "natural" method of acting came into perfect play for Pete Cochran's historic opening running sequences. "I, as an actor, was running away from myself," Cole freely admits, ". . . because I was so unhappy at that point in my life. I grew up without a family. I wasn't close with any of them. And Clarence had his story and Peg had hers" [when it came to the motivation and interpretation for their own running sequences as Linc and Julie].

Today, Cole has millions of fans from around the world, which he calls "friends"—a global community of family members who were inadvertently spawned from a once-painful real-life childhood that blossomed into unforeseen beauty by way of *The Mod Squad*, somehow healing personal rifts in the process and making everyone, off-screen and on, intimate friends or distant fans.

"It makes me want to cry," Cole says in earnest.

The sensitive actor thought it would be truer to the *Mod* characters if they refrained from carrying guns and suggested the idea to Spelling. Toward the end of the show's run, Cole was injured in a severe car accident and almost severed one of his eyelids (and he still has the scar). He maintains close friendships with Williams and Lipton (Andrews died in 1996). Post-*Mod*, Cole had roles in numerous popular TV shows, including *Wonder Woman*, *The Love Boat*, *CHiPs*, *Murder, She Wrote*, *Fantasy Island*, and *Diagnosis Murder*, as well as numerous movies of the week.

In 1987 he secluded himself in a cabin in the Santa Monica Mountains, saying he was "hiding and at the same time looking for myself." After struggling with alcoholism, he was treated at the Betty Ford Clinic in the early 1990s and then went on to make appearances on TV shows like *ER* and in feature films such as *Mr. Brooks* (with Kevin Costner in 2007).

Cole's work on *The Mod Squad*, however, remains a most-treasured time in his life and career. Although he doesn't recall "any episodes that are *not* favorites," a few stand out. First, there was a Christmas story in which Pete Cochran cared for the friend of a little girl. In another episode, Captain Greer was shot, and it was up to Linc to remove the inflicted bullet. That moment caused a particular stir, as it involved an extreme close-up on Linc, who was heavily perspiring. Pete then reached for a cloth to wipe Linc's brow and removed the sweat from his eyes.

At the time of *Squad*'s original airing in the tumultuous mid-60s and early 70s, there were a few network executives who were concerned about such visual biracial bonding between Pete and Linc and more than just a few viewers who objected to the friendship and camaraderie between the two characters from different cultures. That image of Pete wiping Linc's forehead unfortunately proved disconcerting for many narrow-minded viewers, one of whom wrote into the network and complained, "How could a white man mop a black man's brow?"

But the performing actors could not have cared less. In fact, they were thrilled. Says Cole, "I knew we had a hit show when we started to get hate mail. That meant we were on the right track." Upon learning of that one particularly despicable letter, Cole "just screamed at the top of my lungs."

"Yes!" he continued to herald. "What we're doing is right!"

"It was a very proud moment," he says today.

The Mod Squad actors were all too familiar with the challenges of interracial relating, on and off-camera, and experienced various bouts with several forms of prejudice toward race and gender. Peggy Lipton was married to musical genius Quincy Jones, who just so happens to be African American (their daughter is actress Rashida Jones). Clarence Williams later became romantically involved with Caucasian actress Tyne Daly, daughter of actor James Daly (*Medical Center*, CBS, 1969–1976) and sister to actor Tim Daly (*Wings*, 1990–1997). Like Williams, Tyne was also featured in a ground-breaking, classic TV police team drama of her own (*Cagney & Lacey*, CBS, 1982–1988, many episodes of which dealt with gender bias). Williams, like his fellow male *Mod* TV icon Cole, has always lived life to its fullest, breaking professional and personal barriers, from Broadway and beyond, by facing any challenge head-on.

Born August 21, 1939, in New York City, Williams, as a teenager, studied acting at the Harlem YMCA's Little Theater, alongside fellow African-American thespians Cicely Tyson, James Earl Jones, Isabel Sanford, Sidney Poitier, Eartha Kitt, Roscoe Lee Brown, and Danny Glover. His father was Clay Williams; his grandparents were jazz pianist Clarence Williams and blues singer Eva Taylor. He was married to Gloria Foster from 1967 to 1984.

Williams was raised by his grandparents after his parents divorced when he was just an infant. Although jazz was his first artistic love, he became intrigued with acting in 1957, while waiting to borrow twenty dollars from his sister who worked at the Harlem YMCA. While there, he went to a play in the downstairs theater, accidentally walked through a stage door, and found himself in the middle of a scene.

A former paratrooper with the US Air Force, in 1960 Williams made his New York live debut with *The Long Dream* and in 1964 capped his early stage career with a Theatre World Award and Tony nomination for the three-person production *Slow Dance on the Killing Ground* (1964).

An artist-in-residence at Brandeis University, Clarence rejected roles in blaxploitation movies and returned to the stage where he performed alongside Maggie Smith in Tom Stoppard's play *Night and Day* (1979) on Broadway. He later won rave reviews when he starred as Prince's troubled father, Frances L., in the successful 1984 motion picture *Purple Rain*. In the mid-2000s, he costarred in the Hallmark Channel series, *Mystery Woman*, opposite lead Kellie Martin. In 2013 he appeared in the movie *Lee Daniels' The Butler*.

As to his performance as Lincoln Hayes on TV's *The Mod Squad*, he once said:

I know a little about the street. I used to write numbers. I've seen police take bribes. I do know that a lot of officers love to get these jobs in the ghetto because they can shake people down. I know what's going on, but that has nothing to do with a TV show. I'm not appearing on the show each and every week to seduce people into believing in their police departments.

It was a very different role for an African American and a wonderful lead character that a lot of youngsters, black and white, and principally African American youngsters could identify with. I get so much feedback from that show even now and it is almost [fifty] years old.

50

Mike Connors
Mannix

Telly Savalas
Kojak

> Who loves ya, Baby!
>
> —Kojak, as played by Telly Savalas

There's an episode of TV's relatively new classic sitcom *Seinfeld* (NBC, 1989–1998), titled, "The Limo" (Feb. 26. 1992) in which Jerry (Jerry Seinfeld) and his neurotic friend George (Jason Alexander) are in a moving limousine attempting to escape from neo-Nazis. George suggests that he and Jerry leap from the moving vehicle and roll out onto the ground. To which Jerry replies, "Who are you—Mannix?!"

That reference was a true testimonial to the immortal popularity of the classic TV detective series of the same name starring Mike Connors, which originally ran on CBS from 1966 to 1975, Sunday nights. The show was one of the longest-running police crime dramas in TV history, and also stood out because it was the first to feature an Armenian male lead. Along with NBC's *Star Trek* (featuring Nichelle Nichols as communications officer Lt. Uhura) and the network's *Julia* sitcom (starring Diahann Carrol as a nurse), *Mannix* was one of the first shows to feature an African-American actress on a weekly basis: Gail Fisher played Joe's trusted and loyal secretary and friend Peggy Fair, a role for which Nichols had auditioned. Meanwhile, too, both *Trek* and *Mannix* happened to be owned and operated by Lucille Ball's Desilu Productions, which also supervised her *Here's Lucy* CBS comedy, on which Connors played Joe Mannix in a guest appearance. He would reprise the role twice more: in 1997 for an episode of *Diagnosis: Murder* (starring his good friend Dick Van Dyke) and in the 2004 feature film comedy *Nobody Knows Anything*.

According to IMDB, Connors was born Krekor Ohanian, of Armenian descent, on August 15, 1925, in Fresno, California. Tall, athletic, and handsome, he played basketball in college, during which time he was nicknamed "Touch" for his agility at the game. He used Touch Connors as a stage name for early movie appearances like *Sudden Fear* (1952), *The 49th Man* and *Sky Commando* (both in 1953), *Day the World Ended* (1955), *The Ten Commandments* (1956), among others; and for TV shows like *The Ford Television Theatre* (for an episode titled, "Yours for A Dream," his small-screen debut), *City Detective*, *The Lineup*, *The Loretta Young Show*, he was intermittently known as Touch, Mike, Michael, and one time as Jay (for a 1956 episode of *State Trooper*).

After that he was billed as Mike Connors for shows like *The Untouchables*, *Perry Mason*, *Alfred Hitchcock Presents*, *Wagon Train*, and more. Then came *Mannix*, followed by TV-movies like *The Killer Wouldn't Die* (1976), *Long Journey Back* (1978), and *Casino* (1980), followed by one season of ABC's 1981-1982 series, *Today's F.B.I.*, on which he played agent Ben Slater.

Other TV spots included an episode of Steven Spielberg's reboot of *Alfred Hitchcock Presents* (1989), the hit mini-series *War and Remembrance* (1988-1989), the reboot of *Burke's Law* (1994), *The Commish* (1993), *Walker, Texas Ranger* (1998), and a recurring role as Chipacles in the syndicated *Hercules* series starring Kevin Sorbo (1998-1999). His last on-screen performance was for an episode of the CBS sitcom, *Two and a Half Men*, called "Prostitutes and Gelato" (2007), in which he portrayed a character named Hugo.

A very private and dedicated family man, Connors has been married to the same woman, Mary Lou Willey, since September 10, 1949, and they have two children: Matthew Gunner Ohanian (born in 1958) and Dana Lee Connors (born 1960).

Approximately one year following the demise of *Mannix* on TV, another

Mike Connors
Globe Photos

popular guest actor, Telly Savalas, surfaced on an additional CBS police detective show, titled *Kojak* (CBS, 1973–1978), on which he played the hairless and tough-but-lollipop-loving Lt. Theo Kojak (originally spelled "Kojack").

Around the same time, fellow male icons Clint Walker and Darren McGavin starred in new television series also starting and ending with the letter k. Walker was *Kodiak*, which debuted on ABC in the fall of 1973, and McGavin was *Kolchak: The Night Stalker*, also on ABC, but debuting in the fall of 1974; decades later, in 2005, even a short-lived revamp of *Kojak* (starring Ving Rhames) made it to the air.

But none stood the test of time like the show starring Savalas, an original in every sense of the term; someone whose very name (Telly) said "television."

According to Wikipedia, it all began when the actor hosted ABC's *Your Voice of America for the US State Department*, while serving in the US Armed Forces during World War II (1943–1946). He also worked behind-the-scenes as an executive-turned-senior director for other ABC News special events, such as executive producing the network's *Gillette Cavalcade of Sports*, where he subsequently gave Howard Cosell his first TV job.

In 1950 Savalas moderated the New York radio show, *The Coffeehouse*, and seven years later, on January 7, he made his TV acting debut on an episode of the *Armstrong Circle Theatre* anthology series, titled "And Bring Home a Baby." He went on to make two additional *Armstrong* appearances, followed by countless guest-shots on TV shows like *Naked City*, *Arrest and Trial*, *The Eleventh Hour*, *The Untouchables*, *Burke's Law*, *Combat!*, *The Fugitive*, *Bonanza*, *The Man from U.N.C.L.E.*, and *The F.B.I.* Beyond *Kojak*, his most famous TV performance was for a segment of *The Twilight Zone* called "Talking Doll," in which he appeared with hair. Other than that, he had a recurring role as Brother Hendricksen on the popular crime drama series *77 Sunset Strip* and was a regular on the short-lived NBC series *Acapulco*. Post-*Kojak*, he starred in the 1980 TV-film *Alcatraz: The Whole Shocking Story*.

Of Greek heritage, Telly was born Aristotelis Savalas on January 21, 1922, in Garden City, New York, to father Nick, a restaurateur, and his mother, Christina, a New York City artist and native of Sparta. Telly and his brother Gus sold newspapers and shined shoes to help support the family, while attending Sewanhaka High School in Floral Park, New York, from which he received his diploma in 1940. He was then employed briefly as a lifeguard, but was soon devastated after a man drowned on his watch, a tragic incident from which he never fully recovered. He eventually enrolled at Columbia University School of General Studies, where he became versed in the English language and studied psychology and radio, which led to his interest in television and dramatic arts.

Telly Savalas
Globe Photos

In 1960 he portrayed real-life gang-ster Al Capone on the short-lived TV series, *The Witness*, which caught the eye of cinema icon Burt Lancaster, who went on to cast him in several of his films, such as *The Young Savages* (1961) and *Birdman of Alcatraz* (1962; which earned him an Academy Award nom-ination). He played private Detective Charles Sievers in *Cape Fear* (also released in 1962), and three years later he shaved his head for Pontius Pilate in *The Greatest Story Ever Told* (1965). His other movies include *The Dirty Dozen* (1967), and two sequels (1987 and 1988), *The Scalphunters* (1968), *Crooks and Coronets* (1969), and *Kelly's Heroes* (in which he portrayed the tough company sergeant named Big Joe)—all of which led up to his role on *Kojak*, which began as a 1973 CBS-TV-movie called *The Marcus-Nelson Murders* (adapted from the true story of police detective Thomas J. Cavanagh Jr. and the Career Girls Murder case).

Kojak inspired several favorite catchphrases ("Everybody should have a little Greek in them"), and as critic Clive James expressed in his 1977 book, *Visions Before Midnight*, "Telly Savalas can make bad slang sound like good slang and good slang sound like lyric poetry. It isn't what he is, so much as the way he talks, that gets you tuning in."

Today, Rob Ray believes Theo Kojak, as played by Savalas, took his police work very seriously, but also "seemed to have a more playful attitude" than most TV detec-tives of the era, including Mike Connors as *Mannix*.

Comparing Connors to two other television male icons from the 50s, 60s, and 70s–beyond the realm of the crime drama genre, Ray says:

The first word that pops in my head upon thinking of Mike Connors is "integrity." Like Ed Asner and Ralph Waite, Connors presented a seemingly fundamental decent presence on screen.

Asner and his fictional persona of Lou Grant [on both *The Mary Tyler Moore Show* and his sequel series *Lou Grant*] both exude integrity with Lou having a quality of "reluctant fairness." He doesn't want to admit that Mary Richards is doing as good a job as a man would, but when pressed, he will freely admit that. Lou took a paternal pride in Mary's accomplishments. Ed Asner, as an actor, exuded those same qualities of integrity and paternal protectiveness, laced with a strong sense of comic and dramatic timing.

Ralph Waite [the father on *The Waltons*], likewise exuded integrity and a fatherly protectiveness with a gruffness that suggested a sense that there was a stronger force guiding him. In the case of John Walton, that stronger force was undoubtedly his wife, Olivia. In real life, Ralph Waite may have been a bit more complicated. He had been an ordained Presbyterian minister earlier in his life before turning to the stage. And like Ed Asner, he was politically active, running for Congress at one point.

Mike Connors, meanwhile, seemed to represent the best of both Asner and Waite, but positioned in an action-adventure format on *Mannix*.

In all, Mike Connors and Telly Savalas came to define the ultra-cool older brothers not only of all TV detectives and policemen, but seemingly every male TV character in general.

51

Robert Wagner
It Takes a Thief/Switch

My wife [Jill St. John] was a Bond girl in [the 1971 movie] *Diamonds Are Forever*. So, I play James Bond in real life every day.

—Robert Wagner

The words dashing, daring, and debonair were created to describe Robert Wagner. An early film teen sensation along with Robert Conrad, George Hamilton, and Connie Stevens, Wagner first found regular TV stardom in the 60s and 70s as Alexander Mundy on *It Takes a Thief* and as Peterson T. "Pete" Ryan on *Switch*, and later, in the 80s, as Jonathan Hart on *Hart to Hart*. But it was as Alexander where he made his mark. Just how dashing was Wagner? Debonair enough to have cinematic big-screen idol Fred Astaire play his father on *Thief* for a few episodes.

Along with *Mission: Impossible* and *The Man from U.N.C.L.E.*, *It Takes a Thief* debuted in the James Bond super-spy era. While David McCallum and Robert Vaughn tag-teamed on *U.N.C.L.E.* in the adventure drama department, and while Don Adams played the genre for laughs with the half-hour sitcom *Get Smart*, Wagner played it cool as the globe-trotting Mundy on *Thief*.

The popular and successful Wagner has had three hit series and an impressive list of both feature and television films. As a young man under contract to 20th Century Fox, Wagner was cast by Darryl F. Zanuck in *With a Song in My Heart* (1952). Although the part lasted a scant minute, his performance as a crippled soldier responding to the song of Susan Hayward brought immediate public reaction to the studio. Spencer

Tracy saw him in *Beneath the Twelve Mile Reef* (1953) and requested Wagner for the role of his son in *Broken Lance* (1954). Tracy was so impressed with Wagner, he cast him as his brother in *The Mountain* (1956). A small sample of his additional film credits from the 60s through today includes: *Prince Valiant* (1954); *The True Story of Jesse James* (1957); *All the Fine Young Cannibals* (1960); *Harper* (1966); *Midway* (1976); *The Curse of the Pink Panthe*r (1983); *Dragon: The Bruce Lee Story* (1993); *Wild Things* (1998); *Crazy in Alabama* (1999); and his recurring role as Number 2 in the *Austin Powers* movies (1997–2002).

Globe Photos

On television, his roles on *Thief* (for which he was Emmy-nominated), *Switch*, and *Hart* remain legendary. With regard to *Hart to Hart*, he went on to star and produce eight TV-reunion-movies first for NBC then cable's Family Channel. He also starred with Jaclyn Smith in the top-rated miniseries *Windmills of the Gods*, based on Sidney Sheldon's best-selling novel; with Angie Dickinson in the NBC miniseries *Pearl*; with Audrey Hepburn in *Love Among Thieves*; with Lesley Anne Down in *Indiscreet* and in *North and South III*; and with Elizabeth Taylor in *There Must Be a Pony*, all on ABC (and the latter of which he also executive produced).

His other TV credits include the short-lived, but critically-acclaimed ABC series, *Lime Street* (1985-1986); the sitcoms *Hope & Faith* (also on ABC, 2003–2006) and *Two and A Half Men* (CBS, 2007-2008), and what has become TV's #1 show in recent years: *NCIS* (CBS, 2010–2015), on which he portrayed Anthony DiNozzo Sr.

One of Wagner's most destiniguished television appearances occurred when he was selected by Sir Laurence Olivier to star with him in the 1976 adaptation of *Cat on a Hot Tin Roof,* in which he costarred with his wife, the late Natalie Wood. He also teamed up on TV with Olivier for the 1991 remake of *This Gun for Hire*, Danielle Steel's *Jewels* (1992) and *To Catch a King* (1984).

In addition to his film and television ventures, Wagner has toured the world performing A. R. Gurney's *Love Letters*, with his former *Hart* costar Stefanie Powers; they were the first to launch the tour internationally. Currently, Wagner performs *Love Letters* at charity events with his wife, actress Jill St. John.

Wagner enjoys golfing and spending time with his three daughters, Katie (a television personality), Natasha (an actress), and Courtney (an artist).

The modest Wagner credits those creative minds behind the scenes on all of his shows for making him look and sound good, especially those who generated the words he voiced. "It was all about the writing," he says today, with regard to playing Mundy on *It Takes a Thief* (created specifically for Wagner by Roland Kibbee, who wrote for everything from *Alfred Hitchcock Presents* to *The Bob Cummings Show* to *Barney Miller*), Pete Ryan on *Switch* (created by fellow male TV icon Glenn Larson), or even on into the 1980s as Jonathan on *Hart* (created by the prolific novelist-turned-TV-mini-series king Sidney Sheldon, who also created successful sitcoms like *I Dream of Jeannie*). "If the script isn't strong," Wagner intones, "the actor lacks the solid foundation and inspiration to draw and work from. I was lucky. I had good writers to work with each time."

52

Burt Reynolds
Dan August

Rock Hudson
McMillan & Wife

I had to overcome the name Rock. If I'd been as hip then, as I am now, I would have never consented to be named Rock.

—Rock Hudson

Burt Reynolds was a TV star before he became a movie star. Rock Hudson was a movie star before he became a TV star. In the process, both became two of television's top male icons of the 50s, 60s, and 70s.

Reynolds had regular roles in the 50s and early 60s on TV's *Showboat* and *Gunsmoke* before taking the lead in the short-lived but memorable *Dan August* crime-detective series in the early 70s.

Cinema legend Hudson found a second career on television as the star of NBC's *McMillan & Wife*, on which he portrayed San Francisco police commissioner Stuart McMillan. On this show, which was party to NBC's monthly *Mystery Movie* wheel of shows (that also included Peter Falk as *Columbo* and Dennis Weaver as *McCloud*, among others), Hudson shared a winning chemistry not just with Susan Saint James as Sally, his much younger TV wife, but also with Nancy Walker—as their wisecracking housekeeper Mildred, and John Schuck, as Lieutenant Enright, right-hand man to Commissioner McMillan.

Today older-man/younger-woman or older-woman/younger-man couples are pervasive on and off the big and small screens. But in the 70s pairing Hudson, then forty-six, with James, then twenty-five, was unusual, as Mac could have easily been mistaken as father to Sally.

Rock Hudson
Globe Photos

Mac and Sally's age difference became a non-issue, however, because the chemistry and delightful dialogue between Hudson and Saint James was spot-on. Although not every forty-something man looked like Rock Hudson, and not every twenty-something female looked like James, they gelled on screen, and the show worked. Their characters knew each other intimately, and could read each other's thoughts and see through each other's schemes as they tried to stay one step ahead of whatever killer was on the loose this time. Joining them in the witty banter was Schuck's bemused Enright as the audience's surrogate and as more gentle comedy relief, and Walker's nosy Mildred.

Although each episode contained a few violent scenes, it was nowhere near as violent as today's crime-and-mystery dramas, which frequently focus on gore and horrific images. Instead, *McMillan & Wife* concentrated on character interplay, and just plain fun. Characters would be murdered, and mysteries would be created, but the main plot was almost secondary to the characterization and performances by Hudson, James, Schuck, and Walker. Rob Ray offers his usual keen insight, explaining in the process how the old adage, "behind every good man rests a good woman," also applies to fictional TV characters:

> In 1970, the year before *McMillan & Wife* made its debut, the film industry was going through one of the most tumultuous changes in its history. Youth and relevance were in and middle-aged stars who had ruled the box office throughout the 1950s and early 60s were given notice that the times were changing. Hudson, along with so many of his contemporaries, sensed that it was time to follow his fan-base, which was staying home and watching television. On the big screen, the name Rock Hudson was becoming passé, a relic of fifties westerns and some old Doris Day comedies. But to the world of TV, the name Rock Hudson still meant movie-star! The time had come to make the move. And Hudson found the perfect property to do so with *McMillan & Wife*.

The story of a San Francisco police chief who solves murders himself rather than rely on his underlings and who had a young, sexy wife with an insatiable urge to help him [and, like *Perry Mason* and *Ellery Queen*] had its genesis in novels; namely in Dashiell Hammett's classic sleuthing couple, Nick and Nora Charles. In Hammett's initial work, *The Thin Man*, and in a series of six films produced by MGM from 1934 until 1948, Nick and Nora worked as a team, a sometimes reluctant one on Nick's part. William Powell and Myrna Loy achieved cinematic immortality in the roles. A TV adaptation in the fifties with Peter Lawford and Phyllis Kirk didn't click, proving that properties like this have to have that perfect chemistry. Rock Hudson and Susan St. James had it.

Consequently, Mac and Sally were not long away from being newlyweds, and like Nick and Nora, they clearly enjoyed a healthy sex life, as their on-screen foreplay was evident throughout the series (and most productive in the fourth season, when Sally became pregnant—as did James; though once the actress delivered her baby in real life, Sally and Mac's child was never mentioned or seen again). In effect, they made sleuthing *fun*, almost as if it was sexual foreplay itself.

Mac and Sally's chemistry was so crucial to the show's success that, when it was altered, in the sixth and final season (1976-1977), *McMillan & Wife* fell apart. Nancy Walker, for thirty years playing comedy relief on stage, screen, and television, left after finally being granted her own series contract (with ABC, on which her two shows failed), while her housekeeping role on the Hudson/James series was replaced by a mugging Martha Raye as her sister. John Schuck's work brought him to the attention of casting agents, and he also left (like Walker, to do another failed ABC series, this one called *Holmes and YoYo*). But most importantly, Susan Saint James exited over a contract dispute and Sally was killed off, along with the character's unseen newborn son. Audiences could not accept such a downer of a change, particularly as they had watched Sally carrying the couple's son to term throughout the preceding years. The ratings plummeted in the last-season version titled simply *McMillan*, in which Rock Hudson starred alone, proving that chemistry is sometimes everything.

The year Rock Hudson began taking the lead in *McMillan & Wife*, Burt Reynolds was contemplating taking off his clothes for *Cosmopolitan* magazine to become the first nude male centerfold of the print periodical world (and in the process ultimately inspiring *Playgirl* magazine into publication). He had just completed his brief run on *Dan August*—and it was time for a change—or even a complete removal of clothes.

The tall, dark, trim, and sexy actor also found superstardom on the big screen with feature films like *Deliverance* (1972), *The Man Who Loved Cat Dancing* (1973), *The*

Longest Yard (the 1974 original, and the 2005 remake), *Hooper* (1978), *Smokey and the Bandit* (1977), and *Starting Over* (1979), as well as his Golden Globe Award–winning and Oscar-nominated performance in *Boogie Nights* (2005).

But it was on the small screen that Reynolds hit his stride by sliding down the church floor every week in the opening credit sequence of *Dan August* (which costarred Norman Fell, later of the network's *Three's Company* and subsequent *The Ropers* sitcoms).

On the CBS sitcom *Evening Shade* (1990–1994), Reynolds delivered an Emmy-winning interpretation of Wood Newton, an ex–professional football player for the Pittsburgh Steelers who returns to rural Evening Shade, Arkansas, to coach a high school football team with a long losing streak. This show also featured a long list of his closest acting colleagues, such as Charles Durning, Charles Nelson Reilly, Dom DeLuise, and Billy Bob Thornton.

Reynolds's personal appearances on the talk show circuit of the day became nothing less than iconic. Johnny Carson (for whom Reynolds shaved his famous mustache on a dare from Steve Martin), Merv Griffin, Mike Douglas, and certainly

Dinah Shore each . . . um . . . embraced Reynolds in his or her own way. That is to say, his romantic relationship with Shore indeed became the stuff of legends. Ten years his senior, Shore adored Reynolds, the feeling was mutual, and Shore became the first "cougar" of the TV generation.

He may have been *The Man Who Loved Cat Dancing* on the big screen, but on and off any screen, everyone loved Reynolds because of his "everyman" down-home charm. As one reporter pointed out in 2009, "he completely understood that his good ol' boy looks left many women unmoved, although, he added, he loved it when 'women [rushed] across the room at a cocktail party just to say they don't find me attractive.'"

Burt Reynolds
Globe Photos

According to Wikipedia, Reynolds was born February 11, 1936, in Waycross, Georgia, to Burton Mylo Reynolds and Fern H. Reynolds. In his autobiography he explains how his family held residence in Lansing, Michigan, when his father was drafted into the Army. His mother and sister (Nancy Ann Brown) joined the elder Burton at Fort Leonard Wood, where they remained for two years. When Burt's dad was stationed in Europe, the Reynolds brood returned to Lansing. In 1946, they relocated to Riviera Beach, Florida, where his father became chief of police.

During Burt Jr.'s sophomore year at Palm Beach High School (in West Palm Beach, which was up the way a little bit from Riviera Beach), he was named First Team All State and All Southern as a fullback, and received multiple scholarship offers. After his high school graduation, Reynolds attended Florida State University on a football scholarship, and played halfback. He aspired to play professional football, but suffered an injury in the first game of the season, which was exacerbated by a car accident later that year. While he then considered a career in law enforcement, his dad encouraged him to complete his college education and become a parole officer.

To keep up with his studies, he began taking classes at Palm Beach Junior College (PBJC) in neighboring Lake Worth. In his first term at PBJC, Reynolds was in a class taught by Watson B. Duncan III. Duncan suggested Burt audition for a play he was producing, titled *Outward Bound*. Impressed with one of Burt's Shakespeare readings in class, Duncan cast him in the lead. As a result, Reynolds nabbed the 1956 Florida State Drama Award for his *Outward* performance, and to this day, names Duncan as his mentor and the most influential person in his life.

From 1963 to 1965, Reynolds was married to future TV *Laugh-In* performer Judy Carne and, from 1988 to 1993, Reynolds was wed to actress Loni Anderson (from TV's *WKRP in Cincinnati*). Loni and Burt adopted a young son they named Quinton Anderson Reynolds.

At the peak of his career, he opened the Burt Reynolds Dinner Theatre in Jupiter, Florida, and, while in recent years, he has suffered many health and financial hardships, he has still managed to perform in commercials, and on television shows like *The King of Queens*.

According to a report in December 2014, the ailing actor planted the Florida State University team's ceremonial spear at midfield before a game in Tallahassee—and his alma mater was victorious: a significant representation of just how winning Burt Reynolds remains in the eyes of millions of fans of classic television—and every entertainment medium.

53

David Soul and Paul Michael Glaser
Starsky & Hutch

Paul and I were both struggling actors. One night he would serve me in a restaurant, and the next night I would serve him. It was what out-of-work actors did.

—David Soul, talking about life before he and Paul Michael Glaser
were cast on *Starsky & Hutch*

Just how popular were David Soul and Paul Michael Glaser on *Starsky & Hutch*?

Popular enough to inspire Ben Stiller to adapt the successful TV crime show into a major motion picture in 2004 costarring Owen Wilson.

Ten years later, the nostalgic television network, COZI-TV, began airing reruns of the original series, which became such a ratings hit—again—the network produced an all-new special documentary dedicated to the show.

Created by William Blinn, and produced by Aaron Spelling and Leonard Goldberg, *Starsky & Hutch* began as a ninety-minute TV pilot film on ABC's *Movie of the Week* and went on to air as ninety-two weekly episodes between April 30, 1975, and May 15, 1979.

Police detectives David Michael Starsky and Ken "Hutch" Hutchinson were based in Southern California. Glaser played the dark-haired Starsky, who hailed from Brooklyn. He was a veteran of the US Army and possessed a tough but tender intensity. Soul was the blond, more laid-back Hutch from the relatively more tranquil Duluth, Minnesota. They cruised around Bay City, California, in Starsky's two-door, red-and-white Ford Gran Torino, which Hutch dubbed the "Striped Tomato."

Soul was born David Richard Solberg Jr. on August 28, 1943, in Chicago, Illinois, to well-educated parents. His mother was a teacher, and his father, Dr. David Richard Solberg Sr., a Lutheran minister, was a professor of history and political science and director of higher education for the American Lutheran Church. Dr. Solberg was also senior representative for Lutheran World Relief during the reconstruction of Germany following World War II. As a result, the family was in frequent flux during David's youth. After attending Augustana College, University of the Americas in Mexico City, and the University of Minnesota, David, at only nineteen years old, rejected an offer to play professional baseball with the Chicago White Sox to study political

David Soul, left; Paul Michael Glaser, right
Globe Photos

science. While in Mexico, he switched gears again, and this time opted to pursue an interest in music, after learning how to play the guitar. Upon his return to the United States, he made his musical debut in a Minneapolis club called The 10 O'Clock Scholar.

His early TV appearances included *The Merv Griffin Show* in the mid-1960s, during which he performed as the "Covered Man." He wore a mask over his face because he wanted the audience to focus on his music

In 1967 he made his TV acting debut on the half-hour adventure series *Flipper* and on the original *Star Trek* series, in the second-season episode titled, "The Apple." Shortly after, he was cast as Joshua Bolt on TV's *Here Come the Brides*, costarring Robert Brown, Bridget Hanley, and fellow male TV icon Bobby Sherman.

In 1972 Soul costarred with Arthur Hill on *Owen Marshall: Counselor at Law* (which at one point also costarred yet another fellow male TV icon: Lee Majors). Following several additional episodic guest appearances (such as *McMillan & Wife*, *The Rookies,* and *Gunsmoke*), Clint Eastwood cast him in his 1973 feature film *Magnum Force.* Shortly thereafter he was cast in the TV-pilot for *Starsky & Hutch* (for which Soul also helmed three segments).

Soul's other TV work includes guest-spots on *I Dream of Jeannie*, *All in the Family*, and many TV-movies and mini-series like *The Yellow Rose* (airing in 1983, and based on the classic 1942 Humphrey Bogart motion picture, *Casablanca*), and 1980's *Rage*, which was heralded by the US Senate and garnered Soul an Emmy nomination. Soul also appeared in the 1979 TV-miniseries adaptation of Stephen King's vampire story *Salem's Lot* (which was reworked and released in theaters in some foreign markets).

During the mid- to late 1970s, Soul returned to his singing roots. Produced by Tony Macaulay, he recorded hits including "Don't Give Up on Us" (1976), which reached #1 in America and the UK, and "Silver Lady" (1977), which was also a hit in Britain. From 1976 until 1978, the all-around-entertainer had five UK Top 20 singles and two Top 10 albums. Between 1976 and 1982 he toured throughout the United States, Europe, the Far East, and South America. Soul's resume also includes the 1989 movie adaptation of *Agatha Christie's Appointment with Death*, and in the mid-1990s, he formally relocated to London, where he ignited a new career on the West End stage (including a performance as Chandler Tate in *Comic Potential*). Around the same time, he also became involved with the successful 1997 election campaign of Martin Bell, who ran as an MP for Tatton, as well as Bell's failed campaign in Brentwood in Essex in the 2001 General Election. Future productions followed, such as: 2003's BBC's *Little Britain* series (in which he played himself), 2005's *Jerry Springer—The Opera* (he played the lead at the Cambridge Theatre in London), and, in 2006, a revival of Jerry Herman's musical *Mack and Mabel* at the West End's Criterion Theatre.

Paul Michael Glaser was born Paul Manfred Glaser in Cambridge, Massachusetts, the youngest of three children, to Dorothy and Samuel Glaser, an architect. Glaser enrolled at the Buckingham Browne & Nichols School, later transferred to the Cambridge School of Weston, and then on to Tulane University, where he roomed with movie director Bruce Paltrow (father to Gwyneth and husband to Blyth Danner), and in 1966, he earned a master's degree in English and theater. The following year, he acquired an additional master's from Boston University in acting and directing.

After performing in many Broadway plays, Glaser made his movie debut in 1971 as Perchik in the film edition of *Fiddler on the Roof*, followed by performances in acclaimed motion pictures like *Butterflies Are Free* (1972). His initial TV gig was as Dr. Peter Chernak on the daytime soap *Love Is a Many Splendored Thing*, followed by guest spots on series like *The Waltons*, *The Streets of San Francisco*, *Cannon*, *Toma*, *The Sixth Sense*, *Kojak*, and *The Rockford Files*. But it was on *Starsky & Hutch* that he would become his most successful.

After that series ended in 1979, Glaser continued to act in and also direct TV shows *Miami Vice* and *Judging Amy* and movies, such as the 1987 feature *The Running Man* (starring Arnold Schwarzenegger) and 1992's *The Cutting Edge*. In 2004 he returned to acting in *Something's Gotta Give* (playing Diane Keaton's former husband).

Among his diverse appearances on screen and stage, Glaser was featured in a segment of the CBS TV-series *The Mentalist*, called "The Scarlet Letter," which first aired October 1, 2009. In 2013 he made a return-engagement to *Fiddler on the Roof* for a British national stage tour, this time in the main role of Tevye.

A dedicated photographer and poet (presently writing many books for children), the ruggedly handsome actor has been wed twice. In 1980 he married Elizabeth Meyer, who in August 1981 contracted HIV from a blood transfusion while giving birth to their first child (Ariel). Elizabeth did not discover the virus until four years later, when both Ariel and son Jake (born October 1984) were also diagnosed as HIV-positive. Ariel passed away in August 1988; Elizabeth Glaser died in 1994, though not before founding the nonprofit Elizabeth Glaser Pediatric AIDS Foundation.

After Elizabeth's death, Glaser served as chairman of the organization until 2002 and remains its honorary chairman. He has also testified before the US Congress, met with national leaders, and spearheaded annual fundraisers.

Glaser married producer Tracy Barone in 1996; the couple had a daughter, Zoe, on October 7, 1997. Glaser filed for divorce in June 2007.

Starsky & Hutch is still beloved by millions, and Glaser shares that legacy with David Soul. Glaser once credited the now-timeless era in which the series initially aired. "The seventies was a totally different sensibility," he said, "and that allowed us to break new ground on a cop show."

In 2004, when actors Ben Stiller (as Starsky) and Owen Wilson (as Hutch) cleverly resurrected the series as a theatrical motion picture (in which both Glaser and Soul made cameo appearances), Glaser concluded, "I was surprised that the TV series was popular itself, but after that it went on to become more popular over the years and thus it seemed eventually that they would turn it into a movie."

54

Erik Estrada and Larry Wilcox
CHiPs

I owe the public a good performance . . . the best I can give. We really bust our chops on *CHiPs*, but when I go home and get a weekend off, I want to spend it quietly with my lady.

—Larry Wilcox

Besides Paul Michael Glaser and David Soul on *Starsky & Hutch*, two of TV's most popular and macho all-American actors-as-law-enforcement teams (also one blond; one dark-haired) were Larry Wilcox and Erik Estrada, who costarred in yet another police-driven series: *CHiPs*.

This series first aired on NBC from 1976 to 1981—and featured Larry as Officer Jonathan "Jon" Baker, and Erik playing Officer Francis ("Frank") Llewellyn "Ponch" Poncherello—two California highway patrolmen.

Estrada is a native of New York's Spanish Harlem. His first acting break came when a fresh new face was required to costar with Pat Boone in the film, *The Cross and the Switchblade*.

Wilcox was born in San Diego, and brought up in Wyoming, with horseback riding and lasso-rousing as second nature to him. As such, an episode of *CHiPs*, titled, "The Rustling," displayed Larry's rodeo skills, putting him against a steer that had strayed onto the freeway that he patrolled with Estrada on the series.

Many episodes of *CHiPs* utilized the more humanitarian aspects of law enforcement, which contributed a great deal to the show's success. For example, in another episode, titled, "Dog Gone," the two policemen befriended an injured dog named Muffin; while in a segment called "Hitch-Hiking Hitch," Ponch found himself interacting with a slightly larger animal: a St. Bernard. In yet another animal-oriented entry on the show, Erik and Larry met up with an elephant. Additional fun episodes featured other classic TV characters, like the very fictional *H.R. Pufnstuf*, who had his own NBC series—on Saturday mornings (as opposed to Saturday nights, when *CHiPs* mostly aired).

Besides *The Cross and the Switchblade*, Erik appeared on the big screen in movie classics like *The New Centurions*, *Airport '75*, *Midway*, and *Trackdown*. His TV credits include classic shows such as *Hawaii Five-O*, *Mannix*, *Kojak*, *McMillan & Wife*, *The Six Million Dollar Man*, *Medical Center*, and *Police Woman*.

Like Estrada, Larry is a man of many talents. He's a musician (who plays both guitar and piano)—and a genius businessman. Other than *CHiPs*, his acting credits include several groundbreaking TV-movies (one costarring Farrah Fawcett), and several feature films for Walt Disney. He's appeared on many classic TV shows, including *Lassie*, *Police Story*, *M*A*S*H*, and *The Streets of San Francisco*.

Larry Wilcox
Globe Photos

Wilcox wed Judy Vagner, on March 29, 1969, while serving his last months of duty after returning from the Vietnam War. They had two children together: Derek and Heidi. His second marriage was to Dutch native Hannie Strasser, a one-time *CHiPs* assistant sound technician. The wedding took place on April 11, 1980. Their daughter, Wendy, was born in 1982 and they divorced immediately. Wilcox raised Wendy.

On March 22, 1986, Wilcox married Marlene Harmon, a member of the 1980 Olympic heptathlon team. They reside in the San Fernando Valley and have two sons, Chad and Ryan. He assists in caring for his father-in-law, a stroke victim. Wilcox set up an NPO Hub website to benefit police officers killed in the

Erik Estrada
Globe Photos

line of duty and various philanthropic projects.

Estrada was married to Peggy Lynn Rowe, an entertainment executive, songwriter, and producer from 1985 until 1990, when they divorced. The couple had two sons and a daughter, Anthony Erik Estrada (born 1986), and Brandon Michael-Paul Estrada (born 1987), a global track star in his own right, and Lyric Alysia Estrada (born 1996).

In 1997, Estrada wed cinema sound technician Nanette Mirkovich. Their one child, an aspiring actress named Francesca Natalia, was born in 2000, the same year her famous father was named the international "Face" of the D.A.R.E. program (which advocates against substance abuse). Estrada also is an advocate for the American Heart Association, the United Way, and the C.H.P. 11-99 Foundation, a nonprofit that provides benefits and scholarships for real-life California Highway Patrol family members, in addition to helping with funeral costs for fallen officers, as well as several more charities.

Of his on-air *CHiPs* time with Estrada, and their subsequent christening as immortal TV superstars, a modest Wilcox offers this insight:

When I look in the mirror I don't see a male icon. But while we were doing the show, we were supposedly male icons because we starred in a television series and there were then only just three networks, and our Nielson ratings were a high 19 to the 20s . . . numbers that are unheard of today. So, you're reaching millions of people. And I always construed it as the networks spending millions of dollars branding you. So, you should be so lucky to have someone spend 10 or 20 million on your brand. And from that, I felt there was a responsibility as a so-called-male icon. And the responsibility was that those fans out there have a special place in their heart [for Erik and I]. And we were able to serve some kind of meal for the appetite they needed. But I don't think it's about signing autographs and being a "star." It's about serving the hopes, and wishes and spirit of the fans.

One of those fans is Virginia Reeser, a Los Angeles-based communications specialist, who now perfectly summarizes the mainstream appeal of both Larry and Erik as two of classic TV's most popular male personas:

When I think back to watching *CHiPs* in the 1970s, I can only smile. That was really good Sunday night television. Larry Wilcox and Erik Estrada portrayed two brave, kind, charismatic California Highway Patrol motorcycle officers in the mythical land of Los Angeles, California. It was a place where you could drive around on impressive motorcycles in the sunshine, even in February. As a young girl growing up in the snowy Midwest, these sun-soaked adventure scenes in mid-winter seemed just as much fiction as Saturday-afternoon sci-fi television.

Of course, *CHiPs* was actually based in a real location; plus Larry and Erik portrayed everyday heroes. Little did I know that in the future, I, too, would come to understand what it meant when they said someone lived in "The Valley" or "the Foothills." Beyond their characters working in incredible locations, solving curious crimes, and performing heroic rescues, what I admired most about Larry and Erik's portrayal of their characters was their recipe for getting things done together—a fun combination of bravery, teamwork, and charm—all tossed together with charisma and humor. Of course they each had different personalities, but that's what made the team ever better. It showcased the best lesson about working together: as long as you have the same goal, you can have different styles and personalities, and still be a strong, effective team.

Fast forward to modern days. I live in Los Angeles and see the true, brave men and women who are our California Highway Patrol motorcycle officers. I'm impressed every time I see them flying down the highway, off to keep us safe and secure, working as part of an incredible team. And I've even had the honor of meeting Larry Wilcox in person at the Classic Television Preservation Society's 2015 holiday program [held at the Burbank Barnes & Noble, December 4, 2015]. The strong, kind spirit of his character which shone through in the 1970s is still there in his real-life persona today. As a Vietnam War veteran, he's the best kind of modern-day hero, a family man who cares deeply about his children, and continues to serve his fellow war veterans, and the men and women who serve us in the law enforcement fields.

PART VII

THE SUPER MEN

Some could leap tall buildings in a single bound; others were more human (as well as humorous) caped crusaders. Some journeyed to the farthest reaches of the galaxy—and other galaxies relatively far, far away—where no man (and later no one) had gone before. Some offered a fine mix of cowboys and aliens. But all were entertaining, and super men in their own way, playing out-of-this-world characters in either science fiction, fantasy, or general high-concept television series—long before *Marvel's Agents of Shield* hit the small screen, and certainly eons before *Marvel's The Avengers* hit the big screen.

Escapist entertainment has always been a welcome outlet for audience members, going as far back as the 30s and 40s, when film shorts and full-length movies featuring Buck Rogers and Flash Gordon were popular. Once television ignited with its now famous (and first!) Golden Age, the natural progression of technological evolution would transport entertainment properties, including Superman and Batman, onto the small screen. The sci-fi/fantasy craze that ran wild on the big screen in the 50s with the increasing interest in space travel (catapulted on some level by the Atomic Age) also played out in living rooms across the country with shows like *Space Patrol*, *Lost in Space*, and *Star Trek*—the granddaddy of all great televised sci-fi/fantasy. Although the end of World War II set the stage for peace, the Korean War in the 50s, the Vietnam War in the 60s and early 70s, and the general unrest and political turmoil of those last two decades in particular set the stage for massive escapist entertainment, certainly in view of the assassinations of John F. Kennedy, Martin Luther King Jr., and Bobby Kennedy in the 60s.

Simply put: TV audiences of the 50s, 60s, and 70s were looking for a way out. While Elizabeth Montgomery's house-witch Samantha Stephens twitched on *Bewitched*, Barbara Eden's genie blinked her magic on *I Dream of Jeannie*, and Lynda Carter lassoed her way into the hearts of millions of fan-boys and fan-men as *Wonder Woman*, some of the masculine equivalents were George Reeves on *Superman*, Adam West on *Batman*, Robert Conrad as Jim West on *The Wild Wild West*, and Bill Bixby and Lou Ferrigno on *The Incredible Hulk*. While Lindsay Wagner ran in super-lovely slow motion as Jaime Sommers on *The Bionic Woman*, that cybernetic superhero series machinated from the wires that were first weaved by Lee Majors as Col. Steve Austin on *The Six Million Dollar Man*.

Other male TV superheroes included Ron Ely as *Tarzan*, Patrick Duffy as the *Man from Atlantis* (which debuted shortly before his iconic performance as Bobby Ewing on *Dallas*), and even comedic characters from shows like *Captain Nice* and *Mr. Terrific*.

These next chapters explore more closely some of these top super-male TV icons from the 50s, 60s, and 70s.

55

Clayton Moore and Jay Silverheels
The Lone Ranger

Hi Yo, Silver—Away!

—The Lone Ranger, as played by Clayton Moore in the
TV series of the same name.

They were two of TV's most popular and most controversial personas.

Clayton Moore took the lead on TV's *The Lone Ranger*, while Jay Silverheels played his Native American colleague Tonto on ABC from 1949 to 1957.

Their teaming was historic, and nothing but pure magic if littered at times with spots of controversy.

According to his book *I Was That Masked Man*, Moore made a few more westerns and serials, sometimes playing the villain. He was actually fired from the *Ranger* series (and replaced by John Hart), then rehired, and remained with the program until it ended first-run production in 1957. He and Silverheels also starred in two feature-length *Lone Ranger* motion pictures, while Moore appeared in other TV shows including the syndicated western, *The Adventures of Kit Carson*.

After completion of the second feature, *The Lone Ranger and the Lost City of Gold* in 1958, Moore embarked on what would be forty years of personal appearances, TV guest spots, and classic commercials as the legendary masked man. He refused to be seen in public without his mask and was, as a result, periodically perceived as eccentric. Silverheels had joined him for occasional reunions during the early 1960s and, throughout it all, Moore (who died at age 85 in 1999) expressed only respect and love for his former costar.

Jay Silverheels, left; Clayton Moore, right
Globe Photos

Meanwhile, Silverheels, a full-blooded Mohawk, became the first American Indian to costar on a mainstream American television series. Unfortunately, years after the series ended, he felt typecast as an American Indian and confessed to strongly disliking the Tonto role, which he designated as a demeaning character. However, on January 6, 1960, he portrayed an Indian fireman trying to extinguish a forest fire in the episode "Leap of Life" in the syndicated series, *Rescue 8*. Eventually, Silverheels found employment as a salesman to supplement his acting income, began publishing poetry (inspired by his youth on the Six Nations Indian Reserve), and recited his work on television. In 1966 he made a guest appearance as John Tallgrass in the short-lived ABC comedy/western series *The Rounders*, with Ron Hayes, Patrick Wayne, and Chill Wills.

Despite his issues with playing Tonto, Silverheels later satirized his participation in *The Lone Ranger*. In 1969 he played Tonto minus the Ranger in a comedy skit on *The Tonight Show Starring Johnny Carson* (which later appeared on the 1973 record album *Here's Johnny: Magic Moments from the Tonight Show*). One memorable line: "My name is Tonto. I hail from Toronto and I speak Esperanto."

Silverheels further showcased his good sportmanship with a side-splitting take on his Tonto role when he reteamed with Moore for a now-legendary Stan Freberg Jeno's Pizza Rolls TV commercial, and he played opposite Hart in *The Phynx*.

He also appeared in three segments of NBC's *Daniel Boone* (starring Fess Parker as the real-life frontiersman), in an episode of ABC's *The Brady Bunch* (as an Indian who befriends the Bradys in the Grand Canyon), and in sequence for the short-lived *Dusty's Trail* series (starring Bob Denver of *Gilligan's Island*).

In the early 1960s, Silverheels, who died at age sixty-seven in 1980, supported the Indian Actors Workshop, where American Indian actors refined their skills in Echo Park, California. Today the workshop is firmly established.

56

George Reeves
Adventures of Superman

Knock the "t" off the "can't."

—George Reeves

George Reeves remains "the definitive" Clark Kent and "Man of Steel" for the baby boomer generation, according to classic television historian Steve Randisi, who along with Jan Alan Henderson co-authored *Behind the Crimson Cape: The Cinema of George Reeves*. Randisi credits Reeve's talent and charisma with the original and continued success of *Adventures of Superman* (minus the "The"), which began with black-and-white episodes in early 1953 and ended with color segments in 1958. However, the platform for its initial broadcast history is, as Randisi words it, "checkered. Some historians claim it was on ABC in some cities; then it went to syndication, then ABC picked it up briefly in 1957, after which it returned to the syndicated market. Various sources disagree about this. Complicating the story is the fact that the first 52 episodes were shot in 1951, but didn't get shown on TV until February of 1953."

Randisi says the show was "a favorite in both syndicated and network airings, although the network airings were comparatively brief." Since *Superman*'s TV debut, Randisi adds, "all 104 'thrill-packed-adventures' have never been out of circulation. In one form or another, the half-hour [episodes] have remained a profitable commodity through reruns, video and DVD releases, and, more recently, cable network airings.

"George Reeves was an excellent actor," Randisi continues. "Not only did [he] radiate ineffable warmth with his portrayal, he epitomized believability. Reeves made his young audience believe he was Superman. He had a wonderful way of smiling and winking at the camera, thereby acknowledging the fact that viewers were in on his 'secret.' It was only the other characters in the plots that didn't know Clark Kent was Superman. [The perpetually inquisitive Lois Lane often suspected the truth, but could never prove it.]"

"Contrary to popular belief," Randisi clarifies, "George Reeves was not the first live-action Superman. Kirk Alyn had played the role in two movie serials, *Superman* (1948) and *Atom Man vs. Superman* (1950), neither of which played on television in the fifties. And while the Reeves version was seen briefly on the ABC network, it was also one of television's greatest successes in the syndication market. When the films were distributed to local stations in the mid-1960s, viewers were seeing them in color for the first time. The last 52 half hours had been filmed in color, but were originally broadcast in monochrome. And so, when color TV became widespread in the sixties, [the character of] Superman would win a new legion of fans in the process."

Like his noteworthy alter-male-TV-icon-ego (Clark Kent, who was sired as an alien on the planet Krypton and raised by human parents on Earth), Reeves's birth into this world was also extraordinary, relatively speaking.

Born George Keefer Brewer on January 5, 1914, in Woolstock, Iowa, he was the son of Don Brewer and Helen Lescher. Young George arrived five months into their marriage, which is why his mother subsequently claimed an erroneous April birthdate for the infant (a development of which he learned about as an adult). His parents allegedly separated soon after he was born, at which time Helen returned to her home in Galesburg, Illinois. She later relocated to stay with her sister in California, where she met and married Frank Bessolo. In 1925 George's father wed a second Helen, last name Schultz, with whom he had children, while Don Brewer apparently never again laid eyes on his son.

Subsequently, Bessolo became the adopted father of George, who acquired his new stepfather's last name. Frank and Helen divorced after fifteen years. While Reeves was visiting relatives, his mother lied to him, saying that Frank had committed suicide. Reeves's cousin, Catherine Chase, told biographer Jim Beaver that Reeves was unaware for years that Bessolo was still alive and doing well.

With the early melodrama of his pre-teen years behind him, George became interested in theater and music in high school and later attended Pasadena Junior College, where he continued to perform in stage productions. He also had more than a passing interest in amateur boxing (heavyweight class), but his mother forced him out of the sport, fearing he might destroy his handsome face.

In 1939 he was cast in the classic motion picture *Gone with the Wind*, playing one of Scarlett O'Hara's love interests (Stuart Tarleton, falsely listed in the movie's credits as Brent Tarleton). It was a small but significant part, as he and minor-costar Fred Crane, both with brightly dyed red hair (as "the Tarleton Twins"), appeared in the epic film's opening sequences. Soon after, the future Superman was contracted with Warner Bros., who changed his professional name to "George Reeves." Between the start of *Gone*'s production and its release twelve months later, several films on his Warner contract were made and released, making *Gone with the Wind* his first film role, but his fifth film release.

Noel Niell, left; George Reeves, right

Globe Photos

While studying acting at the Pasadena Playhouse, Reeves met his future wife, Ellanora Needles. They married on September 22, 1940, in San Gabriel, California, at the Church of Our Savior. They had no children and divorced ten years later.

Pop-culture historian and author Rick Lertzman summarizes George Reeves's brief, but significant career as such:

> After about a decade of minor roles in films George Reeves finally achieved a dubious type of superstardom as Superman, the idol of every pre-pubescent boy of the 1950s. Such was his fame that when he appeared in character on other shows, such as *I Love Lucy*, he wasn't billed in the credits as George Reeves, but as Superman himself. He *was* Superman to more than one generation, seemingly as broad, strong and sturdy as the Man of Steel himself. But when it was over, sadly his career had nowhere to go. No one suffered a worse case of type-casting than George Reeves. Whether that sad fact had anything to do with his tragic, mysterious death by gunshot [on June 16] 1959 can only be speculated.

Randisi says Reeves's death was "officially ruled a suicide," while "many of those closest to the actor, especially his mother, would challenge that ruling for years."

Reeves's successor as the combined Clark Kent/Superman character was, ironically, an actor with a similar name, Christopher Reeve (in the singular form), who also died a tragic death: a heart-attack at age fifty-two on October 10, 2004, following years of suffering various severe physical complications from a horseback-riding accident May 7, 1995. As the star of the 1978 feature film, *Superman* (aka *Superman: The Movie*), Christopher catapulted the Man of Steel role to new heights of mainstream visability.

When *Superman: The Movie* was released in 1978, it took Joel Eisenberg a while to get used to it. "Make no mistake," he says, "once I did I loved it and saw it repeatedly. But it took me some time to accept the 'Reeve' without the 's.' Why? Because my 14-year-old self did not believe Christopher Reeve was old enough to be a real 'Superman.' He was far too young, barely out of boyhood himself, I thought."

Time then changed his perspective, while his adulation of Reeves remained. "He is, was, and always will be 'Superman' to me," Eisenberg affirms. "George's Clark Kent was relatively serious, not at all campy, though *Adventures of Superman* adapted a more camp sensibility after its first two black and white seasons. While the subsequent color seasons added dimension and humor, George was still George in the dual role; Clark was still Clark and 'Supes' was still 'Supes'. . .thankfully."

Eisenberg heard early on from his parents what happened to Reeves in the end. He grew up with the suicide story before the questions became more public. When he saw *Gone with the Wind* for the first time on television, years after George passed away, he was "stunned to see my 'Superman' in another role" (and then, briefly, in his controversial, and drastically cut, scene in *From Here to Eternity*).

Eisenberg then put the pieces together and began to see why it would be difficult for Reeves to move forward with his career. He would be type-cast. For years he envisioned Reeves, in full Superman regalia, bursting through his living room shutters like he did for Little Ricky during his historic guest-star role on *I Love Lucy*. While that of course never transpired, Reeves did have a history of making similar, real-life appearances, which Eisenberg was happy to see. "George Reeves may have been complex and some say tortured," Eisenberg laments, "but neither diminishes the fact that this was a good man who left us far too soon."

As Steve Randisi concludes, "George Reeves did not live long enough to witness the lasting joy he brought to the world with his portrayal of Krypton's favorite son," and while the actor's real-life-ending adventure "remains one of Hollywood's most tantalizing mysteries, George Reeves, man and Superman, remains an iconic figure to millions."

57

Robert Conrad
The Wild Wild West/Baa Baa Black Sheep/
Black Sheep Squadron

I'm not debonair. I'm not suave. I did wear tight pants, though, because I found out that it worked.

—Robert Conrad

Whether in fiction or in reality, no male TV character of the 50s, 60s, and 70s came any tougher than Robert Conrad as James West on the unique sci-fi western, *The Wild Wild West*, which originally aired on CBS from 1965 to 1969.

The fact that Conrad portrayed a character named West on a series that was set in the Old West served both as a metaphor and as a wink to the program's loyal fan-base who came to love the show's frequent use of self-deprecating humor and style. As Conrad once said about the series, which displayed ingenious, whimsical stories, sets, props, and performances, "It was just so elaborate and so luxurious. We had every gadget imaginable . . . [like] the little gun that [popped] out of [West's] shoe."

The show arrived on TV just as the western genre was giving way to the spy game. In fact, according to Susan E. Kessler's book *The Wild Wild West: The Series*, show creator Michael Garrison once described it as "James Bond on horseback."

Television and media historian James Knuttel credits Conrad's appeal for *Wild*'s success, while comparing the actor's star quality to other small-screen male legends:

I liked Conrad as James West because the role required him to take on two types of heroes rolled into one: the stalwart westerner . . . such as Matt Dillon [as played by James Arness on *Gunsmoke*] and the suave spy/secret agent . . . such as Napoleon Solo [as played by Robert Vaughn on *The Man from U.N.C.L.E.*]. Conrad handled this superbly, being charming with the ladies and tough-as-nails with the bad guys, and he did it in the tongue-in-cheek manner that fit the mood of the series. Likewise, he was a handsome man who looked great in the somewhat dandified outfits that he wore . . . like silk vests, bolero-style jackets, and extremely tight-fitting pants. Add to that, of course, he possessed a muscular physique that made him well up to the challenge of doing a large among of stunt work.

Set during the administration of President Ulysses Grant (1869–1877), *Wild* covered the exploits of a Secret Service agent team headed by Conrad's West and Artemus Gordon, played with amusing aplomb by Ross Martin (and later, Charles Aidman as Jeremy Pike). They deciphered crimes and mysteries, protected the president, and thwarted the schemes of myriad evil opponents, scientists, and the like, each of whom was bent on conquering any or every part of America, if not the world (including the diminutive-in-size but masterfully talented Michael Dunne as the diabolical Dr. Lovelace).

The *Wild* series, with its significant fantasy qualities, and high-tech mechanisms (utilized by heroes and villains alike) became a stand-out TV entertainment showcase. The

use and display of Jules-Verne-like apparatuses, in particular, led some to christen the show as one of the more "visible" origins of the steampunk subculture. Such elements became even more pronounced in director Barry Sonnenfeld's 1999 feature film edition of the series that starred Will Smith and Kevin Kline; a movie that did not at all please Conrad. As the actor explained at the time, he never had anything against Smith. In fact, he once heralded the multitalented music and performing star of TV's *Prince of Bel-Air* as "cool." "My kids [even] have his CDs," Conrad gleamed.

Instead, he pinned what became the film's unsuccessful fate on Sonnenfeld, with whom he had met before the big picture was set in motion. "Barry let his ego go out of control," Conrad recalled. "[Sonnenfeld] told me that he had to do something to make it *his* film." To which the actor replied, "Well, Barry, it's your film. If it rises or falls, you're the man."

The movie fell. It was not the triumphant remake envisioned by anyone, critics or hardcore West fans, much less Sonnenfeld himself (who had faced a similar outcome with his failed attempt to redo ABC's 1977–1984 *Fantasy Island* series for the network's 1998-1999 season).

Conrad stuck to his guns, so to speak, and retained his bold bravado and stoic persona, off-screen. For, like James West, he was never one to back down from confrontation (as evidenced by his famous Eveready battery commercials from the 1980s).

Born Konrad Robert Falkowski on March 1, 1935, in Chicago, Illinois, Conrad attended Northwestern University. His parents were Leonard and Joan Falkowski. He was married twice: Joan Kenlay (from 1952 to 1977) and LaVelda Ione Fann (from 1977 to 2010). His children include: Christian, Nancy, Shane, and Joan Conrad (from first marriage); and Kaja, Camille, and Chelsea Conrad (from second marriage). Before playing James West on *Wild*, he portrayed Tom Lopaka for four seasons of the series *Hawaiian Eye* (1959–1963) and also on some "crossover" episodes of *77 Sunset Strip*. After *Wild*, he was deputy district attorney Paul Ryan for one season of the series *The D.A.* (1971-1972), and Nick Carter in the TV-movie *The Adventures of Nick Carter* (1972). He also later starred as Jake Webster for one season in the series *Assignment Vienna* (1972-1973), and found more consistent success as Major Greg "Pappy" Boyington for two seasons in the series *Baa Baa Black Sheep*, later retitled *The Black Sheep Squadron* (1976–1978).

After that, he was cast as French mountain man Pasquinel in the mini-series *Centennial* (1978-1979) and performed as Thomas Remington Sloane III for one season in the series *A Man Called Sloane* (1979). His last series role was that of Jesse Hawkes for one season in the series *High Mountain Rangers* (1987-1988).

As Conrad once assessed his tough persona, "They only see what I want them to see, what I'm selling—an image."

An iconic image that's held up well over time.

58

Adam West and Burt Ward
Batman

Ol' Chum.

—Batman, as played by Adam West, to Robin, as played by Burt Ward

One of the many positive aspects of classic television remains how the majority of such programming presented uplifting, happy characters. Certainly that is the case when it came to superhero characters like Batman and Robin, as portrayed in the mid-60s on TV with utter joyful precision by Adam West and Burt Ward. Minus the dark, edgy tone and the overt depression, anger, and conflict that embody today's superheroes (ignited in live action on the big screen with Tim Burton's initial 1989 *Batman* feature film), ABC's original live-action *Batman* TV series was played for fun and with satirical genius.

The series benefited immensely from West and Ward's superb twin take in the leads (and in their leotards!). Without them, the show, which debuted on ABC in 1966 and ran until 1968 (initially twice a week), would not have been the same.

According to Jeff Thompson, for many "Bat-fans of a certain age, the Bright Knight trumps the Dark Knight. Before the Caped Crusader returned to his somber roots in the 1970s, ABC-TV's *Batman* exploded with color and camp in the 1960s. At the forefront of this pop phenomenon was Adam West, who *was* and *is* Batman for many Baby Boomers. West appealed both to children, who hung on his every profound word and took *Batman* seriously, and to adults, who enjoyed the show's comedic and satirical elements that were obvious only to them. West as Batman gave a masterful performance of both dogmatic integrity and absurd hilarity. While their parents laughed, Boomer kids learned valuable lessons about safety and honesty from the actor who will always be known and loved as Adam *Batman* West."

As Thompson goes on to explain, Burt Ward held his own playing Robin, opposite West's Batman on their "phenomenal series that mixed earnestness and melodrama with comedy and satire." Ward's appeal, Thompson observes, stems from "his clean-cut looks, his youthful exuberance, and Robin's occasional inexperi-

Adam West, left; Burt Ward, right
Globe Photos

ence, which allowed Batman to teach him—and the young viewers—valuable life lessons. Burt Ward was so popular because he was playing the sidekick that many boys and girls wished *they* could be. Viewers' identification with Robin gave them a closer connection to the Caped Crusader himself. Although Ward and West's working relationship had its ups and downs, their on-screen chemistry as Dick and Bruce, Robin and Batman, was always strong, warm, and inspiring. Their latter-day reunion in *Return to the Batcave: The Misadventures of Adam and Burt* (CBS-TV, 2003) is not to be missed."

Podcaster John S. Drew offers his top pop-culture insight in the particular TV superhero category. "Adam West was, still is, and most likely will always be, my Batman. But more importantly, he will always be my Bruce Wayne. The fact is, as we have seen in other Batman movies, the cape and cowl can be put on anyone . . . even Michael Keaton . . . and the result is still someone convincing enough to resemble the comic book character."

Portraying Bruce Wayne, however, is another matter.

According to Drew, the host of the BatCavePodcast (and many other well-received multimedia shows), West embodies everything that defines Wayne's character. "He is tall, handsome, intelligent looking, and light enough in his presentation to show the difference between [him] and his alter ego."

As Drew sees it, the actor's performance as both characters was his guise. He acted one way as Batman and another as Bruce Wayne creating the illusion needed to fool Gotham City. And this ability served him well in both comedy and drama.

Whether West was playing the doomed captain in the 1964 cinema cult classic *Robinson Crusoe on Mars* or the hapless actor Lookwell in the 1991 satirical sitcom of the same name (written and produced by the comedic duo Conan O'Brien and Robert Smigel), Drew says Adam is a "more than capable actor, something not everyone has always appreciated."

With regard to Burt Ward's interpretation of Robin, as far as Drew is concerned, it was a role the then-teen-actor was "born to play." To help make his case, Drew suggests searching YouTube for the audition footage of Ward and West alongside the auditions by Lyle Wagner as Batman and Peter Deyell as Robin. While Wagner's Batman "might have proved interesting, Peter Deyell just doesn't hold a candle to Burt Ward. It's no wonder Ward may have gotten cocky though in those first months of filming the series. He looked like the character had burst from the pages of the comic. He fit the costume perfectly, better than Adam West did the Batman suit. He had the impressive guns for arms. Add to it the enthusiasm he brought to the role, even when his part was cut back to allow for Yvonne Craig as Batgirl in the show's third season, something he never once wavered in."

Other actors have voiced or played the part of Robin on TV and in theaters since the original *Batman* TV series ended, but as far as Drew is concerned, "None hold a candle to Burt Ward and I seriously doubt anyone ever will."

It doesn't even bother him that many Bat-fans labeled the 1960s TV series as "campy and silly" when it premiered or that it failed to take the caped hero seriously. "There is a great deal of argument that could be made about all that and the comics at the time."

For example, Drew even cites the TV edition of Alfred, millionaire Bruce Wayne's faithful butler who, as played by Alan Napier, "wasn't anything like the comics. Tall, lanky, and somewhat sarcastic at times, Alfred didn't always come across as the gentleman's gentleman as the comics portrayed him as far back as the forties. But Alan Napier made his impact on the role by giving him an air of realism in the insane world of Batman. In many respects, Alfred was us, acting like a Greek chorus, watching all of this and at times commenting on how silly or dangerous it all was. Whether it's his droll remarks about fetching Batman for [the] Commissioner [Gordon, as played by Neil Hamilton, alongside Stafford Repp as Chief O'Hara] as he answers the Bat-phone, or wondering if the life that the two heroes lead may be too dangerous, Alan

Napier injected a level of humanity and realism that took him beyond the comic character."

Drew says, "Napier did this on purpose," which the writers of the series immediately took to and worked into the show. In the end, for Drew, clearly a dedicated follower of all things Batman, Napier, as "the definitive Alfred," became the perfect fit alongside West as Batman and Ward as Robin.

For Joel Eisenberg, it was West who left a lasting bat-impression, reigning supreme in one sequence from the show's pilot, "Hi Diddle Riddle," when, as Batman, the actor performed the now-legendary "Batusi" dance (with guest-star Jill St. John) and once more in the second-season segment, "The Pharaoh's in a Rut." "That inspired a John Travolta dance, for crying out loud," Eisenberg muses.

"You remember it, of course, the one with Uma Thurman in Quentin Tarantino's *Pulp Fiction*," in which Travolta played and danced as Vincent Vega. "The index and middle fingers of each hand, twisting and then pulling away from the eyes . . . West did it first—and best. He was an original, that one. Neither Vinnie Barbarino [Travolta's character in *Welcome Back, Kotter*], nor Tony Manero [*Saturday Night Fever*], nor Danny Zuko [*Grease*] . . . nor Vincent Vega [Travolta's character from *Fiction*] in this case, ever had a chance of out 'Westing' Adam West. His Batman was enduring."

Eisenberg remembers when Tim Burton's initial *Batman* movie was released in 1989. Some of the original TV cast members reunited on a morning news broadcast show, including Cesar Romero, who played the Joker, Batman's number one foil on the 60s series. Eisenberg knew Romero, "a true gentlemen," from the Cauliflower Alley Club (an annual event frequented by notable pro boxers and wrestlers that both he and Romero attended every year back in the 80s). He says Romero and the original *Batman* TV cast discussed "oh so diplomatically" just how "dark" they felt the new Batman films had become. Retaining perspective, Eisenberg believes Burton's first *Batman* movie in particular was "actually a tipping point for superheroes on film. The times they were a-changing. Gone was the camp of the Adam West series. Frank Miller's legendary comic book miniseries 'The Dark Knight Returns' was a dark and horrifying vision of the character that the '89 film took to another level [as did] the subsequent films from there. Superheroes in comics and other media changed to a new shade of gray. Or black. And, for a long time, Bill Dozier's camp classic series became . . . irrelevant."

There were more than a few members of the general public who, like TV's original *Batman* cast, were not at all pleased with Burton's emerging *Batman* film franchise. "Parents and purists were aghast," adds Eisenberg. "We miss our Adam West

'Batman!'" they uttered in discontent. "This is no longer the 'Batman' we grew up with!"

As the years passed, Eisenberg says the original show was rediscovered by many in reruns. "Ill-fated 1970s reunions came and went. But then, the reruns continued as did the appreciation. Adam West became a convention fixture. Fans missed him. They missed the show. The missed the 'light.'"

Today, largely due to what Eisenberg calls "West's utterly charming performance as well as the show's durability," the original TV series' seasons continue in comic book format. "A nice, ironic twist."

"We all loved our Batman, Adam West," Eisenberg intones. "Today, through the continued wonders of that small box, it's as if he's never left."

West himself expresses his appreciation for the "hundreds of sincere letters and stories" he still receives on a regular basis "directly from Bat-fans."

"It is touching and amazing to see the influence our work has had with folks of all walks and persuasions," he says. "Many people tell me how the show changed their lives for the better. That's always good to hear in a troubled world. When I see tears in the eyes of a grown man telling me he had no father, that my Batman became his father and that he's now a police chief, I can't help but feel a little moved."

Another time, a female fan, who grew up watching the series, had once indicated to West how she was somehow later inspired to become a manager for the Internal Revenue Service. "That was a different kind of moment," West muses. "I didn't especially want my performance known for that."

When asked what it's like to be known as an icon, West continues with his trademark sense of humor (which he so perfectly incorporated into his most famous role), and concludes, "I can't lie . . . it does feel good. Sometimes I get a better table. But aren't icons usually older?"

59

Van Williams and Bruce Lee
The Green Hornet

> Always be yourself, express yourself, have faith in yourself; do not go out and
> look for a successful personality and duplicate it.
>
> —Bruce Lee

After *Bewitched* became a hit in its first season on ABC in 1964, NBC became interested in replicating that show's magic popularity with the similarly themed and also female-driven *I Dream of Jeannie*, which debuted the following year.

Such is usually the case on network television. Success in one genre usually breeds and begs repeating. The situation was no different with the ratings TV superhero hit *Batman*, the appeal of which networks started clamoring to copy with shows like *Mr. Terrific* (with Stephen Strimpell on CBS), and *Captain Nice* (starring William Daniels on NBC), both of which premiered January 9, 1967 (and aired only through the end of August of that same year). Then there was *The Green Hornet*.

Hornet, in fact, was brought aboard by *Batman* executive producer William Dozier for the same bat network, ABC in the same bat season (1966-1967). Like *Batman*, *Hornet* also featured a handsome lead, this time in the guise of Van Williams, who up until then, was best known as Ken Madison on TV's *Surfside 6* (1960–1962), which costarred Lee Patterson and Troy Donahue. At his side on *Hornet* was cast future martial arts legend Bruce Lee. Shortly after *Hornet's* brief run, Lee would return to TV again, as yet another sidekick, so to speak, this time to James Franciscus, on yet another short-lived series, ABC's *Longstreet*.

Longstreet debuted as a TV-movie in 1971, one year before David Carradine was cast in the ninety-minute pilot TV-film for *Kung Fu*, the producers for which rejected Lee as the lead (for being *too* tough). Consequently, Lee left American entertainment, and returned to his homeland China, where he became a star in international martial arts films.

But before that, Williams and Lee teamed on *The Green Hornet*, with Williams playing lead to Lee's right-hand man Kato. As Professor Thompson observes:

> Although Van Williams had appeared on *Bourbon Street Beat, Surfside Six,* and *The Tycoon* before 1966, he made his indelible mark that year as the Green Hornet in a series that really should have run longer than one season. Williams's elegant looks and a hard edge that came across in the Green Hornet's body language and voice combined to make Williams convincing and exciting as both the wealthy Britt Reid and the vengeful Green Hornet. Williams always played his dual role straight and seriously—even when he appeared in three episodes (one cameo and a two-parter) of the outrageous *Batman* series. Van Williams's Green Hornet was more like George Reeves's Superman than Adam West's Batman.

According to TVRage.com, Williams was born Van Zant Jarvis Williams, on February 27, 1934, in Fort Worth, Texas. True to his homeland, he had planned to become a cattle rancher, as that was his family's business (he had studied animal husbandry and business at Texas Christian University).

After an early marriage went south, he flew to Hawaii, where he found work as a driving instructor. One of his clients was Mike Todd, the third of six husbands of Elizabeth Taylor, who suggested he utilize his charismatic assets in Hollywood, where Williams eventually landed (after a back injury curtailed other options). As a result, he soon began making guest appearances on various TV series.

Warner Bros. produced many crime dramas, most modeled after their very successful *77 Sunset Strip* show. Williams was cast in one, *Bourbon Street Beat*, with veteran actors Andrew Duggan and Richard Long. The show only lasted one season, but executive producer William Orr took Van's character, Ken Madison, and moved him from the French Quarter of New Orleans to a Miami Beach houseboat, and renamed the show *Surfside 6*, which teamed Van with Lee Patterson and young heartthrob Troy Donahue. While this series only lasted two years, it established Williams as a handsome leading man who could effectively do both drama and comedy, including a guest appearance on *The Dick Van Dyke Show* (playing a former boyfriend to Mary Tyler Moore's Laura Petrie).

By this time, Williams was a husband and a father. He and wife, Vicki, whom he married on New Year's Eve 1959, had a family to care for. Somewhat disgruntled with the instability of acting, Williams began funneling his TCU education and investing his earnings in business and real estate. However, he still continued to act in TV shows like *The Tycoon* (with Walter Brennan).

The role that Williams is best known for came in 1966, when *Batman* producer Dozier decided to bring another comic book crimefighter to life. Williams was cast as newspaper publisher Britt Reid, who fought crime under the name The Green Hornet. To play the role of Kato (which *Kung*

Bruce Lee, left; Van Williams, right
Globe Photos

Fu's Keye Luke had played in two movie serials in the 1940s), Dozier cast the then-unknown Bruce Lee.

The Green Hornet was a success, if with a few issues. Williams felt the thirty-minute format did not allow the series to fully develop the core mythology. The result: The *Hornet* show nested for only twenty-six installments.

Williams continued to act, but his roles were sparse. He starred in a final series—a Saturday morning children's show called *Westwind*—and made a few other TV spots (such as a segment of *Gunsmoke* in 1975, which he considers one of his personal best), and rejected others (like a semi-regular role on TV's *Falcon Crest*). Following a bit part on *The Rockford Files* in 1979, he quit acting, if only to make a cameo in the 1993 Bruce Lee biopic, *Dragon: The Bruce Lee Story*, playing the director of *The Green Hornet*.

During the run of the actual *Hornet* series in 1966, Williams sought more screen time for Lee, both to help his friend, costar, and martial-arts instructor, and to give the show a lift by increasing the visibility of its most popular cast member. But the producers didn't want to deflect attention toward a nonwhite actor. After the series ended, he spent several months a year in Southern California as a reserve deputy with the Malibu station of the Los Angeles County Sheriff's Department.

Williams lives in Ketchum, Idaho, where his neighbor is *Batman* star Adam West. He has three children with wife Vicki, whom he met in Hawaii where she was a surfing pro. He also has twin daughters from a prior marriage.

Lee, meanwhile, died tragically on July 20, 1973, at only age thirty-two, of an accidental shooting during the filming of what became his final martial arts movie: *Enter the Dragon*, released the year of his demise. He left behind two children: Shannon and Brandon Lee, the latter of whom also met a grim death by an accidental shooting at a young age (28) on what would be his last martial arts movie (*The Crow*, 1994). Adding further to the irony was that a few years before, in 1986, Brandon had costarred with David Carradine in the CBS *Kung Fu* TV-reunion film, *Kung Fu: The Movie*. It was a twisted bit of casting, of course, as Lee had originally auditioned for the role of Caine on the original *Kung Fu* series (which was co-created by Ed Spielman and Howard Friedlander, and not by Bruce Lee or the show's producer Jerry Thorpe as has been erroneously reported in the past).

Original *Kung Fu* star Radames Pera shares his thoughts on it all:

Some people say Bruce Lee should have starred in *Kung Fu*, but as has been fairly documented in the past, ABC didn't think the U.S. was ready for "an Asian" in such a leading role. Though they were short-sighted from a cultural perspective, I'm also not so sure Mr. Lee, clearly an innovator and someone much closer to the character himself in terms of inner and outer training, could have brought the subtlety and nuance to the performance that David Carradine did. Certainly the "kung-fu phenomenon" of the era, nor its lasting legacy, would have happened without the one-two punch of the U.S. TV series combined with Bruce's Chinese films. It had to go this way for the greater good. This also paved the way for Brandon Lee, an even better actor than his dad, completing some pretty deep family karma by working alongside David in *Kung Fu: The Movie*. No doubt the two of them learned from each other.

Joel Eisenberg, "a huge fan" of Bruce Lee's films (especially *Enter the Dragon*, as well as 1972's *The Chinese Connection*) had for years believed the reason Bruce Lee died so young was because he "transcended man's physical limitations."

"No kidding," he says. "I was convinced. No one else on the planet could throw so fast a kick or so speedy a punch; no one had ever before exhibited so feral a presence. He became a legend for a reason. He died a legend for a reason and his legend grew still over time. For a reason."

"Before the legend," as Eisenberg puts it, there was a series of early films he made as a child actor in Hong Kong, followed years later by his work on *The Green Hornet*.

Van Williams played the Hornet lead with what Eisenberg calls "a straight-arrow's seriousness and worldly charm," while Lee's "Kato was to be his cohort."

"Turned out," Eisenberg clarifies, "most would say it was the other way around." When Kato fought Burt Ward's Robin in a two-part episode of *Batman*, Eisenberg rooted for Kato. "He was just too cool, too slick and deadly."

Lee's Kato wasn't the costar of *Batman*, as was Ward's Robin, so Eisenberg "had to settle for a *draw*" between the two co-leading characters.

That outcome was somewhat unsettling for Eisenberg, but as he goes on to convey, the moment did not taint his or the world's adulation for Lee:

Bruce was a remarkable athlete, a remarkable performer and a remarkable philosopher. One couldn't help but take him seriously. His influence was supposed to live on, so many years later, in his son Brandon who, like his dad, was gifted with an unnatural charisma. Also like his dad, his death caused him to leave the mortal coil much too early. Some called it *The 'Curse' of the Dragon*, as if any scion of Bruce was fated to an equally untimely end. Regardless, such tragedy only added to the legacy of the family name. Thankfully, however, today Bruce's daughter Shannon carries on her family's tradition of achievement. Shannon continues to thrive as a successful businesswoman and, along with Linda Lee Cadwell, Bruce's widow, ensures that the spirits of her father and her brother will never be forgotten.

60

William Shatner, Leonard Nimoy, and DeForest Kelley
Star Trek

I have found that having is not so pleasing a thing as wanting. It is not logical, but often true.

> —Mr. Spock, as played by Leonard Nimoy in *Star Trek*
> (Episode: "Amok Time")

In original *Star Trek* TV lore they are known as the Triad of Logic, Emotion, and Stability. Or as the Vulcan high priestess in *Star Trek: The Motion Picture* might have said, "Separate yet together."

The sacred troika is best remembered from the initial NBC *Trek* television series, which first aired for only seventy-nine episodes from 1966 to 1969. It was on this show that the world was introduced to William Shatner as Captain James T. Kirk, the stoic leader and median balance point between Leonard Nimoy's computer-minded alien Mr. Spock (from the planet Vulcan) and DeForest Kelley's impassioned American country doctor Leonard "Bones" McCoy. Although Kelley's McCoy was not considered as big a sex symbol as Shatner's Kirk or Nimoy's Spock, he still achieved a significant measure of popularity in the realm of show creator Gene Roddenberry's creative universe.

But it is still Shatner and Nimoy who are best remembered in the mainstream psyche of pop culture. "Two brave men, soul brothers who seem worlds apart yet whose unity has been forged in the fire of danger and whose mission is to go where no one has gone before." Such is the way Kirk and Spock are described in the book, *The 100*

Most Influential People Who Never Lived. Although Kirk and Spock are today portrayed by actors Chris Pine and Zachary Quinto, respectively, in the big-screen *Trek* reincarnated franchise (ignited by J. J. Abrams in 2009), it was Shatner and Nimoy who introduced the heroic characters to millions of small-screen viewers.

Larry Brody worked with both original *Trek* actors on NBC's animated *Star Trek* series, which aired from 1973 to 1975 on Saturday mornings. He shares his unique insight into Shatner and Nimoy, Kirk and Spock, even mind-melding slightly Shatner's Kirk with Kelley's McCoy by way of emotion:

> In person, Nimoy was reserved in that special way that good actors are, a watcher more than a participant, cordial to this particular stranger but far from effusive. Shatner, on the other hand, was filled with smiles and hugs and seemed ready and willing to become my best pal the minute we were introduced.
>
> Their characters were wonderful together. Yin and yang, Brain and emotion. And, to be honest, I found Kirk's idealism and fervor far more appealing than Spock's rationality . . . and I think that part of my own personality was molded by the effect the two characters had on me.

Television historian Ed Robertson, co-author with Judith Barath of *The Ethics of Star Trek,* breaks down *Trek*'s core threesome with a focus on Shatner's Kirk as the most significant performance/character—in the male sector—of the *Trek* universe:

> James T. Kirk was like Jim West and John Wayne rolled into one, a classic American cowboy hero in the world of outer space. Of the five *Star Trek* captains, he was clearly the most impulsive—he was "shoot first, ask questions later"—and while he respected The Prime Directive as ultimate law, he had no problem violating it in the interests of justice or morality, depending on the circumstances. Though a bit of a rogue at times, he was a charming leader with the courage of his convictions and a compassion that extended to not just his crew, but other civilizations. (Then again, Kirk could afford to be impulsive, knowing that he could rely on the wisdom of Spock and McCoy to balance him out when necessary.)
>
> One of Shatner's best performances on *Star Trek* was in "The Enemy Within," the episode that took the divided nature of Kirk to the ultimate extreme. For all the physical bravado that Shatner brought to the show, his ability to convey Kirk's utter helplessness—his inability to make a decision, at a moment when the lives of Sulu and the others lie in the balance—speaks to his depth as an actor.
>
> Though he'll always be known for playing Captain Kirk, Shatner owes his longevity to his ability to reinvent himself. This is particularly true in the case of *T.J.*

Hooker, a show that arrived at a pivotal time in the actor's career. Typecast throughout the 1970s, Shatner leaped at the opportunity to play a tough, conservative police officer—a character who, in many respects, was the polar opposite of James T. Kirk. That proved to be a shrewd decision. The success of *Hooker*, coupled with that of *Star Trek II: The Wrath of Khan*, rejuvenated Shatner's career.

"Depending on the day of the week," either *Star Trek* or *The Six Million Dollar Man* was Joel Eisenberg's favorite television show during his formative years. Both have since become his perennial treasures but regarding *Trek* in particular, "if it wasn't for those three central performances from Shatner, Nimoy, and Kelley," and despite the script quality, Eisenberg might "not have cared as much."

Upon viewing the original series episode "The Enemy Within," Eisenberg says Shatner set the stage for the series.

In "Enemy," Shatner played what Eisenberg calls "a good Kirk and a bad Kirk. I've always said among the qualities of a fearless leader needs to be an element of danger. *The. Shatner. Pauses.* I could never figure what was going on in this actor's head, nor did I have any doubt why he was cast. I would never cross him. Today, Shatner is in his 80s (born March 22, 1931) and working more than ever. No surprise. He is charismatic as hell, and supremely underrated as an actor. *Pauses. Aside.* When he's on-screen, you can never look away."

William Shatner, left; DeForest Kelley, center; Leonard Nimoy, right
NBC/PhotoFest

With regard to Nimoy (born March 26, 1931; died February 27, 2015), Eisenberg references one of the actor's early memoirs, titled *I Am Not Spock*, in which he tried at length to distance himself from his most celebrated role. "Then," as Eisenberg continues to decipher, "when he accepted the fan adulation a bit more, he wrote a follow-up: *I Am Spock*. He asked the producers to kill him off in *The Wrath of Khan*, the second of the *Trek* feature films. Then, second-guessing occurred, [and] they added a shot where he mind-melded McCoy and he said, 'Remember. . .' and yep, he was back for *The Search for Spock*, the next film."

Nimoy clearly had a love-hate relationship with the role that lasted for years. But to Eisenberg, "he will always be Spock. . .and many other things: A Jewish scholar, a director, a photographer . . . a father and husband. He reminded me a good deal of an uncle of mine. I trusted Spock and so I instinctively trusted the actor who portrayed him."

Eisenberg relates a Nimoy/Spock–related anecdote that transpired right before his bar-mitzvah, when his parents invited their rabbi to the apartment for dinner. "We showed him around the house; he saw my big blacklight velvet poster of Mr. Spock on my wall and said, 'Ah, Dr. Spock. I like him.' I turned to the rabbi, aggravated, and said, calmly, 'Rabbi, Dr. Spock is a baby doctor. 'Mr.' Spock is a Vulcan and he's on a TV show called *Star Trek*.'"

Eisenberg still hasn't forgiven him. Why? Because his rabbi insulted one of his favorite actors. "Leonard Nimoy was many things," he muses, "but a 'baby doctor' wasn't one of them."

That label may have periodically been pinned on Dr. Leonard "Bones" McCoy, as played by the late, great DeForest Kelley (born January 20, 1920; died June 11, 1999). As far as Eisenberg is concerned, anything Kelley's McCoy did on *Star Trek* became "instantly memorable" in the psyche of American pop culture, certainly his "I'm a doctor, not a [fill-in-the-blank]!" lines linger through time and space immortal.

"It wasn't so much the character, the good ol' country boy doctor," Eisenberg clarifies. "It was DeForest Kelley himself. Humorous . . . a natural . . . a crank. His interplay with Nimoy and Shatner was both touching and hysterical. Kelley was a remarkable talent."

While Eisenberg can hear the rebel yell now ("I'm a doctor, not an actor!"), he heralds Kelley as "more than an actor. He was an icon for a reason. Anyone who can interact with a green-skinned Vulcan and a hyper macho captain—and hold his own—was okay in my book.

"I wish he was my physician growing up," Eisenberg concludes. "If DeForest Kelley laid it all on the line for me, like he did with Kirk and Spock, I would have trusted him implicitly." As would all who appreciate the media machismo brought to the science fiction/fantasy mainstream by way of *Star Trek*'s holy trio of William Shatner, DeForest Kelley, and Leonard Nimoy.

61

Bill Bixby
My Favorite Martian/The Courtship of Eddie's Father/
The Magician/The Incredible Hulk

Lou Ferrigno
The Incredible Hulk

Brandon!

—Bill Bixby, utterly surprised upon seeing former *Courtship of Eddie's Father*
costar Brandon Cruz on *The Arsenio Hall Show* in 1989

The Incredible Hulk is a big deal on the contemporary big screen, with a reigning popularity that originally stemmed from the unending creative resources of the masterful Marvel comic man Stan Lee. In the last decade or so, Bruce Banner, aka, the Hulk, has been portrayed in motion pictures by Eric Bana, Ed Norton, and Mark Ruffalo.

Introduced to the mainstream media by way of Marvel's comic book, the Hulk made a brief animated appearance on Saturday morning television in the mid-1960s, and then resurfaced with a live-action primetime series in the 70s starring Bill Bixby and bodybuilding champion Lou Ferrigno.

As Rick Lertzman explains, Bixby had for years been a TV staple, a decade before his co-existence with Ferrigno on the *Hulk* TV show that went on to delightfully shake the ratings and TV viewers with green goo and glee:

Bill parlayed his good looks into roles as a leading man with his likeable, amiable presence on television and films for over thirty years. His long television career began with his costarring role as Tim O'Hara [with Ray Walston, an icon in his own right] in the 1960s fantasy classic, *My Favorite Martian*. He followed that as the suave, hip father Tom Corbett in popular *The Courtship of Eddie's Father* in the late 1960s. He then starred in *The Magician* [in the mid-70s] followed by his portrayal as scientist, Dr. David Banner in *The Incredible Hulk*. He was also a popular director of several [later] shows [including *Blossom*] until his untimely death [from prostate cancer] in 1993.

Bill Bixby
NBC/Globe Photos

According to www.imdb.com, Bill was born Wilfred Bailey Bixby on January 22, 1934, in San Francisco, the sixth generation son of a sales clerk and a department store owner. An only child raised by his mother Jane Bixby and same-named father in the 40s and 50s, he attended schools in the same area, and took ballroom dance lessons, before attending Lowell High School, where he excelled in drama. Following his high shcool graduation, he attended San Francisco City College, where he majored in drama. He transferred to the University of California–Berkeley, where he focused on pre-law, but remained interested in acting. After almost graduating, he moved to Los Angeles, where he worked as a lifeguard and a bellhop.

In 1959 two showbiz executives noticed him and hired him instantly for commercial work and modeling in Detroit, Michigan, where he also auditioned for stage roles. He eventually joined the Detroit Civic Theatre Company, making his professional live debut in the musical *The Boy Friend*, while appearing in commercials.

He made his TV debut in an episode of *The Many Loves of Dobie Gillis* (1959), followed by guest performances on programs like *The Joey Bishop Show* (1961), which ultimately led to his being cast in *My Favorite Martian*.

Bixby married three times: Brenda Benet (from 1971 to 1980, when she committed suicide after the death of their son Christopher Bixby), Laura Jane Michael (1990-1991), and Judith Kilban (1993).

Lou Ferrigno
Globe Photos

As documented on Lou Ferrigno's official website, Bixby's hulking costar was born Louis Jude Ferrigno November 9, 1951, in Brooklyn to Victoria and Matty Ferrigno, who was with the police force. Once an International Federation of Bodybuilding and Fitness (IFBB) Mr. America and a two-time winner of IFBB's Mr. Universe title, Lou is now retired from bodybuilding and serves as a motivational speaker and fitness trainer/consultant. He also is still very much an actor, a career formally ignited with *The Incredible Hulk*, following his screen debut in the classic 1977 body-building documentary movie, *Pumping Iron*.

Ferrigno's filmography also includes many European-produced fantasy/adventure productions like *Hercules* (1983) and *Sinbad of the Seven Seas* (1989), as well as 2009's *I Love You, Man*. Beyond his role as the *Hulk*, Lou's TV appearances include the NBC reality series *Celebrity Apprentice* and a semi-regular role on the long-running CBS comedy *The King of Queens*.

Beginning in 1988 with *The Incredible Hulk Returns*, Ferrigno reunited with Bixby for a trilogy of TV reunion movies that ended with *The Death of the Incredible Hulk* in 1990. Beyond that, he provided the voice for the mid-1990s *Hulk* animated series, and the partial voiceover work (in the form of his legendary Hulk grunts) in the recent Marvel feature films.

He's been married twice, first briefly to Susan Groff from 1978 to 1979 and since 1980 to Carla Ferrigno. He has three children: Shannon, Brent, and Louis Ferrigno Jr.

62

David Carradine and Radames Pera
Kung Fu

> I don't need to convince anybody that I know kung-fu. But maybe somebody needs to know that I really can act, without doing a Chinese accent or a funny walk.
>
> —David Carradine

Peggy Herz said that casting David Carradine as Kwai Chang Caine on *Kung Fu* was "a stroke of genius." David, who died tragically on June 3, 2009, in Bangkok, Thailand, was part of the legendary Carradine acting family, which included film star father John Carradine and brother Keith Carradine, both of whom performed with David on *Kung Fu*. John appeared in two episodes as a Presbyterian preacher who lost his sight, and Keith played Caine in the mid-years between David's thirtysomething Caine and young "Grasshopper," as played by Radames Pera (who went on to play John Jr. on TV's *Little House on the Prairie*).

Today, Pera is married to Anne-Sophie Pera since 2015 (previously wed to Marsha Ann Polekoff, 1984 to 2013). And he's still acting and directing. He recalls working with Carradine and the delicate dance surrounding the kind of success that a monumental show like *Kung Fu* creates: "I loved David and observed his struggles with fame as he attempted to live a countercultural lifestyle while working a strict schedule under contract to a couple of giant corporations [Warner Bros. and ABC]. Such a contradiction is simply not sustainable and at one point he decided to sabotage his career, and certainly the show's ratings, by making headlines for an arrest after an LSD-fueled mini-rampage through his Hollywood Hills neighborhood. I always found him more approachable in between bouts of notoriety when his ego was less inflamed. His untimely demise years later followed a pattern of self-abuse and metaphorically playing with fire. Though saddened for his family and fans, I wasn't as shocked, only hoping to glean more about how *not* to blow it like that myself."

Born December 8, 1936, in Hollywood, and later attending several prestigious schools on both American coasts, Carradine spent two years at San Francisco College, where he majored in music. His first taste of acting was at the Theater of the Golden Hind in Berkeley. According to Herz, that seemed to be "just what he was looking for." He quit college to join a few friends in staging a production of William Shakespeare's *Othello* in a little theater in San Francisco. The actor was, as he once said, "one of the first hippies," and periodically was employed in odd jobs (such as selling sewing machines and encyclopedias) while perfecting his craft.

After relocating back to Southern California, he started playing guitar in coffee-houses, only soon to be drafted by the army and, for two years, stationed in Fort Eustis, Virginia. While on leave, he married Donna Brecht, whom he had met while attending high school in Oklahoma, and they had a daughter. After his discharge from the service, he played Laertes in *Hamlet* in Paramus, New Jersey, where an agent noticed him and signed him to a contract. This led to guest appearances on TV shows like *The Armstrong Circle Theatre; East Side, West Side; Wagon Train;* and *The Virginian.*

David Carradine, left; John Carradine, right
Globe Photos

Carradine returned to the New York stage and performed in plays like *The Deputy* and *The Royal Hunt of the Sun*, after which he was cast in the lead for *Shane*, a 1966 TV western eerily similar to the 1972–1975 *Kung Fu* series, if loosely based on the 1953 feature film of the same name. Shane sounded like Caine. Both characters were mysterious quiet types, with one early episode of *Shane* even featuring a dream-type sequence with guest-star Keye Luke, who would frequently appear in flashback episodes of *Kung Fu* as Caine's favorite martial arts monk Master Po (who was blind). But while the *Shane* series was about a gunfighter who helped farmers, and *Kung Fu* was about a man of peace who would also at times assist farmers, or anyone else in need, *Shane* did not capture an audience like *Kung Fu* would later do for three seasons, and lost its battle in the ratings after a mere seventeen weeks on the air. Consequently, David once more returned to performing in off-Broadway plays.

By the time Carradine was cast as Caine in the 1972 pilot TV-movie for *Kung Fu*, he was living in a cabin in the Hollywood Hills, where he painted, wrote, and composed music. He also studied martial arts and, as *Kung Fu* became first a monthly, then weekly series, he sought to incorporate more action sequences into the show—a development that, strangely enough, ultimately worked against the very precepts of the series.

Kung Fu was about a young Shaolin monk who escaped his homeland in China to the American Old West, where he was sought as a fugitive for murdering the Chinese Royal Emperor's nephew who had killed a relatively vulnerable Master Po. The first two seasons of the series focused on Caine's journeys in the West, with flashbacks to his days in China while at the Shaolin Temple. He would only employ his martial arts as a last resort to save the day. By the third season, most of the episodes were set in the Temple of the past, and Caine was seen more frequently utilizing his martial arts skills throughout each episode, minus the slow-motion special effects producers of the show had used to help tone down the violence. As a result, *Kung Fu* lost its original charm and was cancelled by the spring of 1975.

The series lasted only three seasons because, according to what Carradine relayed in *The Kung Fu Book of Caine*, that was his plan all along. "I never wanted to have the series last any longer than that," he said, despite how perfectly cast he was as Caine—a physical role for which his training as a dancer helped him. As to his basic theatrical skills, he told Herz, "Most actors spend a lot of time training themselves to be an actor. And I kind of didn't do that. I just started doing it in front of an audience and had to deliver."

As Michael Cole previously declared about playing Pete Cochran on *The Mod Squad*, Kwai Chang Caine was a role David Carradine was seemingly born to play, although the actor said he'd also thought he would have been a "great Alexander the Great." His demise was controversial, but he once said he never feared death, which he merely defined as an "inconvenience. I have a lot of undone things and it's bound to get in the way. But, no, it doesn't scare me at all."

After *Kung Fu* finished its original run, Carradine went on to appear in motion pictures like *Bound for Glory* (1976, in which he played musician Woody Guthrie);

Radames Pera

Courtesy of Radames Pera

the 1985 TV-reunion film, *Kung Fu: The Movie*; the syndicated sequel series, *Kung Fu: The Legend Continues* (1993–1997); and in the years shortly before he died, *Kill Bill, Volumes 1* (2003) and *2* (2004), both directed by Quentin Tarantino (a huge fan of David's original *Kung Fu* series).

Besides Donna Brecht, to whom Carradine was wed between 1960 and 1968, his wives included Linda Ann Gilbert (1977–1983), Gail Jensen (1986–1997), Marina Anderson (1998–2001), Annie Bierman (2004–2009), while for a time, his unmarried partner was Barbara Hershey (1969–1975), who had also guest-starred on *Kung Fu* (as a female monk). He and Hershey had a son named Free Carradine at birth (born 1972), but who has since changed his name to Tom. David also has two daughters Calista (born 1962) and Kansas (born 1978). Radames Pera nicely sums up the lasting appeal of both his and Carradine's interpretation of Kwai Chang Caine, the life lessons he learned from additional *Kung Fu* actors Keye Luke (who played the visually impaired Master Po), and Philip Ahn (Master Kan), while also addressing his second most famous TV role: John, Jr. on *Little House on the Prairie*:

I was honored to have been a part of two great television Westerns (well, okay, one was an Eastern Western), *Kung Fu* and *Little House on the Prairie*. Both of these shows spoke to the challenges of walking with integrity and putting a set of principles at the center of one's existence.

In *Kung Fu*, Young Caine is an orphaned half-American, half-Chinese monk who represents the innocent seeker inside us all, homing in on the most pertinent questions of human existence: What is love? What is honesty? What is fear? Discerning reality from illusion. The adult Caine takes these lessons learned in the monastery and puts them into practice. The audience shares in his existential dilemmas as he draws from a well of inner strength to do the right thing, taking [control] when needed and also knowing when inaction is best. His universal appeal is as an icon who humbly points the way to a life worth living—and I believe this is why Grasshopper stands the test of time.

From Keye Luke, the sublime, beloved Master Po . . . whom I believe was the inspiration for Yoda [from the *Star Wars* film franchise, which premiered one year after *Kung Fu* was cancelled], I learned what it meant to carry one's self with genuine dignity, to be a consummate professional under great discomfort (those white eyes were large *hard* contact lenses in the early 70s!) and perhaps most importantly to extend the health of my largest organ, my skin, by staying in the shade whenever possible!

A couple of years later, I portrayed the recurring John Jr. on *Little House*. That character, like Caine, also orphaned after his mom [played by the classic film actress Patricia Neal] passes, was a seeker, too. Observing and expressing nature's beauty as a writer/poet John strives to do the right thing, but inadvertently gets disconnected from his roots and loses his way in the confused values of Big City living. He's another archetype relevant to many who genuinely pursue their dreams but who don't realize when they've gone astray.

Lee Majors
The Six Million Dollar Man

The Six Million Dollar Man was one thing. But I wanted to keep my own parts.

—Lee Majors

The TV superhero series was all but dead before Lee Majors reconstructed the genre as half-man/half-machine Steve Austin with expensive, government-funded superhuman "bionic" parts (right arm, two legs, left eye) as *The Six Million Dollar Man*. Based on the science fiction novel *Cyborg* by Martin Caidin, *Six Mill* (as it was known to those who worked on the show), like David Carradine's *Kung Fu* series, began on ABC as a 1973 TV-movie, which spun into monthly ninety-minute installments (produced by Glen A. Larson), then weekly sixty-minute segments (supervised by Harve Bennett, who saved the original *Star Trek* feature film franchise). Originally airing from March 7, 1973, to March 6, 1978, *Six Mill* in turn not only inspired a weekly female edition of itself (starring Lindsay Wagner as Jaime Sommers, *The Bionic Woman*—who cost only five million dollars because her parts were smaller; and costarring Richard Anderson as Oscar Goldman, Steve and Jaime's boss who appeared on both *Man* and *Woman*), but once ABC ignited its cybernetic craze, characters with other superpowers started surfacing on all the networks.

ABC first aired a version of *Wonder Woman* set in the 1940s, but CBS took over and transplanted the exploits of Diana Prince to the 1970s. *The Incredible Hulk* and *Spiderman* also both aired on CBS—which expanded its live-action superhero programming to Saturday morning with *Shazam* (featuring Captain Marvel, as played by Jackson Bostwick and John Davey) and *Isis* (starring Joanna Cameron who had once guest-starred on *The Six Million Dollar Man*). ABC also added to the Saturday morning live-action wonder set with shows like *Electra Woman* and *Dyna Girl* (starring *Days of Our Lives* actress Deidra Hall, and *Room 222*'s Judy Strangis in the respective leads). But it was Lee Majors as bionic man Steve Austin (rebuilt "stronger, faster, better") who started it all.

Popular pop-culture podcaster John S. Drew hosts *The Batcave Podcast*, *The Shazam/Isis Podcast*, *The OSI Files*, *The Home Game Show Podcast*, and *The Chronic Rift*. He also served as moderator for the Bionic Reunion, featuring Majors, Wagner, and Anderson, at the 2015 Mid-Atlantic Nostalgic Convention, which was held at the Hunt Valley Wyndham Hotel in Hunt Valley, Maryland.

Globe Photos

Like many *Six Million Dollar Man* fans, Drew, as a child, "tried desperately to emulate" Majors' portrayal of Austin. He doesn't just mean moving in slow motion, as though he were bionic, and mimicking the special visual and sound effects that were utilized on the series. Drew's fandom for Majors reached beyond the average Austin antics. Even though he found himself dressing (in tan and beige clothing) and parting his hair (to the right) as Lee's Austin was often seen on *Six Mill*, Drew was generally "fascinated" with Majors' general appearance. The future podcaster believed the actor's look served him well for every TV show in which he performed, be it Austin, or his previous role as Heath Barkely on *The Big Valley* (ABC, 1965–1969), as Jess Brandon on *Owen Marshall, Counselor at Law* (ABC, 1971–1974), or later, as Colt Seavers on *The Fall Guy* (ABC, 1981–1986). As Drew explains, besides Brandon on *Marshall*, Majors frequently seemed to portray the interloper. "Heath was the bastard child, trying to be accepted but still being his own man . . . Steve Austin struggled with keeping his humanity while dealing with his bionic limbs. And Colt Seavers was an older man trying to make it in a world where the stuntman was not as respected as he should be. There's a common theme in all his shows—the outsider."

All of which resonated with Drew. "As a kid growing up, I felt like the outsider myself and Lee Majors as any of his characters was one to give me hope because even though he was the outsider, he still maintained a dignity that served him well. I honestly can say that part of my moral compass was directed by his manner . . . as well as my fashion sense."

Joel Eisenberg can relate on a similar level. When he was a teen he, too, wanted to be Colonel Steve Austin, *The Six Million Dollar Man*. He ran track in high school and had the show's theme song running through his head during all of the exercises. When he began his writing career, Austin figured prominently in some of his early fan fiction.

Like Drew, Eisenberg dressed like the Austin character. "What style! What grace! Leisure suits became my second skin," he joyfully admits. As he matured, however, the future-scribe realized why he appreciated the *Six Mill* series. Again, like Drew, it wasn't so much the character of Steve Austin, as it was the actor Lee Majors who portrayed the role.

Eisenberg explains:

During the 1970s, there were many macho guys on television with porn star mustaches and grizzly bear chests. Lee Majors, I believed then as now, put so much of "himself" in the role, it was no accident he inspired millions of young fans around the globe. He was macho without being threatening, strong and yet possessed of a monster-sized heart. A down to earth Midwest guy who could steal your girlfriend and lift cars with one hand. If it wasn't for Lee, who somehow made these qualities "believable," the series would not have lasted for as long as it has, nor have had half the impact.

A closer look at Majors's life history may provide some insight into the strong impression he made on many of his loyal fans, as well as the "loner" aspect that be brought to Steve Austin and his other most famous TV roles.

Born Harvey Lee Yeary II on April 23, 1939, in Wyandotte, Michigan, Majors was raised in Middlesboro, Kentucky. Like his most famous TV counterpart Steve Austin, Lee's biological father died when he was an infant. By the age of three, he lost his biological mother as well and was adopted (which he didn't discover until he was twelve). As an adult, the not-yet-aspiring actor arrived in Los Angeles with the initial intent to become a high school football coach. In Middlesboro, he was a star athlete in high school and a member of the Kentucky All-State Football team. His physical agility earned him an athletic scholarship to the University of Indiana.

Shortly after his arrival at Indiana, the actor sustained a serious injury and was kept out of competition for the next three years. He moved closer to home, to Eastern Kentucky State, for his senior year, where he resumed his football training in earnest. That's where the St. Louis Cardinals spotted him and made an offer.

But his professional sports career fell by the wayside when he became a Hollywood film extra, and his interest in acting increased. Among the auditions that beckoned: a chance to play Heath Barkley, the illegitimate son of Barbara Stanwyck, matriarch of the old Western TV family on *The Big Valley*. Lee not only won the role, but his soft-spoken, attractive, confident, and polite manner beat out over four hundred additional aspirants.

While performing in *Valley*, Lee made his feature film debut in 1968's minor classic, *Will Penny*, starring Charlton Heston and Joan Hackett. In 1970 ABC reworked the premise of a creaky NBC western called *The Virginian* and transformed it into *The Men from Shiloh*, on which Lee was hired as a regular. *Shiloh* survived only one season on the TV plain, and Lee was swiftly cast as Jess Brandon, a contemporary attorney on *Owen Marshall: Counselor At Law* (starring Arthur Hill, it was the crossover legal cousin to producer David Victor's *Marcus Welby, M.D.* medical show, which also aired on ABC).

John S. Drew explains *Marshall*'s supporting cast history that involves not only Majors, but fellow male TV icons Reni Santoni (who went on to find fame some twenty years later as Poppi on *Seinfeld*) and David Soul (later cast with Paul Michael Glaser on *Starsky & Hutch*):

Lee was there from the start in the fall of 1971 and played partner Jess Brandon until December of 1973. Interestingly enough, probably because of the way some episodes were often held until later in the season, Lee's last episode was in February of 1974, when he was well into *The Six Million Dollar Man*. As a result, many people say he was working two series at the same time. Viewers were treated to Lee twice that week as he played Steve Austin in "Day of the Robot" that Friday night of February 8, 1974, and then Jess Brandon in "A Killer with a Badge" on Saturday night in an episode guest-starring Richard Anderson and Ford Rainey!

Reni appeared as Danny Paterno in only six episodes of *Owen Marshall* starting in October 1973, most with Lee Majors making some sort of an appearance. "The Camerons are a Special Clan" is the only solo episode Santoni did without Majors . . . although Lee was still in the opening credits. His final story was the previously mentioned "A Killer with a Badge," which lends even more credibility to the idea that this story is out of production order as Santoni's previous appearance was December 12, 1973, in "The Prowler."

David Soul first appeared on *Owen Marshall* in two early episodes playing two different characters in the first and second seasons. He would then play the character Ted Warwick in three episodes of the final season in 1974 after Lee Majors had left the series. His first episode was the week following Lee's last, February 16, 1974, "The Sterilization of Judy Simpson," He would then appear in two more episodes, every other week, "I've Promised You a Father," the second half of a *Marcus Welby* cross-over and "The Desertion of Keith Ryder" both in March of 1974. He didn't appear in the series finale. I guess Owen went it alone.

When Majors appeared in the initial 1973 *Six Mill* 90-minute movie pilot, he inherently knew he was making more than just a motion picture for television. When the film debuted, "It seemed like it would become a regular show, and that felt great," he revealed in *The Bionic Book*. "I was excited. I had been in a lot of other shows as a supporting player. Finally, I had the lead, which is every actor's fantasy, whether they admit that or not." With the modesty Majors is known for, he added, "My dream came true."

The Six Million Dollar pilot was a slam-dunk in the ratings. King sci-fi-novelist Martin Caidin, who wrote *Cyborg*, the novel that spawned the first *Million Dollar* movie, was also interviewed for *The Bionic Book*. "There was an incredible reaction to the show," he said. "Mail, calls, telegrams, and an avalanche of favorable reviews. The director, Dick Irving, wanted as much reality as possible, and he was a very tough taskmaster." ABC timidly commissioned Universal Studios and producer Glen A. Larson to manufacture two more ninety-minute *Six Mill* segments that would be screened in the *Suspense Movie* weekly time-slot for the following September. The series then turned weekly in January 1974, with the network's former *Mod Squad* supervisor Harve Bennett replacing Larson at the bionic helm.

When not working on *Man*, Majors enjoyed the company of his superstar-actress wife, Farrah Fawcett who, during the peak of her husband's bionic popularity, became TV's top blonde bombshell by way of *Charlie's Angels*. Debuting on ABC in 1975, and originally costarring Kate Jackson and Jaclyn Smith, *Angels* catapulted Fawcett into a stratospheric success, crowning both her and Majors as Hollywood royalty, ultimately becoming the Brad Pitt and Angelina Jolie of their TV era. Although in an interview with Fox News in 2013, Lee phrased it slightly differently. When the network's reporter called him and Farrah "a glamorous couple, like a real-life Ken and Barbie," Majors replied:

It was quite the extreme. It was probably like Brad and Jennifer when they were together. The press was all over us and of course she was doing a show also which was pretty popular. Naturally we really couldn't go anywhere. Back then you were working so hard you didn't even realize how popular the show was.

Unfortunately, the Majors-Fawcett marriage crumbled, in part due to Ryan O'Neal's romantic interest in Farrah, whom he later married after she divorced Lee. It was a tough triangle, mostly because Ryan and Majors had once been close friends. As Fawcett said during the challenging transition, "I feel so bad for Lee. Our relationship has got to be different because I am different. But it's so hard for him to understand." Lee relayed at the time, "If you have ever loved something, you know that sometimes you just have to set it free—no matter how much it hurts."

Despite the personal challenges, Majors, who was married to Farrah from 1973 to 1982, continued to work and succeed without really trying.

From 1981 to 1986, he was Colt Seavers on *The Fall Guy* (an episode of which reunited the actor with his former bionic costar—and on-screen love-interest—Lindsay Wagner).

In the late 80s and 90s, he reprised his Austin-powerful bionic role in a series of TV-movies with Wagner, and he also delivered many additional *Six Million-Dollar*-geared supporting, recurring, and cameo appearances in feature films, various animated TV shows, commercials, and video games. In recent years, he guest-starred on TV series like NBC's *Community* and TNT's reboot of the CBS classic *Dallas* show, both editions of which starred his good friend and fellow male TV icon Larry Hagman.

Besides Fawcett, Lee has married Kathy Robinson (1961 to 1964), Karen Velez (1988 to 1994), and Faith Majors (since 2002). His children include: Lee Majors II, Nikki, Trey Kulley, and Dane Luke Majors.

Of his life and career overall, he once concluded, "I've had disappointments and heartbreaks and setbacks and roles I didn't get, but something always came along that either made me better or was an even better role. Acting is a tough business, and the percentage of people who make it is very low—it's about 1 percent."

Odds that clearly worked in his bionic favor.

Ricardo Montalban
Fantasy Island

Because we should always respect other nationalities, I have always tried to play them with dignity.

—Ricardo Montalban

In 1975, Erik Estrada as Frank Poncherello on *CHiPs* became the first Latin actor to land a series-lead since Desi Arnaz on *I Love Lucy*. Around the same time, veteran Latin leading man Ricardo Montalban (who died in 2009) was making headway with his legendary performance as the mysterious but ever-dapper Mr. Roark on TV's *Fantasy Island* (ABC, 1977–1984) years after his debut as the diabolical Khan in the 1967 "Space Seed" segment of the original *Star Trek*.

Rick Lertzman comments on the diverse and significant career of Montalban, who was born Ricardo Gonzalo Pedro Montalbán y Merino, on November 25, 1920, in Mexico City, Mexico:

Ricardo Montalban was a film star for several decades when in 1977 he starred as Mr. Roarke in the Aaron Spelling television series, *Fantasy Island*. Herve Villechaize portrayed his sidekick, Tattoo. The series, which endured [on ABC] for seven years [until 1984], was immensely popular. Montalban, who was born in Mexico, was proud of his Latino heritage. He founded the Nosotros ("We") Foundation in 1970 to advocate for Latino actors. He also was known to a generation of *Star Trek* followers for his role as Khan Noonien Singh in the *Star Trek* TV series and the [1982] film, *Star Trek II: The Wrath of Khan*. He also became identified as the longtime spokesperson for the Chrysler automobile, the Cordoba, and was remembered for his unique pronunciation of its "soft Corinthian leather."

Twenty years after *Wrath*'s debut, Paramount Studios presented in Hollywood a special twentieth anniversary screening of the movie, hosted by the film's director, Nicholas Meyer, featuring a special guest appearance by Montalban who by then was in a wheelchair. For years, many of his fans were unaware that he was fitted with an artificial leg. But at the time he attended this special event, his increased disability did not detract from his charisma and still potent ability to connect with his multitude of admirers. The press had documented his appearance as a monumental moment in entertainment history, one

Globe Photos

that will most likely never be repeated again, certainly not in today's TV environment.

Beyond his *Trek* and *Fantasy* performances Montalban (who was married to the same woman, Georgiana Beltzer, from 1944 to his death in 2007) made countless other appearances on the big and small screens, including a guest-shot on an episode of TV's *The Name of the Game*, which originally aired on NBC from 1968 to 1971. This series, one of the more unique entries in TV history, featured a rotating cast, like that of the network's original *Sunday Mystery Movie* wheel of shows (1971–1977, including *McMillan & Wife*, *Columbo*, and *McCloud*, among others). Unlike those showcased on the *Mystery* series, the revolving weekly characters on *Game* (which also happened to air on Sundays) were interlocked by a singular plot device: They worked alternately for a publishing firm in Los Angeles. A set number of characters were played by Robert Stack (post–*The Untouchables*), Gene Barry (post–*Burke's Law*), and Tony Franciosa (pre–*Matt Helm*).

Montalban appeared in one of the Stack segments called "Echo of a Nightmare," an average story (about a kidnapper freed from prison) that was outweighed by another one of Ricardo's above-average performances. Yet, his *Game* performance is note-worthy not only due to his stellar talents, but because of his mere participation. While filming the *Game* Montalban was in his forties. Years later, when he was Mr. Roark on *Fantasy Island*, and returned to playing *Trek*'s Khan (in *Wrath*), he was by then a senior citizen in his late fifties and early sixties. As a disabled Latino senior, he was three times a minority, but still an outstanding sought-after actor—as well as a male TV icon.

He once said, "Hollywood does not write parts for people like me, an elderly gentleman, and when they find out you're crippled, forget about it. No, I'll never work again."

But he continues to work. His energy never wavered, and he was never defined by his disabilities, which were surpassed by his abilities. He had a strength of character in his very being that he carried with grace and elegance throughout his entire life, a trait which he credited to his mother and father. "There couldn't be better parents than mine," he said, "loving yet strict. They disciplined with love. A child without discipline is, in a way, a lost child. You cannot have freedom without discipline."

Such discipline paved the way for substantial success, spanning decades, from count-less Latin and American motion pictures in the 40s and 50s, to countless more TV performances throughout the 60s, 70s, 80s, and beyond. As he also said, "It is to TV that I owe my freedom from bondage of the Latin lover roles. Television came along and gave me parts to chew on. It gave me wings as an actor."

THE DOCTORS, THE DEFENDERS, AND THE DEPENDABLES

They made you feel safe, more so than any other of the male icons of television of the 50s, 60s, and 70s. They were the intelligent, even-tempered, trustworthy professionals of every vocation, be they medical doctors or attorneys; architects or insurance salesmen; single, married, or family men. They worked for the government downtown, in bright, shiny new office buildings, or they possibly supervised a home office with a small staff in a small-town neighborhood.

Prime examples are characters portrayed by David Hartman, Hal Holbrook, E. G. Marshall, John Saxon, and others on *The Bold Ones*, which debuted on NBC in 1969; the same year ABC premiered *Marcus Welby, M.D.*, starring Robert Young and James Brolin, and CBS constructed its *Medical Center*, starring Chad Everett and James Daly.

The Bold Ones remains an anomaly in the history of classic television, as it ignited an ever-popular "wheel" format that both NBC and Universal would later utilize to its fullest extent for their hit *Sunday Night Mystery* series of rotating shows that would include *McMillan & Wife*, *Columbo*, *McCloud*, and more. But before *Sunday Night Mystery* began airing in 1971, *The Bold Ones* pioneered a similar format with four different shows that aired on a rotating basis, three of which alternated each year:

1. *The Doctors* (1969–1973) starred Marshall, Hartman, and Saxon (who was replaced by Robert Walden in the final season).
2. *The Lawyers* (1969–1972) starred Burl Ives, Joseph Campanella, and James Farentino (based on the TV-movies *The Sound of Anger* and *The Whole World Is Watching*).
3. *The Protectors* (1969-1970) starred Leslie Nielsen and Hari Rhodes as a police official and district attorney who frequently butted heads (based on the TV-movie *Deadlock*).
4. *The Senator* (1970-1971) starred Hal Holbrook (based on the TV movie *A Clear and Present Danger*).

It soon became clear which of the wheel installments were the most popular, and which professional group would be best defined as *The Bold Ones*. The father-son–like relationship between Marshall and Hartman was more in line with the association between Young and Brolin on *Welby*, as well as between Daly and Everett on *Center*, not to mention how *Bold* harkened back to Marshall's on-screen association with TV son Robert Reed on *The Defenders*, which aired on CBS from 1961 to 1965 (and which the network semi-remade in 2010 with James Belushi and Jerry O'Connell).

Reed would go on to find an even greater fame as family man Mike Brady, who supervised *The Brady Bunch*, which debuted on ABC the same year NBC aired *The Bold Ones*, and which went on to become a pop-culture phenomenon with countless sequels.

While John Saxon may have later left *The Bold Ones*, his strong, physically-fit and steel-jawed good-looks secured for him a steady taste of success as a martial arts film star, and one singular performance as an evil android on an episode of TV's *The Six Million Dollar Man*. On *The Bold Ones*, Hartman's amiable persona played off well against Saxon's intensity, resulting, however briefly, in an appealing dichotomy that contributed to the show's groundbreaking reality-geared premise.

Before Reed played top-dog-dad Mr. Brady, a plethora of noteworthy patriarchs ran the gamut on television, including Ozzie Nelson on *The Adventures of Ozzie and Harriet*, Robert Young on *Father Knows Best*, Carl Betz on *The Donna Reed Show* (after which he played an attorney for one season in 1967 on ABC's *Judd for the*

Defense), Fred MacMurray on *My Three Sons*, and John Forsythe on *Bachelor Father* (ABC, 1957–1962).

Fame arrived relatively late for Forsythe, who had been a working actor for years. He enjoyed a measure of success with feature films like *The Trouble with Harry* (1955), but it wasn't until he applied his thespian talents to the small screen that he became firmly planted within the radar of the pop-culture continuum. On *Bachelor Father*, he was a doting dad to his on-screen niece played by Noreen Corcoran. *Father* became the only primetime series in history to run in consecutive years on all the then-only three major television networks (ABC, CBS and NBC), and his presence there was somewhat of a precursor to Brian Keith on *Family Affair* (which Forsythe's subsequent 1969–1971 ABC series *To Rome With Love* certainly owed a morsel of homage).

A decade or so later, in 1981, and when he was much older still, Forsythe began performing on ABC's *Dynasty*, this time playing Denver oil mogul Blake Carrington (a refined replicant of Larry Hagman's Texan J. R. Ewing from CBS's *Dallas*). As Forsythe once observed, ever so modestly, "It's rather amusing at my advanced age to become a sex symbol. I figure there are a few actors like Marlon Brando, George C. Scott, and Laurence Olivier who have been touched by the hand of God. I'm in the next bunch. Part of my strength as an actor comes from what I've learned all these years: when you play a villain, you try to get the light touches; when you play a hero, you try to get in some of the warts."

According to Rob Ray, who serves on the board of directors for the Classic TV Preservation Society, a nonprofit that seeks to close the gap between popular culture and education, Forsythe was not only the definitive TV dad, but the definitive dependable male TV iconic persona in general:

> John Forsythe was benignly genial. His character, very much like Brian Keith's Uncle Bill on the similarly-themed *Family Affair* was supposed to be a playboy who never seriously entertained thoughts of marriage. I suspect the fact that the censors and sponsors may have been a little worried about this aspect of the leading character made them go with someone who had John Forsythe's qualities—the same qualities he would bring to *Dynasty* later—integrity, honesty, geniality. And he was handsome without being overtly sexual about it.
>
> He and Bob Cummings were the two confirmed bachelors in the staid television comedy world of the 1950s. But John's Bentley Gregg was less farcical and had the great responsibility of raising a teen-age daughter. (That job was left to Bob's sister on *The Bob Cummings Show*.)

I haven't seen the show itself in over 50 years and would like to revisit it (I have about four episodes on one DVD), but Wikipedia tells me that they scrupulously tried to make the Asian man-servant played by Sammie Tong a three dimensional character who avoided stereotyping. As such, the Wikipedia author writes, "Casting his houseboy was difficult as well with Tong being cast based primarily on his experience as a stand-up comedian." Forsythe believed much of the program's success resulted from the interaction between Tong and himself and that Tong was gifted with great comic timing. He also stated that Tong's character was unique for the time and that he was not the "typical" Asian house servant. Forsythe insisted on Tong being a major character on the program. As such, Tong (Forsythe and Corcoran as well) appears in all 157 episodes. Several of the program plots center around Tong, many dealing with his attempts to improve his position in life. Although none ever pan out (much like Bentley or Kelly) he does develop as a character through the life of the program.

The dependable male role on television in the 50s, 60s, and 70s came in all shapes, sizes, and colors. A closer look at a few more such wonderful figures helps to focus on this particular professional sector of manly TV characters.

65

Richard Chamberlain
Dr. Kildare

Vince Edwards
Ben Casey

> I pattern my actions and life after what I want. No two people are alike. You might admire attributes in others, but use these only as a guide in improving yourself in your own unique way. I don't go for carbon copies. Individualism is sacred!
>
> —Richard Chamberlain

We all know the commercial. "I'm not a doctor. I just play one on TV."

That certainly was and remains the case for a number of actors best known for portraying physicians on television's most prominent medical shows through the years, beginning with *Dr. Kildare* and *Ben Casey*, from the early 1960s all the way up to more contemporary ventures like *ER* and *House*.

Kildare and *Casey* were two of the first TV doctors to earn a strong medicinal-like following from the home viewer. Both premiering in the fall of 1961, *Kildare*, starring Richard Chamberlain (on NBC), and *Casey*, starring Vince Edwards (on ABC), proved to be a one-two thumpity-thump on the hearts of TV fans across the country.

On *Kildare*, Chamberlain portrayed the dashing (first name, James) young lead doctor who set hearts afire, on screen and off. Author John Javna, in his book, *Cult TV*, said it perfectly: Kildare was "every mother's dream, and every girl's desire," as he fought nobly to "save human lives every week." By his side as mentor: the much-older Dr. James Leonard Gillespie, played by Raymond Massey. President John F. Kennedy was inaugurated in 1961 and, as Javna assessed, a new era of politics, and a fresh spirit of "optimism and idealism" was delivered to America, encouraging the country's

Richard Chamberlain
Globe Photos

youth to "get involved" . . . "make a difference" and to create life-changing interest groups and organizations like the Peace Corps.

Dr. Kildare, the character, was "the first bona fide TV hero of the 60s," Javna assessed: someone who represented the "best hopes" of this new generation. "Young, intelligent, committed, the evil he fought was disease. His weapons were a good education and a willingness to care about people. Teenagers loved him [over 2 million watched him every week]. His popularity also reflected the growing esteem in which doctors were being held. America was turning to science for salvation, and doctors were the new gods."

The silver-tongued Kildare was so popular, in fact, that Chamberlain received more fan mail than silver screen legend Clark Gable (and three times as much as Vince Edwards and *Ben Casey*). Chamberlain also had a hit record with a lyric-based edition of the show's theme, while his likeness was spread across a *Kildare* comic book that sold over five hundred thousand copies in six months. The show's adventures were even popular abroad, in quite surprising places like behind the Iron Curtain, where the Polish Communist Party rescheduled its meetings from Wednesday to Thursday because, on Wednesday, all eyes were glued to viewing *Kildare* on the tube—and no one attending their meetings. Now that's popular!

On *Ben Casey*, Edwards played the straightforward, yet unconventional lead neurosurgeon at County General Hospital. He was more rugged-looking and less classically handsome than Chamberlain, but like Kildare, had a mentor—this one named Dr. David Zorba, as portrayed by Sam Jaffe (and whose voiceover, "Man, woman, birth, death, infinity," opened every episode). As Javna went on to observe, "Casey wasn't just a doctor—he was a macho doctor. His shirt was always open, revealing a thick mat of chest hair. He didn't respect authority, and he didn't kowtow to anyone. The only man who could talk to him was the wise old grandfatherly Dr. Zorba."

In comparing *Casey* to *Kildare*, the former had almost the exact same run as the latter. *Casey* debuted only a month after *Kildare* and was cancelled only five months earlier. Thirty-two million people watched *Casey* every week, while Edwards became as big a sex symbol as Chamberlain. Both had paraphernalia like pins that said things like "Doctor Kildare Is a Doll" and "I've Got a Case on Ben Casey." There were even competing board games, The *Ben Casey, M.D.* Game—The Drama of Life in a Big Metropolitan Hospital and *Dr. Kildare*: Medical Game for the Young. As with *Kildare*, the *Casey* theme song became a hit record, sung by Valjean (a pop-artist of the day). The only main difference is that Casey had a shirt named after him . . . a replica of which he adorned on a weekly basis.

Javna, for one, doubted whether *Casey* would have found an audience, had not *Kildare* been along for the ride. "But you really can't separate them," he said. "They were always thought of by viewers as a single unit. Together, they were the most visible manifestation of an early 60s phenomenon—the emergence of doctors as media heroes."

Pop-culture scholar Jeff Thompson says:

Ben Casey was a full-fledged medical doctor whereas James Kildare was an intern. Dr. Kildare was a softly handsome blond and Ben Casey was darkly handsome. Or to use a seventies analogy, one was more the Robert Redford type to the other's Burt Reynolds.

Historian/author Rick Lertzman concludes:

When Richard Chamberlain assumed the role of Dr. Kildare in 1961, he possessed many of the qualities of his pre-

Vince Edwards
Globe Photos

decessor in the role, Lew Ayres, who was the star of the MGM motion picture series [1938–1942] of the same name. Chamberlain was handsome, tall and charismatic. Despite his youthful appearance, he seemed far older than his chronological age. He oozed class, manner and elegance. As Dr. James Kildare, Chamberlain portrayed an idealist that directly conflicted with his ability as a skilled internist. Unlike many of his contemporaries starring in television dramas (including Vince Edwards as Ben Casey), Chamberlain's James Kildare represented the optimism of the Kennedy era. As a member of the Camelot generation, his Kildare mirrored the youthful exuberance of our young President.

A classically trained actor, Chamberlain brought a realism to his role that appealed to viewers of all ages. *Dr. Kildare* still resonates with viewers who remember this well crafted program and its leading man, Richard Chamberlain.

66

Alan Alda
M*A*S*H

> Be brave enough to live life creatively. The creative place where no one else has ever been.
>
> — Alan Alda

It's difficult not to address *M*A*S*H* when referencing actor/director/writer Alan Alda, and vice versa. The two are forever intertwined, particularly when it comes to discussing all things sincerely defined as masculine in the media, and certainly when it comes to profiling male icons of television. As such, it's best to commence a discussion about Alda with a full introduction to the media sensation known as *M*A*S*H*, which debuted on CBS in the fall of 1972—and which went on to become one of the most legendary television series of all time (military-based or otherwise).

The armed forces have been represented on television in many different incarnations including both dramatic and comedic shows. In the drama department, there has been *Combat* (ABC, 1962–1967), *JAG* (CBS, 1995–2005), *NCIS* (CBS, 2003–present), and *Army Wives* (Lifetime, 2007–2014). The war comedy category dates back to *The Phil Silvers Show/Sgt. Bilko* (CBS, 1955–1959), *McHale's Navy* (CBS, 1962–1966), *Gomer Pyle, U.S.M.C.* (CBS, 1964–1969), *Hogan's Heroes* (CBS, 1965–1971), and *M*A*S*H*, the latter of which is most certainly the most popular military-geared series, if with a medical slant, in history.

The show's special two-hour finale in the spring of 1983 proved as much. Titled "Goodbye, Farewell, and Amen," this segment remains the highest-rated TV show episode ever documented.

"We wanted the series to say that war is destructive, wasteful, and stupid—and [that] there are better ways to solve problems." So told *M*A*S*H* producer/director Gene Reynolds to author Peggy Herz in her book, *All About M*A*S*H*. Reynolds, who had worked on *Room 222*, and later *Touched by an Angel*, had partnered with writer Larry Gelbart (responsible for feature films like 1982's *Tootsie*) to develop

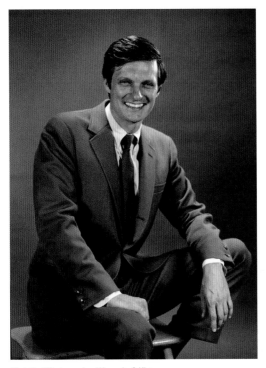

PhotoFest/Photographer: Warnecke & Klein

and produce CBS-TV's *M*A*S*H*. The show's title took its name from *Mobile Army Surgical Hospital*, and centered on a medical war unit called the 4077th—stationed in Korea during the Korean War. Like *222* before it, *M*A*S*H* was a half-hour dramedy, although with a laugh-track (which *222* did not have) at least in its first few seasons. Three years after it debuted in 1972, the series became less humor-bound (but no less tragic in premise). Its original competition were long-running hit shows like *The FBI* on ABC and *The Wonderful World of Disney* on NBC. By the end of its initial year, *M*A*S*H* ranked at #46 in the Nielsen ratings.

But CBS remained loyal to the series. For the show's second season, the network scheduled it on Saturday night, following its mega-hit *All in the Family*. The result: By the end of that year, *M*A*S*H* became a bona fide hit (if at the sacrifice of *Bridget Loves Bernie*, which it replaced).

The show began as a novel by Richard Hooker (1968) and adapted into a hit feature film in 1970 starring Donald Sutherland and Elliott Gould as unconventional doctors Hawkeye Pierce and Trapper John—characters later played by Alan Alda and Wayne Rogers in the small-screen edition. Also in the TV edition: McLean Stevenson as Colonel Henry Blake; Loretta Swit as Margaret "Hot Lips" Houlihan; Larry Linville as her stuffed-shirt lover, Major Frank Burns; Jamie Farr as the gender-bending Corporal Clinger; William Christopher as Father Mulcahy; and Gary Burghoff as naïve but daring Radar (the only casting carried over from the motion picture).

At first there were roadblocks to the TV version. According to Herz, the language and "antics" of the medical personnel depicted may have been acceptable for adults in a movie theater, but the standards and practices of television at the time were much more restrictive than motion picture codes. "The movie was probably the funniest film of the year," wrote Herz, but it was also "the bloodiest . . . The operating scenes were ghastly, and they were meant to be. If there's one thing that turns TV executives pale, it's the sight of too much blood on the home screen." (That was then, and certainly not now, where blood and gore are the mainstay on today's primetime shows like *The Walking Dead* or *Breaking Bad*.)

But Alda wasn't certain he wanted in on the show or any TV series, especially a comedy about war. As Reynolds told Herz, "[Alan] wanted to know our point of view. His concern was that the show should not glorify war or make it appear romantic. He wanted the humanity of the doctors to be emphasized." After reading the pilot script and meeting with Reynolds and Gelbart, Alda agreed to appear on *M*A*S*H*, because of its unique point of view on war. "It was probably the best television script I'd ever seen. But before agreeing to do it, I needed some assurance that they would show war as it really was. I didn't want to get into a fun-and-games war without meaning or content or reality. But I didn't have to worry. Larry and Gene had the same idea."

Reynolds said the series was a "good example of theatre of the absurd . . . the whole effort of these doctors [played by Alda, Rogers, et al.] is fruitless. They repair lives that are then sent back [into combat] to be destroyed . . . We show war for what it is—tragedy. That doesn't mean that people in the situation don't behave in very amusing ways. They use humor as a defense mechanism. If the sum total of the show were to say that war is fun—that would be wrong."

Herz agreed. *M*A*S*H* owed its success to several factors. "Brilliant writing, directing and acting . . . made it hilariously funny . . . [with] . . . a constant barrage of one-line jokes." Yet, with all of its "irreverence," there was also "a lot of heart . . . an undercurrent of caring. There is no moralizing or sermonizing—yet it is probably the most moral show on TV."

Alda threw himself into the role of Hawkeye, the core voice in the series. He enjoyed the character's candid outlook and verbiage, and straight-out moxie, and described him as possessing "some kind of caring at heart. It's a nice role to play. [He] steps out and takes over—and that rubs off on me. I always find that certain elements of the characters I play accrue to me. That's a way of growth."

As the series progressed, Alda became increasingly satisfied with what he called a "deepening" in the episodes. "We tried to make [them] more interesting by going deeper into the characters and the situations. We don't make war funny on *M*A*S*H*. We show the effects of war. People get hurt. In one episode, a guy died on the operating table. That's unusual for a comedy show—or even a medical show. We're not trying to get gruesome, but we want the show to be more real." For him the show's humor arose from how the characters responded to war, which he called "a hurtful thing. I was in ROTC in college and was a second lieutenant in the reserves. I was on active duty six months, but I didn't have to kill anybody. I was very disturbed by the whole experience.

"Basically," he decided, "any play, especially comedy, must be based on real people. We're trying to see all these characters as real people."

A respected stage actor, and son of cinema B-list actor Robert Alda, Alan had made various guest-star TV appearances on everything from the aforementioned *Phil Silvers Show* in 1958 to a series titled *The Doctors and Nurses* in 1963. Other pre-*M*A*S*H* television appearances included *The Trials of O'Brien* and *East Side/West Side*. When *M*A*S*H* debuted in 1972, he continued performing elsewhere on the small screen, in TV-movies like *Isn't it Shocking?* and *The Glass House*. He also made several noteworthy feature films, before and after *M*A*S*H*, such as *The Seduction of Joe Tynan* (1979), *The Four Seasons* (1981), which he wrote and directed, and which costarred his good friend Carol Burnett, and *Crimes and Misdemeanors* (1989), among several more. In recent years, he's been cast in regular roles on highly regarded TV shows like *The Blacklist* and *The Big C*.

However, it's through his experience of playing the sensitive and intelligent doctor Hawkeye Pierce on *M*A*S*H* with which he made his monumental lasting impression as a male television icon . . . and as a human being. As he once concluded, "No man or woman of the humblest sort can really be strong, gentle and good, without the world being better for it, without somebody being helped and comforted by the very existence of that goodness. . . . A really great actor, in a lucky performance, can transform himself or herself. I've seen actors do that. But often it's a mechanical transformation, which isn't as interesting, and you've got to be careful how you go about something like that, I think . . . You have to leave the city of your comfort and go into the wilderness of your intuition. What you'll discover will be wonderful. What you'll discover is yourself."

Alda on *M*A*S*H* played himself—and the TV audience loved him. And they still do.

Born January 28, 1936, to actor Robert Alda and Joan Brown, parents who also gave birth to his brother Antony, Alan has been married to Arlene Alda since 1957, and they have three daughters: Beatrice, Elizabeth, and Eve.

67

James Brolin
Marcus Welby, M.D.

Chad Everett
Medical Center

People named their kids after me!

—Chad Everett

While Alan Alda was playing doctor from a more sensitive angle on *M*A*S*H*, and before Gregory Harrison donned his dashing beard and motorcycle on *Trapper John, M.D.* (CBS, 1979 to 1986, a decades-later *M*A*S*H* sequel starring Pernell Roberts [*Bonanza*] in the Wayne Rogers role), James Brolin and Chad Everett cornered the market on young, hip, and handsome primetime doctors with their twin gigs on *Marcus Welby, M.D.* (ABC, 1969 to 1975) and *Medical Center* (CBS, 1969 to 1975).

Brolin played second fiddle Dr. James Kiley to lead doctor Robert Young on *Welby*, while on *Center* Everett starred opposite second banana James Daly (father to Tim *Wings* Daly, and brother to Tyne *Cagney & Lacey* Daly). All four men remained dashing, daring, and debonair via their respective shows, but it was Brolin and Everett whose media machismo set hearts aflutter in living rooms (and assumedly, a few bedrooms, too!) around the country.

Rob Ray says, "Brolin personified the post-Kennedy era generation of physicians. He was more rebellious, rash and questioning of authority. But still ruggedly handsome in the process." Adds Professor Jeff Thompson:

James Brolin provided the perfect balance—and foil—to Robert Young's older, more traditional Dr. Welby. The extremely handsome Brolin won the hearts of the audience with the very first regular episode, "Hello, Good-Bye, Hello," in which Dr.

Kiley developed feelings for a terminally ill schoolteacher, played by Susan Clark. Brolin's sensitive performance was a highlight of this, one of the very few Welby episodes that had a downbeat ending. Whether riding his motorcycle to Dr. Welby's clinic, flashing a smile at his patient, or solving a medical problem, James Brolin as Steve Kiley exuded a charm that made him irresistible to viewers.

Thompson goes on to observe:

While *Welby* starred the older physician (Young) and costarred the younger (James Brolin), *Medical Center* starred the younger doctor (Everett) and costarred the older (James Daly)—just as Dr. Kildare and Ben Casey (both 1961–1966) had done. Chad Everett and his popular character Dr. Joe Gannon propelled *Medical Center* through seven successful seasons of medical drama because of Everett's rugged good looks, winning smile, and serious, authentic approach to his role as the heroic surgeon. Everett was perhaps at his most compassionate and endearing in "Judgment," a fourth-season episode guest-starring Ruth Buzzi as a hopelessly lonely hospital volunteer who fabricates a full, happy life for herself until Dr. Gannon uncovers the sad truth.

Everett was born Raymon Lee Cramton on June 11, 1937, in South Bend, Indiana. He attended Wayne State University. His parents were Virdeen Ruth (née Hopper) and Harry Clyde "Ted" Cramton. He was married to Shelby Grant from 1966 until her death in 2011, and he had two daughters, Shannon Everett and Katherine Everett.

He began acting in television in 1961, making guest appearances through 1969 in *Maverick*, *Bronco*, *77 Sunset Strip*, *Cheyenne*, *Surfside 6*, *Hawaiian Eye*, *Route 66*, *Combat!*, *The Man from U.N.C.L.E.*, *The FBI*, and *Ironside*.

Between 1962 and 1969 he appeared in motion pictures like *The Chapman Report*, *Get Yourself a College Girl*, *Made in Paris*, *The Singing Nun*, *Johnny Tiger*, *First to Fight*, *Return of the Gunfighter*, *The Last Challenge*, *The Impossible Years*, and *Journey to Midnight*.

In 1963 he portrayed Deputy Del Stark for one season in the western series *The Dakotas*. The series was reputedly cancelled after only nineteen episodes due to viewers' protesting one episode where lawmen gunned down outlaws inside a church.

Three years after CBS closed *Medical Center* in 1976, Chad was cast as Major Maxwell Mercy in the epic NBC mini-series *Centennial*. Other roles included: Harold Columbine in the mini-series *The French Atlantic Affair* (1979), Paul Hagen for one season on the series *Hagen* (1980), Wyatt Earp III for one season in the series *The*

Rousters (1983-1984), Jack McKenna for one season in the series *McKenna* (1994-1995), Thomas Sterling in four episodes of *Melrose Place* (1998), and Jake Manhattan for one season in the short-lived series *Manhattan, AZ* (2000).

Between 1977 and 2012 Everett appeared in TV-movies such as *In the Glitter Palace*, *The Intruder Within*, *When Time Expires*, and *Hard to Forget*, and guest-starred in numerous series including *Police Story*, *Cybill*, *Touched by an Angel*, *Diagnosis Murder*, *Just Shoot Me!*, *Melrose Place*, *The Nanny*, *Love Boat: The Next Wave*, *Cold Case*, *Without a Trace*, *Castle*, and *Saturday Night Live*.

"I went into acting because I'm easily bored," Everett once deciphered. "Acting seemed to give vent to a lot of different feelings."

James Brolin
Globe Photos

James Brolin was born Craig Kenneth Bruderlin on July 18, 1940, in Los Angeles, California. He graduated from University High School and attended Santa Monica City College and UCLA. His parents were Helen Sue Mansur and Henry Hurst Bruderlin, and he has three siblings: Brian, Sue, and Barbara Bruderlin.

Beyond playing Dr. Steven Kiley on *Marcus Welby*, his second-most-famous TV role was that of hotel manager Peter McDermott in the TV series *Hotel* (ABC, 1983–1988).

Brolin first became interested with all things Hollywood when he toured a film studio at fifteen. After that, he bought his first camera and started making movies. Brolin attended high school with actor Ryan O'Neal, who encouraged him to get into acting. At eighteen, James was stopped on the street by someone who asked if he would like to do a commercial. He accepted and made four hundred dollars for a non-speaking role driving a Dodge truck. He appeared in the hit TV series *Batman* (ABC, 1966–1968) as one of Catwoman's henchmen. There he met his future wife Jane Cameron Agee on the set, where she was working as a casting executive.

Chad Everett
Globe Photos

The original premise for *Marcus Welby, M.D.* had initially pitted Brolin's young Dr. Kiley and his new views on medicine against Young's elder Dr. Welby and his more orthodox treatments. For his part as Kiley, Brolin won an Emmy Award for Outstanding Performance by an Actor in a Supporting Role in 1970 and received three additional nominations.

In 1973 Brolin starred in the film *Capricorn One* with actor Elliott Gould, who was once married to Brolin's future wife, singer/actress Barbra Streisand. Brolin acted in a makeup test for *Planet of the Apes* (1968) as "Cornelius," the chimpanzee scientist later portrayed in the film by Roddy McDowall. He was considered to play James Bond in the 1981 movie *For Your Eyes Only* and screen tested for the 1983 movie *Octopussy*, but didn't get the role either time when Roger Moore decided to return to the series. Brolin recently had a recurring role, as Richard Castle's CIA operative father Jackson Hunt, on ABC's contemporary hit show *Castle* and presently stars in the new CBS series, *Life in Pieces*.

Brolin once said, "I think you can have a whole terrific, smart career as a second and third banana and work more and have much less risk than the lead guy. But I like being the lead guy."

On working with Young on *Welby*, he said: "I never had dinner with Robert Young once. Never. He was very private. Never a problem, but there was a 'pheasant-under-glass' element to him. If he wasn't working, he'd be locked in his trailer with curtains pulled. In the morning in makeup, we were very careful not to ask him a question because that would lead to one hour of monologue."

Near the end of *Welby*'s run, the show began to falter in the ratings. Producers decided to stir up the pot a little bit and opted to marry off Brolin's Dr. Kiley. As the actor recalled, he suggested Farrah Fawcett as a TV wife possibility. "But they felt she couldn't act. So we bring in Pamela Hensley. The night we were married was maybe the highest-rated show we'd ever had. Number one. And the next week we dropped to like number 79 or something. Anticipation rules. So keep dangling the carrot and make it sexy!"

In real life, Brolin married three times: Jane Cameron Agee (1966 to 1984), Jan Smithers (*WKRP in Cincinnati*; 1986 to 1995), and since 1998, Barbra Streisand. He has three children: actor Josh Brolin, Molly Elizabeth Brolin, and J. Brolin.

Chad Everett died on July 24, 2012, at age seventy-five in Los Angeles, California, from lung cancer.

68

Raymond Burr
Perry Mason/Ironside

> My greatest satisfaction in acting on television is to have the opportunity to communicate with the world.
>
> —Raymond Burr

Raymond Burr as the star of *Perry Mason* became embedded in the minds of millions of TV viewers as the ultimate trusted attorney in the legal series that began in the 1950s and was resurrected in the 1980s for a series of TV-reunion movies that lasted throughout the 1990s, even after Burr's demise in 1993. Certainly remembered, too, is Burr's portrayal as the physically disabled but mentally superior police detective Robert T. Ironside on *Ironside* (NBC, 1967–1975).

Burr was particularly proud of his monumental *Mason* series, which ended its original run in 1966. Monte Markham and CBS resurrected it as a *New Perry Mason* series in 1973–1974. As he once said, "*Perry Mason* is a marvelous show because it has so much to do with peoples' lives and television. People were buying television sets when Perry Mason first went on, and it all goes back to that nostalgia."

On reprising his role as Mason for the mid-80s reunion movies, he said: "When I sat down at the defense table again, it was as if 25 years had been taken off my life. I don't think there's anything wrong with returning to a character. I played Macbeth when I was 19, and I would do it again. But of course, I wouldn't do it exactly the same way. Similarly, I hope there's been a progression in the way I play Perry Mason."

Jeff Thompson explains the seamless transitions of Burr's charisma that stretched over two extremely popular classic TV shows over several decades, as both *Mason* and *Ironside* gave birth to popular reunion movies years after their original runs:

CBS/PhotoFest

A beloved mainstay on television for decades, Raymond Burr portrayed Perry Mason in the 1950s, 1960s, 1980s, and 1990s, and he played Robert Ironside in the 1960s, 1970s, and 1990s. Originally in *noir*-ish black-and-white on CBS, Burr, as Mason, won every case with shrewd deduction and dramatic flair. "Brought to you in living color on NBC," Burr, as *Ironside*, exhibited grit and determination, along with just a touch of smugness. The secret of Raymond Burr's appeal was that he allowed viewers to see beyond his often gruff, imposing exterior to the gentler, more compassionate person underneath. Raymond Burr's expressive eyes always told the real story.

TV scholar Ed Robertson and Bill Sullivan co-authored *The Case of the Alliterative Attorney: Guide to the Perry Mason TV Series and TV-Movies.* As Robertson conveys:

Defense attorneys have an odious reputation, particularly in criminal cases. After all, it's their job to protect the rights of people accused of murder and other heinous crimes.

What made Perry Mason different, of course, is that we knew, beyond a reasonable doubt, that every person he defended in court was in fact innocent. That made him about as noble as a defense attorney can be.

Perry Mason was an idealized portrayal of our legal system—a reminder that, in the end, what matters is that justice is truly served. We saw that illustrated every week, not only in Perry's dedication to clearing his client's name, but in the way he, Della and Paul always cooperated with the police and the District Attorney's office over the course of each episode. While I think some of that was a natural extension of how much the cast members of Perry Mason genuinely liked Raymond Burr off-screen and enjoyed working with each other, there was a mutual respect and collegiality between Perry and Hamilton Burger on-screen that rarely exists between opposing counsels. [Besides, Perry may have dispelled Burger's case against his client, but in exposing the real killer every week he also gave the D.A. a rock-solid case that would stand up in court.]

Nine years is a long run for any network series. As the show progressed Perry Mason added wrinkles to keep the format fresh, and the Mason character interesting. One such example appears at the beginning of "The Case of the Witless Witness," the final episode of the sixth season. After losing an appeal (one of the few times we actually saw Mason fail in court), Perry engages the appellate court judge in a respectful exchange on the merits of precedent. When the judge reminds Perry that the court's ruling "is the law," Perry replies, "The law is simply words on paper—the oxcart in an Atomic Age. The law is more than a record of upheld decisions. It's a testament to the people who created those words."

That bit of dialogue speaks to the appeal of not only *Perry Mason* as a series, but Burr's portrayal of the Mason character. Burr was an imposing figure, but he gave Perry compassion, a burning desire for justice, and a tireless dedication to the people who put their life in his hands. He took that "testament to the people" seriously, without being sanctimonious. That's what made him a great character.

Robert Young
Father Knows Best/Marcus Welby, M.D.

Fred MacMurray
My Three Sons

> Margaret—I'm home!
>
> —Jim Anderson, as played by Robert Young opposite his TV wife
> played by Jane Wyatt on TV's family classic *Father Knows Best*

In the 50s and 60s, television audiences would be hard put to find two more perfectly suited (literally and figuratively) father figures than Robert Young on *Father Knows Best* (ABC/CBS/NBC, 1954–1960) and Fred MacMurray on *My Three Sons* (CBS, 1960–1972). As the guiding forces of their given TV families, Young and MacMurray imbued the essence of personable leadership, loving-kindness, wisdom, protection, and trust.

Both Young and MacMurray enjoyed significantly successful careers in the 30s and 40s; and certainly MacMurray continued to enjoy a measure of popularity on the big screen with Walt Disney movies like *The Absent-Minded Professor* (1961). But ultimately, he and Young received a steadier paycheck via TV in their later years. As Young once assessed, "The kind of role I was supposedly best suited for—light romantic comedy leads [in motion pictures]—no longer existed. There wasn't a place for me. Feature films, you might say, passed me by."

However, such was not the case with TV. Says Jeff Thompson,

Lightning struck twice for Robert Young, who played two extremely beloved TV characters. Young portrayed Jim Anderson of *Father Knows Best* on both radio and television and later returned as the title character of the hugely popular *Marcus Welby,*

M.D. On the latter series, viewers were attracted to Young's patience, compassion, and self-assurance as Dr. Welby. The seasoned general practitioner Welby seemed to really *listen* to his patients and went the extra mile to help them solve their complex and dramatic problems. Loyal viewers of the Tuesday-night TV staple tuned in to see America's doctor find a remedy or a cure for almost every patient's malady.

No two ways about it: Young nailed it with his extremely accessible performances on both *Father* and *Welby*. While he turned in two very different interpretations of two very different characters, either show could have easily been renamed *Doctor Knows Best*, or *Jim Anderson, M.D.* On one level the characters were interchangeable, while on an entirely different level, they were not.

The overlap between Young's Anderson and Marcus roles was never more apparent as when, shortly after he finished his run as Dr. Welby, the actor reunited with *Father* costars Jane Wyatt, Elinor Donahue, Billy Gray, and Lauren Chapin for two very successful Anderson family TV reunions: *The Father Knows Best Reunion* and *Father Knows Best: Home for Christmas*, both screened on NBC during the November/December holiday season of 1977. In the second-aired *Home for Christmas*, Young was spot-on with his return to playing an older Jim Anderson. In the first film, the actor seemed to be channeling Marcus Welby instead of Jim Anderson. Both films were ratings winners, and allegedly were to pave the way for a new *Father Knows Best* that unfortunately never came to fruition.

Fred MacMurray
Globe Photos

With an amiable, straight-to-the-point–type presence on screen, Young started making movies in 1931 and continued for a little over two decades. He was the carefree but practical All-American male. Like MacMurray, Young made the transition from film to TV with ease. Although not as successful in films as MacMurray, and many times confused with Robert Montgomery, another film-turned-TV star (and father to *Bewitched* star Elizabeth Montgomery), Young was not considered as serious a presence on the big screen as James Stewart or Henry Fonda (both of whom failed in late career attempts on television).

After the *Welby* series folded in 1975, and besides the *Father* reunion movies, Young returned to television with a few *Welby* reunion films, another series attempt (*Little Women*, NBC, 1979), and the occasional role against-type (as mercy killer Roswell Gilbert in *Mercy or Murder?* in 1987). He also utilized his likable and comfortable core screen presence in a series of TV commercials (for products like Sanka Coffee).

In retrospect, one episode of *Marcus Welby, M.D.* holds significant status in the history of Young's career. The segment featured a young woman who had experienced a substantial weight loss. In doing so, and by today's standards, she would have been considered physically attractive. The episode cast as the girl's parents a pre–*Mary Tyler Moore Show* Cloris Leachman and the iconic William Schallert, who for years played a comforting TV dad himself on *The Patty Duke Show* (and later a strong father-figure presence on *The Waltons*, after Ralph Waite left that series).

The young girl in the *Welby* episode—directed by the late, great Leo Penn (father of Sean)—was called Cathy, the same name of Lauren Chapin's young character on *Father Knows Best*, and the moniker given to one of Patty Duke's twin-personas on *The Patty Duke Show*.

Now, here they all were together, led by Robert Young—and the episode remains a stand-out in the *Welby* series. Penn's direction was exceptional, and the turmoil and tribulations of the young girl, who was once considered unattractive and now "easy," was played so convincingly well (by Lee Purcell). Leachman gave her usual A-list performance, this time as a self-absorbed mom—and Schallert was signature perfect as usual.

It was a quality segment of a quality series that perfectly represented the high quality and standards that Robert Young insisted upon throughout his entire career.

As was the case with Fred MacMurray on *My Three Sons*, Young, on both *Welby* and *Father Knows Best*, represented everything that was right about television.

Says Rob Ray:

Fred MacMurray was a family man off the screen and, as Nanette Fabray once told me, 'The camera never lies. He was kind, gentle, a bit of a square as Lucille Ball once described him, but nonetheless very underrated as an actor, as his image-shattering performances for Billy Wilder in *Double Indemnity* [1944] and *The Apartment* [1960] prove. He was perfectly cast as the widowed father of three boys in *My Three Sons*. In real life, his first wife had died suddenly in 1953 and he thought he would never marry again before finding love a second time just a year later with June Haver, who had briefly left Hollywood to join a convent before returning and marrying Fred in 1954.

He was honest, fair and loving without being overly expressive about it, much like a young boy's own Dad might be at times. There was a slight sense of distance in his love. This quality was exploited by Disney in the 1959 hit, *The Shaggy Dog*, where he played a somewhat cool, distant though ultimately loving father to Tommy Kirk. He also had a certain clueless absent-minded quality about him. Once again Disney made good use of this quality in the concurrent sixties hit, *The Absent-Minded Professor* [1961].

All of these qualities came to play in his role as Steve Douglas on [TV's] *My Three Sons*.

MacMurray found everlasting fame on the long-running family sitcom, *My Three Sons*, in which he portrayed a widowed dad to TV sons played by Tim Considine, real-life brothers Stanley and Barry Livingston (the latter of whom joined the series in its later years), and fellow male TV icon Don Grady. Also in the family: William Frawley as Uncle "Bub," and later William Demarest as Uncle Charley.

MacMurray's cordial nature and persona fit the cozy, down-home accessibility that the smaller screen then more easily invited. As popular-culture scholar Jeff Thompson puts it, the affable actor performed on *Sons* "for a remarkable twelve years with his easygoing manner and his quiet, reassuring way . . . *My Three Sons* became a comedic *One Man's Family* as MacMurray's TV relatives grew up, married, and had children of their own." Thompson goes on to explain how even Steve Douglas, Fred's alter TV ego, wed Barbara Harper, played by Beverly Garland, which allowed for "yet another side of MacMurray's likable, comforting patriarch persona."

MacMurray was married to Lillian Lamont from 1936 to 1953, and actress June Haver (Danny Thomas's first TV wife on *Make Room For Daddy/The Danny Thomas Show*) and, ironically, did not have any children of his own.

As *TV Guide* journalist Dwight Whitney observed in 1965, MacMurray (who died of pneumonia on November 5, 1991) was "Neat. Very safe. Conservative, as befits a conservative man. The common touch must remain common and uncloying."

"I've been lucky," Fred told Whitney, as he discussed *Sons*' original popularity. "If there is an explanation, it is the all-male, motherless family that Don Fedderson [the show's executive producer, who would later preside over CBS's *Family Affair* from 1966 to 1971] and George Tibbles [who penned the pilot] devised. Five men without a woman lend themselves to a lot of funny things."

During Fred's interview with *TV Guide*, the actor reached for his pipe, which Dwight described as "that marvelously reassuring instrument which he is forever cleaning, tamping, lighting and relighting," and which only added to the welcoming presence MacMurray displayed on *Sons*. "The father in our show isn't a dope," Fred said. "He can handle things better than I can at home. Then, too, we don't have any big messages. No dramatic problems. I play myself. Most actors do. Maybe I happen to be the kind of fellow I'm playing. I don't tell jokes. I react to jokes. I'm not really a very funny fellow. I've threatened to retire. Particularly after the second year I thought I had enough. Then it all got a little easier. Now I probably never will. I think if I had to be *Perry Mason* [like fellow male TV icon Raymond Burr]

Clockwise from left: Lauren Chapin, Elinor Donahue, Robert Young, Billy Gray, Jane Wyatt
NBC/PhotoFest

doing all those long-winded speeches to the jury, I wouldn't be here today.

"You stop being Fred MacMurray and become Steve Douglas," the actor himself concluded. "A lot of people who think they're pretty knowledgeable TV watchers don't even know your name. It's 'Hiya, Steve! How're the kids? What's Uncle Charley cooking up for supper tonight?'

"Fred MacMurray? Who the heck is he?"

Jeff Thompson says Fred "proved his versatility in *My Three Sons*' last season by portraying a different character, Fergus McBain Douglas (whose love interest, Terri Dowling, was played by Anne Francis)." But it was still MacMurray's core Steve Douglas interpretation that small-screen viewers will always hold dear "as one of television's most beloved fathers"—as well as one of TV's greatest male icons.

MacMurray died in 1991 at the age of eighty-three, ultimately from pneumonia (after various battles with cancer).

Young died in 1998 at age ninety from complications from Alzheimer's disease.

Robert Reed
The Brady Bunch

Ralph Waite
The Waltons

Dick Van Patten
Eight Is Enough

I have a vanity and greed enough for one person. But at the same time, I feel in my bones you lose a lot of life's value if you don't see yourself as a member of the family of man.

—Ralph Waite

Continuing the tradition of Fred MacMurray's monumental portrayal of Steve Douglas on *My Three Sons*, everyone in the TV audience wanted their dads to be like Robert Reed's Mike Brady from *The Brady Bunch* (ABC, 1969–1974), Ralph Waite's John Walton on *The Waltons* (CBS, 1972–1981), or Dick Van Patten's Dick Bradford on *Eight Is Enough* (ABC, 1977–1981). Some viewers who were fathers themselves even sought to emulate the characters these three male icons presented on screen.

While MacMurray's Douglas presided over a core family of only three children (the number of which was later extended via various adoptions and additions to the *Sons* brood), Reed's top dad Brady had a supersized gang of six from the beginning (three biological sons plus three stepdaughters via Florence Henderson's Carol Ann Tyler Martin Brady); Waite's fully-dimensional Poppa Walton corralled seven (four sons/ three daughters, all biological via Michael Learned's Olivia Walton), and Van Patten's

Mr. Bradford circled eight (three sons/five daughters, also all biological—from first TV wife, Joan Bradford, as played by Diana Hyland—who died of cancer after completing only the first four episodes of the series and was then replaced by Betty Buckley as stepmom Abby Bradford).

No matter the number or diversity of their on-screen children, each of these fine gents were television patriarchs who displayed a caring but firm hand over their various significantly large families.

Van Patten (brother to actress Joyce Van Patten), born December 9, 1928, and died June 23, 2015, had been acting since he was a child. He made his first of twenty-seven Broadway appearances at age seven in *Tapestry in Grey*, and began his television career in the early days of the medium performing in a different family arena on 1949's *Mama* series (starring Peggy Wood). In real life, he married former June Taylor dancer Pat Poole, and they recently celebrated their sixtieth wedding anniversary. They have three sons, Nels, Jimmy, and Vincent, the latter of whom was cast as one of Ronny Cox's sons on the short-lived CBS 70s family series, *Apple's Way* (created by *The Waltons'* Earl Hamner). Vince also played the lead in the failed ABC pilot, *The Bionic Boy* (an intended sequel to *The Six Million Dollar Man*).

Waite was born in White Plains, New York, on June 22, 1928, and educated at Bucknell University where he graduated with a bachelor of arts degree. He worked as a social worker, religious editor for Harper & Row, and even as a Presbyterian minister after spending three years at the Yale School of Divinity. It wasn't until he was thirty years old that he discovered his true calling as an actor. In 1960, he made his professional theatrical debut in a stage production of *The Balcony* at the Circle in the Square in New York, and was later seen on Broadway in *Blues for Mister Charlie* before earning fine reviews in 1965 along-side Faye Dunaway in *Hogan's Goat*.

Robert Reed
Globe Photos

Ralph Waite
PhotoFest

Consequently, Ralph was inspired to relocate to Hollywood, where he was cast in small roles in big films such as *Cool Hand Luke* (1967) and *Five Easy Pieces* (1970). One of those motion pictures, the coming-of-age *Last Summer* (1969), starred an up-and-coming talent named Richard Thomas, who would later portray Waite's number one son, John-Boy, on *The Waltons*—a series that apparently helped to mend Waite's broken heart and ultimately save his life from years of alcohol abuse brought on by the death of his nine-year-old daughter in 1964. Married three times, to Beverly Waite (1951–1966), Kerry Sheare Waite (1977–1981), and Linda East Waite (1982–2014), Ralph Waite continued as a working actor (playing dad to Mark Harmon on *NCIS*) until his sudden passing on February 13, 2014, at age eighty-five in the Palm Desert, California, home he shared with his third spouse, Linda.

Before playing architect dad Mike Brady on *The Brady Bunch*, Robert Reed, who was gay, and who died tragically of AIDS, portrayed the young son and protégé attorney opposite his TV father-colleague played by E. G. Marshall on *The Defenders* (CBS, 1961–1965), and a somewhat stern younger brotherly-type opposite Mike Connors on *Mannix* (CBS, 1967–1975).

In 1988 Reed talked about accepting the role as the Brady daddy after it was presented to him by show creator Sherwood Schwartz (*Gilligan's Island*). As Reed once recalled:

Sherwood gave me the plot that sounded wonderful. He put together statistics of broken families, so I said, "It was going to be comedic, but not . . . it's going to be life-like. But then, I got the script of it, and it was one gag after another, and I thought, "I don't think this has much of a chance, but they tell me, you can either do this or *Mission: Impossible*." Anyway, I did this. That was what got me *The Defenders* job. There were literally hundreds of young actors around, and the reason the producers looked at [scenes from *The Defenders*] was because they were looking for a young lawyer, and they knew that there was a young actor playing a lawyer in it. Obviously, they couldn't see everyone. So that was my lucky break.

Although Reed first made a TV name for himself as the younger half of *The Defenders*, he will always be known and loved as architect Mike Brady, the patriarch of the original *Brady* sitcom, which spawned countless TV and movie sequels. "Several generations of viewers have come to love Reed in the endless *Brady* reruns and revivals," Jeff Thompson says. As to the main reason why TV audiences flocked to Reed's fatherly persona, Thompson references the show's opening theme lyrics:

Dick Van Patton
Globe Photos

Here's the story of Robert Reed's appeal: he truly loved his TV children. He relished serving as a second father to the six young actors; he even took them on vacations with him. Reed's genuine love for the youngsters (although not always for the *Brady* TV series itself) came across to the viewers and allowed them to think of him as a real father and perhaps the *ideal* easygoing, understanding, adoring father.

The same could certainly be said for Ralph Waite and Dick Van Patten.

Acknowledgments

The author would like to thank each of the actors, writers, directors, and journalists who granted exclusive interviews and commentaries for *Dashing, Daring and Debonair* (as listed in the Introduction), particularly Adam West, who wrote the Foreword, and Joel Eisenberg, who penned the Preface.

Deepest gratitude is also extended to all the top professionals at Rowman & Littlefield / Taylor Trade / Globe Pequot, including Rick Rinehart, Evan Helmlinger, Julie Marsh, Jason Rock, Sharon Kunz, Karie Simpson, and Kalen Landow.

Thanks also to Melissa McComas, who expertly negotiated the deal for this book; top-notch researchers and entertainment historians Ken Gehrig, Mary Holm, James Knuttel, and Rob Ray; as well as the following individuals who generously contributed their time, talent, efforts, and support to this publication in a variety of ways: Dottie Clark, Bobby Leaf, David Leaf, Pamela Mastrosimone, Sam Mastrosimone, Sammy Mastrosimone, Pierre Patrick, Rudi Rudenski, Fred Westbrook, and Eva Lois Easton-Leaf.

Chapter Notes

A list of source material and/or quotes that are not specifically attributed within the text of the given chapter.

Chapter 1: Jack Webb
www.emergencyfans.com/people/jack_webb
.htm

Chapter 2: Desi Arnaz
www.brainyquote.com/quotes/authors/d/desi
_arnaz.html#TYhutJmjVRfS7Jt7.99

Chapter 3: Nat King Cole
www.brainyquote.com/quotes/authors/n/
nat_king_cole.html
www.wikipedia.org
www.biography.com

Chapter 4: Danny Thomas
www.brainyquote.com/quotes/quotes/d/
dannythoma187291.html

Chapter 5: Dick Van Dyke
http://parade.condenast.com/170961/linzlowe/
who-almost-played-the-lead-on-the-dick
-van-dyke-show/
www.emmytvlegends.org/blog/?p=3849

www.esquire.com/features/what-ive-learned/
ESQ0207dickvandyke

Chapter 6: Johnny Carson
www.notable-quotes.com/c/carson_johnny
.html#W5efGA4JEG3bXu7x.99
www.notable-quotes.com/c/carson_johnny
.html

Chapter 8: Gene Roddenberry
www.goodreads.com/author/quotes/43942
.Gene_Roddenberry
www.biography.com/people/gene--9461573

Chapter 9: Norman Lear
www.goodreads.com/author/quotes/2899420
.Norman_Lear
www.searchquotes.com/quotes/author/
Norman_Lear/

Chapter 10: Sonny Bono
www.brainyquote.com/quotes/authors/s/
sonny_bono.html

Late Night with David Letterman, November 13, 1987

Chapter 12: John Ritter
www.brainyquote.com/quotes/authors/j/ john_ritter.html

Chapter 14: Bob Crane and Darren McGavin
www.thecabinet.com/horrortelevisiondatabase

Chapter 15: Dwayne Hickman and Bob Denver
Loyola Marymount University Magazine, November 17, 2011
www.brainyquote.com/quotes/authors/d/ dwayne_hickman.html
Bob Denver on *The Rosie O'Donnell Show*, November 10, 1997

Chapter 16: Andy Griffith and Don Knotts
www.great-quotes.com/quotes/movie/ The+Andy+Griffith+Show

Chapter 17: Dick York and Dick Sargent
The Bewitched Book by Herbie J Pilato

Chapter 18: Larry Hagman
www.brainyquote.com/quotes/authors/l/larry _hagman.html

Chapter 19: Don Adams
Golden Years of Television (1988) Channel 9 Melbourne broadcast

Chapter 23: Ricky Nelson
www.brainyquote.com/quotes/authors/r/ ricky_nelson.html

Chapter 27: David Hedison
www.classicfilmtvcafe.com/2013/03/david -hedison-talks-with-cafe-about.html
http://herocomplex.latimes.com/tv/voyage-to -the-bottom-of-the-sea-david-hedison-looks -back-on-periscope-days/

http://cjonline.com/life/arts-entertainment/ 2014-03-20/voyage-skipper-david-hedison -discusses-his-lifes-journeys
www.universalexports.net/interviews/hedison .shtml

Chapter 28: Desi Arnaz Jr.
www.lasvegasbackstagetalk.com.

Chapter 29: Bobby Sherman
www.brainyquote.com/quotes/authors/b/ bobby_sherman.html
http://articles.latimes.com/1998/jul/21/ entertainment/ca-5548
http://articles.latimes.com/1993-01-28/local/ me-2432_1_bobby-sherman

Chapter 30: Christopher Knight and Barry Williams
http://thinkexist.com/quotation/i-don-t-think -of-myself-as-a-role-model-i-do-try/368901 .html
www.biography.com/people/christopher -knight-591412
www.huffingtonpost.com/2013/08/28/ christopher-knight-peter-brady_n_3824796 .html
www.nndb.com/people/535/000025460/
www.brainyquote.com/quotes/authors/b/ barry_williams.html

Chapter 31: David Cassidy
http://m.imdb.com/name/nm0144180/quotes
www.davidcassidy.com/fansite/ BiographyPages/InterestingFacts.html
The New Musical Experience Magazine, October 1972
www.brainyquote.com/quotes/authors/d/ david_cassidy.html

Chapter 32: Donny Osmond
Grove, Martin A. "A Candid Conversation with the Osmonds: What It's Like To Star in

a Hit TV Show." *TV Stars Today*—Special. Summer 1978.

Chapter 33: Shaun Cassidy and Parker Stevenson
TV Stars Today. Bluegrass Publishing Company, August 1978.

Chapter 34: James Arness
www.great-quotes.com/quotes/author/James/Arness

Chapter 35: Michael Landon
http://religiondispatches.org/touched-by-a-michael-landon-americas-jewish-angel/

Chapter 37: Clint Eastwood and Clint Walker
images.search.yahoo.com/search/images/quotes/Eastwood/Walker

Chapter 40: John Schneider and Tom Wopat
www.brainyquote.com/quotes/authors/j/john_schneider.html#I2seFJccrK8DDuff.99

Chapter 41: George Maharis and Martin Milner
www.brainyquote.com/quotes/authors/m/martin_milner.html

Chapter 43: Henry Winkler
www.brainyquote.com/quotes/authors/h/henry_winkler.html

Chapter 46: Efrem Zimbalist Jr.
www.brainyquote.com/quotes/authors/e/efrem_zimbalist_jr.html

Chapter 47: Peter Graves, Martin Landau, Greg Morris, Peter Lupus
Chapter 48: Robert Vaughn, David McCallum, Patrick McGoohan
www.wikipedia.org
www.brainyquotes.com

Chapter 49: Michael Cole and Clarence Williams III
www.chezgrae.com/modsquad/media/tvguide69-12Jul.pdf
www.people.com/people/article/0,,20127923,00.html
www.tvguide.com/celebrities/michael-cole/bio/165981
lacrossetribune.com/couleenews/news/local/the-book-on-madison-s-mod-squad-star-michael-cole/article_68865610-ee90-547b-905e-f9890bb9c3ec.html
www.wikipedia.org, Michael Cole (actor)
http://articles.latimes.com/1994-02-27/news/tv-27672_1_clarence-williams-iii
http://articles.latimes.com/1995-06-03/entertainment/ca-8911_1_clarence-williams-iii
www.chezgrae.com/modsquad/media/tvguide70-28Feb.pdf
http://articles.latimes.com/2003/aug/31/entertainment/ca-boehm31
www.tvguide.com/celebrities/clarence-williams-iii/bio/189704
http://articles.latimes.com/2003/aug/31/entertainment/ca-boehm31

Chapter 52: Burt Reynolds
The Globe, December 15, 2014

Chapter 53: David Soul and Paul Michael Glaser
Chapter 54: Erik Estrada and Larry Wilcox
Chapter 55: Clayton Moore and Jay Silverheels
Chapter 56: George Reeves
Chapter 57: Robert Conrad
Chapter 58: Adam West and Burt Ward
www.imdb.com
www.brainyquotes.com
www.wikipedia.org

Chapter 59: Van Williams and Bruce Lee
www.tvrage.com/person/id-15046/Van+Williams

www.brainyquote.com/quotes/authors/b/
bruce_lee.html

Chapter 62: David Carradine
www.brainyquote.com/quotes/quotes/d/
davidcarra330400.html
www.brainyquote.com/quotes/authors/b/
bruce_lee.html

Chapter 63: Lee Majors
*Celebrate the 70s: Stars and Fads from an
Amazing Decade* (People Books, 2009).
FoxNews.com, March 18, 2013.
www.brainyquote.com/quotes/authors/l/
lee_majors.html
IMDB.com
Ultimate70s.com
*The Complete Directory to Prime Time
Network and Cable TV Shows 1946-Present
- Sixth Edition, 1995* by Tim Brooks and
Earle Marsh

Chapter 64: Ricardo Montalban
http://thinkexist.com/quotation/true-love
-doesn-t-happen-right-away-it-s-an-ever/
389499.html
www.brainyquote.com/quotes/authors/r/
ricardo_montalban.html

PART 8: The Doctors, the Defenders, and the
Dependables
www.brainyquote.com/quotes/authors/j/john
_forsythe.html

Chapter 65: Richard Chamberlain and Vince
Edwards

www.brainyquote.com/quotes/authors/r/
richard_chamberlain.html

Chapter 66: Alan Alda
www.brainyquote.com/quotes/authors/a/
alan_alda.html
www.goodreads.com/quotes/46196-be-brave
-enough-to-live-creatively

Chapter 67: James Brolin and Chad Everett
www.tvguide.com/News/Castle-James
-Brolin-1075907.aspx
www.tvguide.com/celebrities/james-brolin/
bio/155307
http://articles.latimes.com/2009/aug/12/
entertainment/et-classichollywood12

Chapter 68: Raymond Burr
www.brainyquote.com/quotes/authors/r/
raymond_burr.html

Chapter 69: Robert Young and Fred
MacMurray
www.imdb.com/name/nm0001870/bio?ref
_=nm_dyk_qt_sm#quotes
http://quotes.famousfix.com/tpx_14088/fred
-macmurray/quotes
www.enewsreference.com/actors/robert_young
.html

Chapter 70: Robert Reed, Ralph Waite, and
Dick Van Patten
www.brainyquote.com/quotes/authors/r/
ralph_waite.html
http://m.imdb.com/name/nm0001658/quotes

Index

About the Author

Herbie J Pilato is the author of several pop-culture/media tie-books, including: *Glamour, Gidgets, and the Girl Next Door*, *The Essential Elizabeth Montgomery*, *Twitch Upon a Star: The Bewitched Life and Career of Elizabeth Montgomery*, *Bewitched Forever*, *The Kung Fu Book of Caine*, *The Kung Fu Book of Wisdom*, *The Bionic Book*, *Life Story—The Book of Life Goes On*, and *NBC & ME: My Life As A Page In A Book*. He has made hundreds of TV and radio appearances, including those on *Entertainment Tonight*, and E!; and has produced and/or appeared as a cultural commentator on Bravo's hit five-part series *The 100 Greatest TV Characters*, the TV Guide Network's *100 Greatest Moments of Television*, TLC's *Behind the Fame* specials on *The Mary Tyler Moore Show*, *The Bob Newhart Show*, *Hill Street Blues* and *L.A. Law*, as well as the DVD releases for *CHiPs*, *Bewitched*, *Kung Fu*, and *The Six Million Dollar Man*. He's also written about classic TV for various magazines, including: *Sci-Fi Entertainment*, *Starlog*, *Sci-Fi Universe*, and *Starlog*.

Herbie J presently contributes to www.Emmys.org (owned and operated by the Television Academy of Arts and Sciences), and Larry Brody's prestigious *TVWriter*

.net, and has written *The Retro Report* for www.forcesofgeek.com. He periodically hosts classic TV events at the Paley Center of Media in Beverly Hills while, as the founder and executive director of the Classic TV Preservation Society (a formal 501(c)3 nonprofit organization dedicated to the positive social influence of classic television programming), he offers Classic TV & Self-Esteem Seminars to schools, colleges, and community, senior, and business centers around the country.

In 2015 he began presenting *Throwback Thursdays with Herbie J Pilato*, a popular live event at the Burbank (California) Barnes & Noble Media Center, which featured classic TV guest stars like Cindy Williams (*Laverne & Shirley*), Kathy Garver (*Family Affair*), Lydia Cornell (*Too Close For Comfort*), Ed Spielman (creator of *Kung Fu*), Anson Williams (*Happy Days*), and Dawn Wells (*Gilligan's Island*). His production company, Television, Ink., recently teamed with Mirkwood Partners for *Herbie J Pilato's Now & Then* TV talk show that will be geared toward classic television.